ARKANSAS MADE

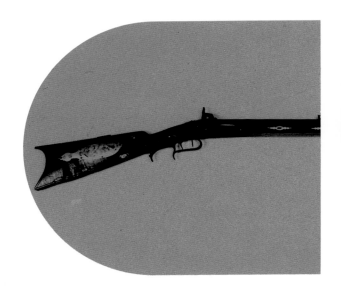
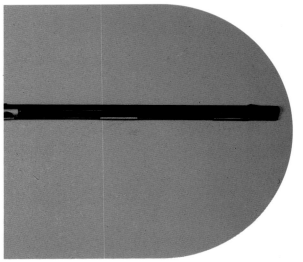

Swannee Bennett
&
William B. Worthen

The University of Arkansas Press

Fayetteville   1990   London

ARKANSAS MADE

A Survey of the Decorative, Mechanical, and Fine Arts Produced in Arkansas, 1819–1870

Volume One

Furniture • Quilts • Silver • Pottery • Firearms

DESIGNER: *Ch. H. Russell*
TYPEFACE: *Linotron 202 Trump Mediaeval*

This project was funded in part by a grant from the Arkansas Endowment for the Humanities.

The paper used in this publication meets the minimum requirements of the American National Standard for Permanence of Paper for Printed Library Materials Z39.48-1984. ∞

Library of Congress Cataloging-in-Publication Data

Bennett, Swannee, 1949–
     Arkansas made : a survey of the decorative, mechanical, and fine arts produced in
  Arkansas, 1819–1870 / by Swannee Bennett and William B. Worthen.
        p.   cm.
     Includes bibliographical references.
     ISBN 1-55728-138-6 (alk. paper) (v. 1.). — ISBN 1-55728-139-4 (pbk.: alk. paper) (v. 1.)
     1. Decorative arts—Arkansas—History—19th century.
   2. Folk art—Arkansas—History—19th century.   I. Worthen, William B., 1947–.   II. Title.
NK835.A8B4   1990
709'.767'09034—dc20   89-20508
                                                                                  CIP

Contents

Introduction 3

ARKANSAS FURNITURE

Furnituremaking in Arkansas 9
A Biographical Appendix of Arkansas Furnituremakers 19
An Illustrated Catalog of Arkansas Furniture 46

ARKANSAS QUILTS

Quiltmaking in Arkansas 83
An Illustrated Catalog of Arkansas Quilts 90

ARKANSAS SILVER

Silversmithing, Goldsmithing, Clockmaking, Jewelrymaking,
and Watchmaking in Arkansas 111
A Biographical Appendix of Arkansas Silversmiths, Goldsmiths,
Clockmakers, Jewelers, and Watchmakers 119
An Illustrated Catalog of Arkansas Silver 132

ARKANSAS POTTERY

Potterymaking in Arkansas 145
A Biographical Appendix of Arkansas Potters 152
An Illustrated Catalog of Arkansas Pottery 156

ARKANSAS FIREARMS

Gunsmithing in Arkansas   *167*
A Biographical Appendix of Arkansas Gunsmiths   *177*
An Illustrated Catalog of Arkansas Firearms   *192*

Glossary   *207*
Key to Abbreviations   *213*
Acknowledgments   *215*
Bibliography   *217*

ARKANSAS MADE

Introduction

The first arrival of the Overland Mail Stage in 1858 provided the opportunity for a parade in Ft. Smith. Soldiers, Odd Fellows in full regalia, the Hook and Ladder Company, mechanics, farmers, and others made up the procession.

> The mechanics with praiseworthy zeal and energy, had platforms erected upon wagons and while the procession moved onward, worked at their trades.
>
> Upon one platform we noticed our venerable friend F. H. Wolfe with hammer, moulds, etc., engaged in making work in his line of Gold and Silver Smith, and his son Geo. Wolf, binding books. The platform was tastefully decorated with flags and banners bearing appropriate mottos. . . .
>
> There were the Carpenters and house joiners, wheelrights, wagon makers and cabinetmakers all carrying on their trades during the progress of the procession. Young America was aptly illustrated by young Pearson with his one horse wagon, containing the sign and tools of his father [gunsmith John Pearson]. We regret our inability to do full justice to the procession and the various branches of art and industry represented. No town in the Union can show a greater number of intelligent and industrious mechanics than Fort Smith.[1]

Here the editor chronicled the frontier promise fulfilled: artisans moving west for the opportunity Arkansas offered and participating in the carving of community out of the wilderness. It was no small accomplishment, and in the period from 1819 to 1870 hundreds of creative individuals transformed Fort Smith, and the entire state.

So why are we only now rediscovering this creative legacy? Why for a century have early Arkansas's artists and artisans remained hidden from the public eye and the state's consciousness? The answer lies in an image of Arkansas that has obscured a much more interesting reality. When Thomas W. Jackson selected a title for what was to become the best selling joke book in American history, he chose *On a Slow Train through Arkansaw.* Not Mississippi, Kansas, Idaho, or Texas. Were the jokes about Arkansas? Not especially. The use of Arkansas in the title was a marketing decision based upon a well-established image of what "Arkansaw" was. Half a century earlier, Frederika Bremmer used the same image to bemoan Arkansas's lack of "spiritual and material culture," without ever setting foot in the state.

It's not that these and dozens of other commentators didn't find an element of truth in their rough and crude version of Arkansas. Friedrich Gerstäcker's stories of "bad characters, gamblers, drunkards, thieves, murderers" contain glimpses of real frontier society, before the civilizing influence of lawyers, women, and preachers could be felt in earnest.

Evidence could also be found of more appealing characters for whom "civilized" might be a generous term. On September 9, 1829, the *Arkansas Gazette* printed this letter to a Crawford County merchant:

> "Mr. ———. Dear sir i want you to let my son have one hat and i will pay for the same before i return home i have not got the money to pay the account that i have with you at this time but i have a prety wife a nice daughter a fast horse and a good Raccon dog and i will see you before i go home—i am Dear sir yours with more than common Rispect."

The values reflected in this letter should gain universal admiration, but, to the Little Rock editor, their statement betrays a rustic perspective. The frontier, rough and rowdy, or rustic and unrefined, is still the frontier. Therein is the source of Arkansas's persistent image; even today it has a frontier flavor.

Such conclusions are easily reached, especially when reinforced by learned outside sources. A recent and otherwise excellent survey of the art and architecture of the Old South excluded only one of the states of the Confederacy: Arkansas.

The problem isn't just with Arkansas. There is a tendency to focus on big names and famous places. How natural it is to overlook the edges of civilization when looking for the fruits of that civilization. Places such as Arkansas became the backdrop providing little more than contrast to the "truly significant" locations of American history.

Arkansas's image grew so pervasive that it became easy to expect little of the state's history. So easy, in fact, that the State Board of Education has only recently decided to require the teaching of Arkansas history in our schools. Generations of Arkansas school children have grown up assuming that their state's history wasn't worth studying. Not surprisingly, quality textbooks have been few and far between.

Not above being a victim itself, the Arkansas Territorial Restoration backed into the study that resulted in this book. The subject of the institution's energy is Arkansas's frontier period, which for practical purposes lasted until the Civil War. After all, foreign soil touched the state until 1845 when Texas was admitted to the Union, and the telegraph and railroad, those tentacles of civilization, arrived only just before the conflict began.

This research project began as a necessary supplement to the reinterpretation of the institution's museum houses. Just how should these structures of pre–Civil War Little Rock be furnished? The National Endowment for the Humanities assisted in the project, and the houses have seen substantive changes based upon the research. Changed also was the institution's vision of early Arkansas's material culture: silversmiths, gunsmiths, cabinetmakers, and other skilled artists and artisans were waiting patiently to be discovered. Frederika Bremer, and those of like mind, would have been pleasantly surprised.

The museum, finding a vast hole in the state's already neglected history, set out to fill it. The research project was continued, and the established goal was not less than the listing of every artist or artisan engaged in his or her vocation in Arkansas from 1819 to 1870. Volunteers and paid staff members surveyed every census taken in Arkansas in 1870 and before and the advertisements in every Arkansas newspaper of the period. Letters, diaries, the standard history texts, and county journals were scoured for references. Researchers reviewed all of the probate inventories of several counties and traced many subjects through tax records and deed books. Many trails wandered back to the East and across the Atlantic. The introduction to the bibliography reviews the research project in some depth.

The field portion of the project took curator, photographer, and staff researcher (sometimes three in one) to all corners of the state and beyond, peering into chests of drawers and behind family portraits, measuring pots, and hoping for makers' marks. Letters and speakers were used to appeal to county historical societies, feature articles promoted the project, and the search relied heavily on the person who knew the person who knew the person. Many generous people cooperated, including several whose own interest and commitment to specific fields had anticipated such a project as this.

Research discovered a solid artisan tradition in Arkansas. Certain groups proved easiest to categorize. Gunsmiths, silversmiths (etc.), potters, and cabinetmakers were in clearly defined national traditions and appropriately enumerated in censuses. Then came the photographers and portrait, landscape, and genre artists, which will be covered in volume two of *Arkansas Made.*

At the heart of this publication are the biographical appendices—lists of artisans and some information about each. The raw number of listings in these categories might be surprising: cabinetmakers, 436; gunsmiths, 224; potters, 29; and silversmiths, 183. Add to these lists the quilters and the visual artists mentioned in the text, and it becomes clear that a significant part of the creative community of frontier Arkansas has been overlooked.

The physical legacy is a mixed one: solid cabinetmaking, fine portraiture, well-made silver and guns, beautiful quilts. But little is so grand as the best of that which was produced in major manufacturing centers and available to one of means. New Orleans was not alone in serving Arkansas. Cincinnati, Pittsburgh, New York, Philadelphia—this list could go on—found a ready market on the frontier. The tension between the local artisan and the distant factory was present in the early days of the territory. This was the story of the artisan tradition in nineteenth-century America, and Arkansas artists and artisans shared the fate of others throughout the country. The point of this on-going study is not necessarily to find the finest, but to discover what was available. Indigenous manufacture in Arkansas may have never equaled that of Philadelphia or New Orleans, but it was *there.* The image of Arkansas might not be transformed by such findings, but it can be supplemented.

This ambitious but understaffed research project could not achieve the broad comprehension to which it aspired. The 1870 cutoff, while perfect for some trades, has proven less ideal for those artisans who lingered on through the rest of the century. Certain trades have been disappointing in the number or quality of the products found up to the present. For example, rumors of Arkansas-made silver tea services surfaced with some regularity, but none were actually located. Researchers in the field over weeks and months, able to follow up on leads, will make this project much more thorough in the future. A rich and only partially tapped resource is the quantity of probate inventories—so many unindexed—waiting for the patient researcher. Finally, certain creative products—coverlets, clothing, mortuary art, tin and ironware, etc.—have not been touched, and many issues regarding the economic impact and status of artists and artisans, as well as style, tradition, etc., await further study.

The concerns stated above are tempered by the understanding that this book is only a beginning, an invitation. Sources will undoubtedly come to light; makers will be added to the lists; theories will be developed, and explanations offered. But the first step must be taken. The breadth of the omission from our history needs to be acknowledged and the Arkansas artist and artisan welcomed back.

Notes

1. *Arkansas Gazette,* 23 October 1858.

1870 Map of Arkansas

ARKANSAS FURNITURE

Furnituremaking in Arkansas

Materials

In 1819 Thomas Nuttall, the celebrated American naturalist, wrote of the vast, primordial woods near the Arkansas Post: "Nothing yet appears but one vast trackless wilderness of trees, a dead solemnity, where the human voice is never heard to echo. . . . All is rude nature . . . preserving its primeval type, its unreclaimed exuberance."[1] Authorities estimate that when the first large-scale migration of white settlers began to arrive in Arkansas, such forest blanketed 85 percent of the land.

Since wood is the primary material used in the construction of furniture, the nineteenth-century Arkansas cabinetmaker chose from a stunning array of raw materials from the state's almost limitless hardwood and pine forests. The wooded regions of Arkansas are divided into several natural areas including the Mississippi Alluvial Plain, called the Delta, in eastern Arkansas; Crowley's Ridge, contained within the Delta and extending from southern Missouri down through eastern Arkansas to Helena; the West Gulf Coastal Plain to the south and west; the Ouachita Mountains, stretching across west-central Arkansas and bordered on the north by the Arkansas River valley, on the south by the Gulf Coastal Plain, and on the east by the Alluvial Plain; the Arkansas River valley; and the Ozark Mountains in the northwest.[2]

The Mississippi Alluvial Plain is a flat region containing a variety of bottom-land woods including bald cypress, water-tupelo, swamp cottonwood, pin, Nuttall, and willow oaks, water hickory, and green and Carolina ash. Also found in these low, poorly drained soils are persimmon, winged elm, and red maple. On higher, better drained ridge soil, sweet gum, green and willow oaks, and a rare loblolly pine find suitable homes. The swamp chestnut, hickory, and blackgum are also native to the area.[3]

Crowley's Ridge is hardly more than 250 feet in height at any one place and ranges in width from one to twelve miles.[4] According to geographers Hanson and Stroud, this area is "distinctly different in that its forests are more closely related to the tulip tree-oak forest of the Tennessee hills and other areas to the east than to the oak-hickory forest of the Ozarks to the west."[5] On the ridge, local artisans found a rich assortment of trees including tulip poplar; cucumber tree; basswood; white, northern, red, and chinkapin oaks; several kinds of hickory; ashes; maples; cherry; walnut; and butternut. The area was also the only region in the state where the tulip tree (tulip poplar) grew naturally.[6]

The most distinctive features of the Gulf Coastal Plain are the loblolly pine forests, although shortleaf pine also exists on the higher elevations. Interspersed among the predominant pines are strands of shumard, chinkapin, and white oaks, and the butternut, shagbark, and mockernut hickories.[7] Along major streams are a wide variety of bottom-land hardwoods. The oak-hickory-gum type also occurs on the best sites of this area while willow-oak forests are found commonly in flat, poorly drained soils.[8]

In the Ouachita mountains, the predominant forest tree is the shortleaf pine, along with bottom-land hardwoods, which are located in flat, poorly drained valley floors and along the numerous streams that course through the rugged terrain. The bottom-land and hardwoods most commonly found are the willow, water, overcup, and southern red oaks, along with sweet and black gum, red maple, elms, sugarberry, beech, hickories, and, at one time, chestnut.[9]

The Ozark Mountains are located in the northwestern part of the state and are bounded by the Alluvial Plain on the east, the Arkansas River valley and the Ouachita Mountains on the south, while continuing northward into Missouri and west into Oklahoma. Dr. Rudy Moore, an expert on the region, describes the natural vegetation as primarily upland hardwood of the oak, ash, and hickory varieties, and a very good admixture of shortleaf pine. Also in evidence are the American and slippery elms, white ash, black gum, basswood, hackberry, chinkapin, black walnut, black cherry, yellowwood, and beech, as well as numerous other varieties in lesser quantities. Hawthorn, persimmon, ash juniper, and eastern red cedar are often found together in the eastern areas of the Ozarks near the White River, while silver maple, river birch, elm, pecan, sweet gum, sycamore, and various oaks are located in many of the Ozarks' stream valleys.[10]

The *U.S. Census for Products of Industry* for 1850, 1860, and 1870 lists the kinds of woods each Arkansas cabinetmaking shop utilized. These woods were most often walnut, cherry, pine, sweet gum, mahogany, oak, and cypress. For the most part, wood used by Arkansas cabinetmakers was indigenous, and, except for mahogany, there is no documentation of furniture wood importation into Arkansas. The state's forests afforded an average maker as wide a selection of suitable lumber as he might find anywhere in the country. The only conspicuous scarcity was in the yellow or tulip poplar wood favored by American woodworkers for cabinets. In Arkansas, its growth was confined to Crowley's Ridge, and local craftsmen like L. F. Walker of Phillips County used it for their work. Walker advertised that he would use poplar, as well as other woods, to make "coffins of any size or quality. . . ."[11]

The Migrants

America, with its long tradition of economic and social mobility, was in more than the usual state of flux during the nineteenth century. Americans were on the move then, economically, socially, and geographically. They were searching for a home, an opportunity, an escape. Along the way, some of them found Arkansas.

On January 16, 1827, the following notice appeared in the *Arkansas Gazette:* "John Onstot, Carver and Cabinetmaker has opened a shop at the Post of Arkansas, where he intends carrying on the above business, in all its various branches."[12] The documented history of Arkansas's cabinetmaking began with this advertisement. It was not a success story, at least not in 1827.

By that year Arkansas Post, once a bustling territorial capital, had languished into a dilapidated rural county seat. The Post, situated just above the confluence of the Arkansas and White rivers, had few remaining business houses after the first quarter of the century and even fewer patrons for an ambitious artisan. Onstot was aware of this situation, and in his advertisement he indicated he intended to send some of his work to Little Rock.

Indeed, by mid-1827, Onstot himself had gone to the newer, faster-paced, and more prosperous town. Although he moved to Little Rock for business reasons, the available evidence indicates that opportunities to make a reasonable living as an artisan were few, even in the new capital city. By 1840 Onstot had moved again and had even changed jobs. This time he located in the northwestern hillside village of Fayetteville, where he opened the "cheap house of entertainment" that provided his primary source of employment at least until 1860.[13]

His peregrinations in Arkansas and his change in occupation illustrate the fact that Onstot was a product of the age in which he lived. As such, he would have been possessed by what Arkansas humorist C. F. M. Noland called "a disposition to be ever going toward the setting sun." In the nineteenth century, men of ambition, thwarted in their advance, could always look outward toward the West to an opportunity-filled frontier.[14] Yet, a closer examination of Onstot's meandering reveals more complex motives at work in his life than a cultural predilection for mobility and his own locomotive disposition.

Everywhere in America, the competitive nature of the handicraft trades forced artisans into constant relocations. On the east coast, competition compelled both impoverished journeymen and more prosperous masters to abandon shop. These men often moved west, providing competition to local craftsmen.

Work in the West especially seemed alluring when compared with conditions on the eastern seaboard where, as one New Yorker described the situation: "We worked ourselves at the bench with 2 or 3 hired men and could hardly make so much as our men, which was a dollar a day . . . we economized where we could and held on hoping for better times to come."[15]

Better times seldom came for nineteenth-century artisans. These were years of rampant business consolidation and, by the 1840s, combination had badly eroded wages and status in the crafts. Under these conditions, the cabinet-maker's kitchen garden often became the family farm. Historian Carl Bridenbaugh has pointed out that in the eighteenth century, "nearly all craftsmen were inexorably drawn into planting or farming because they could not fain a living from their trades."[16] This was no less the case a hundred years later. "In 1844 the same amount of labor that had once produced for the mechanic and his family a comfortable subsistence was inadequate to maintain his standards, and his only alternative was increased effort or a reduction of his wants."[17]

Should his wants be irreducible, a mechanic could always find a solution by maintaining two jobs. In the country, he could farm as well as build furniture. Thus, the craftsman-farmer became a common frontier phenomenon well into

the latter half of the nineteenth century. Arkansas cabinetmakers serve as a case in point. A majority of them owned land other than town lots and probably supplemented their market baskets by means of that land.[18] Finally, some even did as Onstot was forced to do and gave up cabinetry altogether. During the period from 1840–1870, northwest Arkansas's Benton County had a population of at least thirty-one woodworkers. Records for those thirty years show that approximately one-third of them either added to their woodworking income by farming or changed their occupation.[19]

Documents also indicate that the cabinetmaking industry in Arkansas was typical, subject to the same competitive pressures and economic stringencies that existed elsewhere in America. The times were tough for tradesmen, and fortunes on the frontier appear to have been as variable as those in the city. However, if times were as bad in Arkansas as elsewhere, why did more than four hundred artisans pack their planes and chisels and come to the state between 1827 and 1870?

Many came to the less populated hinterland with the idea of having adventure in a more wide-open venue. On the edge of civilization, some believed, lay an abundance of opportunity, and a man with initiative could prosper in proportion to his effort, regardless of wealth or status. Historians have argued that one key concept in nineteenth-century thought was the awesome potential of the New Eden, and the idea of frontier openness and plenty provided a base upon which all nineteenth-century American culture was organized.[20]

Juxtaposed with the promise of a mythic American wilderness were the difficulties of life in the older settled areas. Craftsmen of every type crowded each other as the economic depression of the late 1830s and 1840s left large segments of the population unemployed. In cities like New York, as much as 30 percent of the work force went jobless and, for those who did work, wages declined by 30 to 50 percent.[21] As far west as Cincinnati, the times were "as bad as [they] could be. Merchants traded with one another by barter. Transportation was costly . . . [with] no markets except at prohibitive [shipping] prices."[22]

Although economic dislocation was nation-wide, economic problems were especially acute in the South. This section of America faced mid-century with political and economic woes rooted in its slave legacy and its predominately agricultural base, and the greater proportion of Arkansas's woodworkers fled to the state from other areas in the South.

Along with other difficulties, one of the problems that faced white Southern craftsmen in Arkansas and elsewhere centered on competition from slave artisans. They were viewed as a real threat, likely to supplant free competitors and steal their livelihood. White mechanics in the South continually asked for security in the form of laws that would keep slaves from competing with them for scarce jobs. But, even as craftsmen agitated for anti-slave legislation, other Southerners, especially farmers, encouraged black tradesmen and spoke of slavery as a "bulwark against extortion and our safeguard against the turbulence of white mechanics, as seen in the great city strikes both in England and in the North, and [as] . . . the only protection we have in any possible struggle between capital and white labor."[23]

In Arkansas, this debate generated a furor among the ranks of Little Rock and Washington County's mechanical associations. In the late 1850s, after more than a decade of complaints against unfair competition by prison mechanics, Arkansas's artisans banded together to confront the added threat of black rivals. "By coupling and yoking the hired slave mechanic with the white mechanic you elevate the former to a white artisan, while you degrade the latter to a hired slave mechanic,"[24] one participant wrote. To confront encroachment by slave artisans, Arkansas's mechanics warned their fellows: "You who have wives to support, and children to feed and educate, look to it that you vote not for some candidate who is the owner of Negro mechanics and who in defiance of justice and reason, and of every right, has placed them in competition with you. . . ."[25]

The state's politicians were occasionally threatened with defeat over this issue. Fellow artisans were at risk, too, menaced by the specter of ostracism should they hire out their slaves to do a craftsman's job. Yet, overall in Arkansas, the slave labor debate was not significant. The frontier, with its cheap or even free acreage, served as an escape valve for discontent, and the compensation of life in a land of opportunity proved more important than the fear of exclusion or racial rivalry to Southern cabinetmakers.

Many Southern artisans came to Arkansas from Tennessee and North Carolina, states famed for their furniture production. These individuals provided more than one-third of Arkansas's cabinetmaking migrants. They must have found a special grace in an area southern enough for Delta and cotton-land pilgrims and still unrestricted enough to give them scope for future success.

European cabinetmakers also came to Arkansas in large numbers. At a time when native-born craftsmen were vying with each other in a poor market for a finite number of jobs, immigration worsened their chances for success. By 1850, 10 percent of the nation's work force was comprised of immigrant labor, and the new German-American woodworkers were especially competitive. These artisans, fleeing poverty and political strife at home, might be hired for as little as twenty dollars a year, straight off the ship that brought them to their new home.[26]

Under such conditions, cabinetmakers from Germany became plentiful in the East. They comprised thirty-two percent of all Philadelphia joiners in 1850 and were half the work force by 1870.[27] They also appeared as a major force in the history of crafts in Arkansas. As early as 1839, they were noticeable in Little Rock, causing one traveler to remark, "several Germans inhabit the town and neighborhood."[28] Native-born Germans eventually came to represent a substantial proportion of the state's artisans and a smaller but still significant statewide subculture.

The Germans who immigrated to Arkansas were joined by a smaller number of their English, Irish, and Scandinavian counterparts. But whatever land the European travelers called home, the interior of America looked promising to them, especially an isolated area like Arkansas, which the outsiders perceived as an untapped market filled with prosperous farmers, all in need of the goods and services European artisans could offer. Popular wisdom held this to be so, and many of the immigrating European cabinetmakers discovered it was, at least in part, true.

The Market

In any Arkansas county during the nineteenth century, the agricultural population was never less than 90 percent of the total. While there were numerous farmers, there was also a chronic insufficiency of specie. Moreover, European as well as local craftsmen encountered unexpected competition from a substantial group of merchants. These merchants carried goods from furniture factories up the Arkansas River in riverboats and provided a wide choice of merchandise at low prices. J. Bigelow, a canny Fort Smith businessman, could get his customers in a buying mood before he tempted them with a Cincinnati bedstead or some other item. In a newspaper advertisement from the era, Bigelow informed potential customers that he had received "a large fresh supply of GROCERIES—Cognac, Brandy, Holland Gin, Jamaica Rum, Rye Whiskey, Madiera . . . also FURNITURE, consisting of bedsteads, bureaus, tables, etc."[29]

To sharpen the keen, if not always sober, contest, Arkansas retailers tried a new system of sales, which gained in popularity at mid-century. Rather than dealing directly with furnituremakers and manufacturers, they bought job lots of furniture from wholesalers who did, and at lower prices. Urban centers such as Cincinnati saw jobbers become commonplace. A job lot seller with his plentiful inventory could advertise, as Winthrop Orr did, an overwhelming "1300 chairs suitable for down river trade."[30] The change in marketing technique was profound enough to cause a cabinetmaker to remark, "manufacturing [was] fast getting to be a separate business from selling." Moreover, it presented a problem for the local woodworker. He had to meet or beat high volume prices on furniture produced efficiently with up-to-date tools or by cheap labor.[31]

The inundation of the Arkansas market by machine-made furniture had an adverse effect on home manufacture in many areas, especially those close to steamboat-navigable streams. Most artisans simply made the best of the situation, while a few fought back. Among this latter group was Thomas Spotswood Blennerhassett of Fayetteville. If the local citizens were price-conscious and fickle, he could give them what they wanted.

"I challenge the competition in quality and style of work," he stated in an 1854 advertisement that revealed his own frustration. "For independence is the soul of ambition; and I will try to prove it by manufacturing all kinds of CABINET WORK At such prices that will convince the Public that Cincinnati Galvanized Furniture, or work made at any of the Hessian Abolition Factories is no value for money. Every little helps, and if the people will only patronize their own Mechanics so as to keep the money here. . . ."[32]

Despite Blennerhassett's protests, competing mechanics themselves were not above selling eastern-made tables and bedsteads alongside their own. Before 1870, the most successful of these merchant mechanics was Little Rock's Stephen S. Sanger. Sanger was also among the first to open, in April, 1850, what he advertised as his "new and commodious furniture warerooms . . . where he intends to keep constantly on hand a large and well-selected assortment of fine and plain FURNITURE of his own manufacture, and from the most FASHIONABLE Manufactories at the EAST."[33]

Furniture or cabinet showrooms like Sanger's were a novelty in 1850 Arkansas, but they were a common merchandising tool in larger cities to the east, south, and west. St. Louis, Vicksburg, and New Orleans all had warerooms that gave a vendor the ability to display and produce goods on demand. This was a new, potent weapon in the selling wars, and it gave the stylish big-city salesmen a competitive edge in the battle for impulse buyers. Early on, Philadelphia, Cincinnati, and New York show rooms pressured small local businessmen to keep a variety of finished furniture if they wished to compete.

An inventory of ready-made goods, however, was not enough. Local merchants also had to deal with unscrupulous auctioneers, who liquidated estates, purchased furniture from eastern factories, and took goods from these factories on consignment. Auction sales were seductive to customers. An auction promised bargains for the bidding and a good show, both of which were difficult to resist. Local merchant-artisans were not insensible to the threat of a showboat auctioneer stealing their customers. One such showman was James D. Fitzgerald, who practiced his flamboyant trade in Little Rock. A number of successful sales campaigns in the 1850s and 1860s gave him a substantial share of the capital's market and irritated hometown rivals. They were further galled by his advertisements, such as this one from 1859: "Just received per steamer Henry Fitzhugh, . . . 50 doz. Cane, wood seat, rush & split bottoms, rocking & children's [chairs] . . . a variety of bureaus, center tables, wash stands, cribs, fine cupboard & drawer safes, etc. . . . which will be sold low for cash, at private sale."[34]

Even as commercial rivalry heated up in Arkansas, it was obvious that the centers of power in cabinetry were located elsewhere. New Orleans had long been a well-used entrepôt for European wares, and other cities, north and east, had thriving furniture factories manufacturing goods for western markets. Boston, for example, had 324 furniture establishments by 1869, while the number of furniture workmen in Philadelphia increased from 2260 to 3700 in the twenty years after 1850.[35] By 1846, however, the center of American furniture manufacturing had shifted to Cincinnati, where it remained until the last quarter of the century, when that honor was captured by Grand Rapids, Michigan.

The business of furnituremaking never existed in Arkansas on a large scale, but some furniture was made in Arkansas. The pieces were made by local craftsmen who worked the indigenous woods. Some of the cabinetmakers who built this furniture were prosperous, although most artisans simply sought out a living, and some only made furniture as a hobby. Yet, even though some local artisans subsisted by their craft, it is difficult to recreate exactly what their finished pieces, working conditions, work place, or pay were like because nineteenth-century Arkansas woodworkers left few records.

The Merchandise

To study Arkansas furniture is not to roam in elegant plantations amidst the sophistication of the Rocaille. Nor does it consist of a sojourn through mahogany expanses of Classical Revival. Studying Arkansas furniture more resembles a hike in the hills.

In the nineteenth century, 90 percent of Arkansas's population fell into the yeoman farmer and small tradesman class, and most furniture made in the state went to furnish their homes. This historically voiceless majority had simple tastes, limited means, and lives on the frontier, away from the mainstream of popular taste and consumption. They wanted their furniture to be well-constructed and functional. In such venue, settlers had more of a need of housewrights, carpenters, and blacksmiths than of cabinetmakers. So, while a few larger manufactories did exist, most cabinet shops were small struggling operations.

Early newspaper advertising by cabinetmakers was also sparse. However, the advertisements that were printed reveal the variety of furniture forms that were offered, at least in the more populous towns across the state. For example, William M. Bowers and John Buie's firm in Fayetteville, Washington County, advertised they would "manufacture to order . . . bureaus, bedstead, tables, center tables, wardrobes, secretaries, safes, wash stands, etc."[36]

This list was typical of the era, and furniture made in Arkansas did not vary greatly from that manufactured in other Southern states. The majority of Arkansas's woodworkmen hailed from the South. There is no evidence that when they came to the state they were moved to develop a new style of furniture—they did not alter time-honored designs and techniques, they simply made Southern furniture in Arkansas.

Of the furniture forms routinely associated with the South, a few small-scale sideboards, often called slabs, liquor storage case pieces or cellarettes, and sugar chests still exist in Arkansas. Their scarcity attests to the fact that all such case furniture would have commonly been found in the homes of the wealthy, and Arkansas did not boast an affluent population. In fact, before 1870, county estate inventories, auction records, and advertisements surveyed contained no adjectives to describe ornate furniture styles.

To understand Arkansas furniture styles, county records, inventories, and newspaper advertisements are invaluable. For example, wardrobes for clothes storage were referred to by Arkansans as wardrobes; chests of drawers were listed as bureaus; and sideboards remained sideboards in

Arkansas, even if they were chiffonniers or slabs in Georgia. In chair styles, ladderbacks in Arkansas were called common chairs, while the painted and ornamented variety, known today as Hitchcocks, were known as fancy chairs.

Whether they made fancy chairs or sideboards, furnituremakers in Arkansas produced almost identical sorts of furniture. Bedsteads and work and dining tables were the most popular items, and most often pieces were manufactured to fill basic needs. In frontier life, the amenities were few, and eating, sleeping, storage, and work-related gear were the priorities.

Only a few different forms were created in the state, and the amount of Arkansas furniture produced was also limited. From 1850–1870, the output of most shops was moderate. The Hempstead County firm of Skinner and Arnett typified this trend. According to *Products of Industry,* their 1860 yield, using a three-man workforce, totaled a marginal thirty bureaus, twenty wardrobes, five fine tables, sixty bedsteads, and forty coffins.

Slim production was coupled with minimal cash returns. In the same year, the firm grossed only $2,940. Even at this low figure, they had the second highest total in the state. Only Samuel Daugherty and Henry Glass of Crawford County bested them, and then by only sixty dollars.

The Makers:

In order to see how Arkansas's cabinetmakers dealt with the twin necessities of making a living and providing a wide range of products, one representative of that group, George Berryman, provides an excellent illustration. Berryman was a nineteenth-century Pulaski County cabinetmaker, and the records of his estate, tax records, and advertisements from the *Arkansas Gazette* indicate what the life of this Arkansas artisan was like.

He was first a maker of furniture, from sofas to bedsteads, of fine quality and "warranted superior to any imported articles."[37] But he also repaired everything from parasols to guns. He could also be counted on for bucket handles and some light-running soldering on stoves and the like. Berryman further supplemented his income with a rent house and had a second career as an undertaker. These many efforts did not go unrewarded in that Berryman possessed, according to the 1840 tax records, an extra carriage, a cow, and gold jewelry valued at $150.

Yet, the posthumous tally of his shop's contents was not considerable. Besides the tools of his trade, he had some unfinished pieces, one complete "bedsted," and assorted materials for his business. The furnishings of both his home and shop were old and, if not sparse, certainly not sumptuous.

A chilly wind whipped the remaining fall leaves against the corners of Berryman's modest home and shop on the day the three appraisers made their meticulous catalog of its contents. It must have been an unpleasant task for the men, rummaging through the personal effects of an old friend. Unfortunately, Berryman had not made a will. Still, the men were officers of the county probate court, and the court had ordered Berryman's goods and gear sold at public auction to satisfy his outstanding debts. At least they could see to it that their friend's tools and household goods were carefully listed and given fair value. The men moved on, evaluating, writing, organizing what was left of their companion's craft and capital.

However distressed they might have been at Berryman's death, his friends did their job well. Their inventory survives and provides an excellent idea of what tools, raw materials, and products might have been found in a small-town cabinetmaker's shop during the nineteenth century. The appraisers' inventory indicates the shop was self-sufficient, containing a variety of tools that allowed Berryman to produce completed merchandise from raw materials. In a shop such as this, he would have been able to make not only furniture but a wide range of other wood products.

Normally woodworkers repaired furniture and built coffins, but Berryman also dug graves and owned a hearse to carry his customers to their final rest. A review of his receipts indicates that in the five years before his death, Berryman's business was almost equally divided between cabinetmaking and undertaking. In this respect, he illustrates what had become a norm for wood craftsmen of his era. He had, like many of his peers, taken on the position of de facto funeral director for his community, and in this way he and other nineteenth-century artisan-undertakers fathered the burial business in America.[38]

Cabinetmakers, Locations in Arkansas

County	Date Founded	Number of Makers
Arkansas	1813	8
Ashley	1848	3
Benton	1836	31
Boone	1869	3
Bradley	1840	6
Calhoun	1850	
Carroll	1833	7
Chicot	1823	1
Clark	1818	10
Columbia	1852	3
Conway	1825	1
Craighead	1859	9
Crawford	1820	17
Crittenden	1825	2
Cross	1862	
Dallas	1845	12
Desha	1838	
Drew	1846	9
Franklin	1837	2
Fulton	1842	1
Grant	1869	
Greene	1833	9
Hempstead	1818	22
Hot Spring	1829	6
Independence	1820	21
Izard	1825	4
Jackson	1829	6
Jefferson	1829	8
Johnson	1833	10
Lafayette	1827	3
Lawrence	1815	6
Little River	1867	
Madison	1836	16
Marion	1836	2
Miller	1820	
Mississippi	1844	1

County	Date Founded	Number of Makers
Monroe	1829	
Montgomery	1842	3
Newton	1842	1
Ouachita	1842	11
Perry	1840	
Phillips	1820	21
Pike	1833	3
Poinsett	1838	2
Polk	1844	2
Pope	1829	11
Prairie	1846	3
Pulaski	1818	59
Randolph	1835	4
Saline	1835	2
Scott	1833	3
Searcy	1835	2
Sebastian	1851	19
Sevier	1828	12
Sharp	1868	1
St. Francis	1827	1
Union	1829	1
Van Buren	1833	3
Washington	1828	30
White	1835	3
Woodruff	1862	1
Yell	1840	4

Total number of locations listed: 441
Total number of listings in biographical appendix: 436

Only eight of the sixty-two counties existing by 1870 do not have at least one cabinetmaker listed here. Thus was the universality of the market. Benton and Washington counties of the northwest show a strong cabinetmaking tradition. One of the few artisans who showed the mobility to require listing more than once was John Onstot. He moved across the state like the frontier, first at Arkansas Post, then in Little Rock, and, finally, he finished up as an innkeeper in Washington County. Since he was documented as a cabinetmaker at the first two locations, those are included here. The purpose of this listing is to suggest the extent that cabinetmaking touched Arkansas.

Count of Arkansas Cabinetmakers by Place of Birth

AMERICAN BORN

Alabama	16
Arkansas	13
Connecticut	2
Georgia	17
Illinois	5
Indiana	5
Kentucky	24
Massachusetts	2
Maryland	3
Michigan	1
Mississippi	7
Missouri	13
New Jersey	2
New York	8
North Carolina	44
Ohio	10
Pennsylvania	9
Rhode Island	1
South Carolina	26
Tennessee	74
Vermont	1
Virginia	26
Washington, D.C.	4

FOREIGN BORN

Canada	1
England	3
France	5
Germany	27
Hungary	1
Ireland	4
Scotland	1
Sweden	2
Switzerland	2

Total number of cabinetmakers documented as to birth place: 359

This information came primarily from censuses. The birthplaces of cabinetmakers show an especially strong geographic connection directly to eastern sections of the South. From Tennessee, North Carolina, South Carolina, Virginia, and Kentucky came a healthy majority of the artisans. Thirteen percent of these makers whose birthplaces are known were foreign born. Cabinetmakers were listed here only when a source claimed to provide an actual birth place, as opposed to asserting that "he was from . . . ," or the equivalent.

NOTES

1. Reuben Gold Thwaites, *Early Western Travels, 1748– 1846: A Series of Annotated Reprints . . . , Nuttall's Travels into the Arkansa Territory, 1819.* Volume XIII (Cleveland, Ohio: The Authur H. Clark Company, 1905) 101.

2. Hubert B. Stroud and Gerald T. Hanson, *Arkansas Geography: The Physical Landscape and the Historical-Cultural Setting* (Little Rock: Rose Publishing Company, 1981) 27.

3. Dwight Munson Moore, *Trees of Arkansas* (Little Rock: Arkansas Forestry Commission, 1972) 27.

4. Stroud, 16, 29.

5. Ibid.

6. Moore, 8.

7. Ibid., 6.

8. Stroud, 30.

9. David Dale Owen, *First Report of a Geological Reconnoissance of the Northern Counties of Arkansas 1857–58* (Little Rock: Johnson & Yerkes, 1858) 112–45.

10. Stroud, 34; Moore, 5.

11. *Southern Shield,* 27 September 1851.

12. *Arkansas Gazette;* 16 January 1827.

13. Ibid., 19 February 1840. Onstot does not appear in Washington County census records after 1860.

14. Ibid., 26 March 1852.

15. Elizabeth A. Ingerman, "Personal Experience of an Old New York Cabinetmaker," *Antiques* (November 1963): 580.

16. Carl Bridenbaugh, *The Colonial Craftsman* (Chicago: The University of Chicago Press, 1950) 31.

17. Wendell Garrett, "The Matter of Consumer's Taste," in *Country Cabinetwork and Simple City Furniture,* ed. John D. Morse (Charlottesville: University Press of Virginia, 1970) 225–26.

18. Unpublished survey of all householders included in the 1850 and 1860 United States Census Schedules of Population for Pulaski, Independence, Benton, and Dallas counties. Data available from the Arkansas Territorial Restoration.

19. A survey of Benton County Tax Assessment 1840–70 U.S. Census 7–9. Benton County.

20. Frederick Jackson Turner, "The Significance of the American Frontier in American History," Paper delivered to the American Historical Association, Chicago, 1893.

21. Garrett, 225–26.

22. Irving H. Bartlett, *The American Mind in the Mid-Nineteenth Century* (New York: Thomas Y. Crowell Company, 1967) 41.

23. *Charleston Courier*, 12 December 1840.

24. *Arkansas Gazette*, 9 October 1858.

25. Ibid., 31 July 1858.

26. Garrett, 228.

27. Page Talbot, "Philadelphia Furnituremakers and Manufacturers, 1850–1880," in *Victorian Furniture: Essays from a Victorian Society Autumn Symposium*, ed. Kenneth L. Ames (Philadelphia: The Victorian Society in America, 1982) 90–91.

28. Friedrich Gerstäcker, *Wild Sports in the Far West*, eds. E. L. Steeves and H. R. Steeves (Durham: Duke University Press, 1968) 201.

29. *Arkansas Gazette*, 7 October 1834.

30. Jane E. Sikes, *The Furniture Makers of Cincinnati 1790 to 1849* (Cincinnati: Jane Sikes, 1976) 46.

31. Ibid., 48.

32. *Southwest Independent*, 28 January 1854.

33. *Arkansas Gazette*, 8 February 1850.

34. Ibid., 16 July 1854.

35. Talbot, 91; Jan M. Seidler, "A Tradition in Transition: The Boston Furniture Industry, 1840–1880," in Ames ed., 82.

36. Seidler, 82.

37. Probate file, Pulaski County 1855, Arkansas History Commission.

38. Robert W. Haberstein and William M. Lamere, *The History of American Funeral Directing* (Milwaukee: Bulfin Printers, 1955) 225–37.

Biographical Appendix of Arkansas Furnituremakers

Abbey, O. L.

"Abbey, O. L. cabinet maker, bds 301 Center." LRCD, 1871, 33.

Agnew, Andrew

Cabinetmaker, A.67, B.SC: MCR 1850 Washington Co., Roll 31, AHC. Cabinetmaker, A.77, B.SC: MCR 1860 Washington Co., Roll 52, AHC. Also listed in WCTR 1844–46, Roll 61, 1847–49, and 1851–55, Roll 62, and 1861, Roll 63, AHC.

Alberty, E. F.

Cabinetmaker, A.49, B.Germany: MCR 1860 Arkansas Co., Roll 37, AHC.

Alexander, D. E.

Alexander made Desks, & etc. for the Legislature at Washington, Arkansas, warrant 113, State Auditors Office, 10–1–64. He also made 4 chests and a desk for Sec of State, warrant 28. State Auditors Office, 1–24–65.

Allen, H. J.

Master Carpenter, A.30, B.TN: MCR 1860 Clark Co., Roll 39, AHC. "Cabinet Shop. . . . The Principle articles which he intends manufacturing are . . . Sideboards, Secretaries, Escrutoirs, Desks, Bureaus, Ladies Dressing do., Column do., Plain do. Sofas, Lounges, Wardrobes, Cases . . . Tables and Bedsteads of Every Quality and Price. . . . his work, which embraces a great variety from Cradle to the Coffin. . . . Funerals furnished. Also old Furniture Repaired with neatness and dispatch." *OCJ* 7–14–61.

Allen, Jethro

Mattressmaker, A.26, B.TN: MCR 1860 Clark Co., Roll 39, AHC.

Anderson, Armstead

Cabinetmaker, A.46, B.TN: MCR 1870 Carroll Co., Roll 49, AHC.

Anderson, William

Cabinetmaker, A.21, B.MO: MCR 1870 Carroll Co., Roll 49, AHC.

Annear, William

Cabinetmaker, A.33, B.England: MCR 1850 Pulaski Co., Roll 29, AHC. "Furniture Manufactory." *AG* 2–8–50. Also listed in PCTR 1840–48 (pt.), Roll 1; 1848 (pt.)–56, Roll 2; and 1857–58, Roll 3, ATR.

Anschutz, John

Cabinetmaker, A.41, B.MS: MCR 1850 Jackson Co., Roll 27, AHC.

Archer, Dennis

Chairmaker, A.45, B.TN: MCR 1850 Hempstead Co., Roll 26, AHC.

Armstrong, John

Cabinetmaker, A.22, B.Sweden: MCR 1870 Pulaski Co., Roll 62, AHC.

Arnett, ?

Cabinetmaker, A.Unknown, B.GA: MCR 1860 Sevier Co., Roll 51, AHC.

Arnett, John C.

[Cabinetmaker] Carpenter, A.47, B.KY: MCR 1850 Hempstead Co., Roll 26, AHC. "New Cabinet Shop!! Skinner and Arnett." *WT* 12–22–58. Skinner and Arnett, cabinetmakers; Hempstead Co., Ark., *Products of Industry* 1860, Roll 16, AHC. Also listed in HCTR 1848–54, Roll 74, and 1857–65, Roll 75, AHC.

Arnold, James

Cabinet workman, A.27, B.GA: MCR 1860 Sevier Co., Roll 51, AHC.

Arnold, William

Cabinetmaker, A.33, B.GA: MCR 1860 Sevier Co., Roll 51, AHC.

Bade, Jaeb

Cabinetmaker, A.40, B.Switzerland: MCR 1870 Crawford Co., Roll 51, AHC.

Badgett, Rev. Joel L.

[Cabinetmaker] Secondary Source: Rev. Badgett was born in Mississippi in 1837. His family moved to Arkansas in 1841, first settling in Saline Co., and in 1845 in Cleveland Co. [Rison]. In 1861 he worked in his father's [Silas Badgett's] cabinetshop for one year. After the Civil War he worked as a carpenter and stock dealer in Little Rock. In 1871 he settled in Rison to farm, and in 1884 he began his ministry. *Goodspeed Southern Arkansas*, 598–99.

Badgett, Silas

Cabinetmaker, A.60, B.NC: MCR 1860 Bradley Co., Roll 38, AHC. *See* Joel Badgett

Baer, Ferdinand

"Furniture Repaired. F. Baer & C. Turkies Main St. Little Rock. . . . Have on hand Bureaus, bedsteads, chairs, tables, washstands, cribs, etc. . . . Coffins of all descriptions furnished at the shortest notice. . . ." *UU* 9–14–65. Also listed in Pulaski Co. tax records 1863–68, Roll 175, AHC. "Cabinetmakers & Undertakers F. Baer & T. Thomas . . . Old furniture neatly repaired, varnished, etc. . . . Particular attention given to burials . . . Hearse and carriage furnished. . . ." *AG* 8–18–69.

Baggett, John

Cabinetmaker, A.27, B.AL: MCR 1860 Bradley Co., Roll 38, AHC.

Baker, John

Cabinetmaker, A.30, B.England: MCR 1860 Sevier Co., Roll 51, AHC.

Banister, W. L.

Cabinetmaker, A.21, B.SC: MCR 1860 Drew Co. (Monticello), Roll 41, AHC.

Banzer, Lorenz

Cabinetmaker, A.30, B.Switzerland: MCR 1860 Jefferson Co., Roll 44, AHC.

Barnes, Harvey

Cabinetmaker, A.38, B.CT: MCR 1850 Madison Co., Roll 27, AHC.

Barnes, Henry

Cabinetmaker, A.27, B.Prussia: MCR 1860 Benton Co., Roll 37, AHC.

Bassham, ?

Secondary Source: Brother and partner of Joseph P. Bassham in a cabinet shop at Clarksville which was in business ca. 1854–57. *Goodspeed Northwestern Arkansas,* 1288.

Bassham, Jonathan

Secondary Source: Jonathan Bassham was born in Franklin County, Virginia, around 1796. He was a soldier in the War of 1812 and a cabinetmaker and farmer. He moved to Johnson County, Arkansas, in 1839 from Virginia and remained there until his death in 1848. *Goodspeed Northwestern Arkansas,* 1288.

Bassham, Joseph P.

Secondary Source: The son of Jonathan Bassham, Joseph Bassham was born in Tazewell, West Virginia, May 12, 1827. He was a cabinetmaker and farmer and married three times, fathering nineteen children. He and a brother opened a cabinet shop in Clarksville, which they managed until 1857. Bassham then moved to Sebastian County, and on October 8, 1863, he enlisted in Company F, Second Arkansas Volunteer Infantry, U.S. Army, and received an appointment as an orderly. After the Civil War he returned to Sebastian County and engaged in farming. *Goodspeed Northwestern Arkansas,* 1288–89.

Bates, Daniel

Cabinet workman, A.25, B.GA: MCR 1860 Sevier Co., Roll 51, AHC.

Baxter, M. M.

Secondary Source: A cabinetmaker, born March 15, 1834, in Georgia, Baxter came to Hempstead Co., Arkansas from Indiana in 1869. He earned the reputation as an exceptionally fine cabinetmaker and millwright. *Goodspeed Southern Arkansas,* 390.

Beam, J.

"Turning and Cabinet Business. The undersigned carries on extensively the above business at Madden's Mills, on Big Piney, where he will be pleased to fill any orders for cabinet Work or Turning. . . . Orders for turning columns from Little Rock, or any other part of the state, will be punctually attented to. Orders to be sent to the subscriber at Clifton Post Office, Johnson County, Ark. J. Beam." *AG* 6–11–38.

Beaumister (Baumeister), Henry

Cabinettmaker, A.27, B.Prussia: MCR 1860 Benton Co., Roll 37, AHC. Also listed in BCTR 1860, Roll 39; 1867, Roll 40; and 1868 and 1869, Roll 41, AHC. Secondary Source: In 1860 Bentonville contained five general stores in addition to the furniture store of Henry Beaumister. *Goodspeed Northwestern Arkansas,* 96.

Beaver, M. V.

Cabinetmaker, A.22, B.NC: MCR 1860 Madison Co., Roll 45, AHC.

Bentley, Joseph E.

Cabinetmaker, A.44, B.VA: MCR 1850 Independence Co., Roll 26, AHC. Also listed in ICTR 1842–49, Roll 56, and 1850–52, Roll 59, AHC.

Berryman, George

"Cabinet Manufactory. Berryman & Ostwald." *AG* 8–20–49. "Furniture Manufactory. Ostwald & Berryman Cabinet and Chair-Makers." *AG* 5–24–50. Cabinetmaker, A.48, B.VA: MCR 1850 Pulaski Co., Roll 29, AHC. Also listed in PCTR 1840, 1843, and 1845–48(pt.), Roll 1, and 1848(pt.)–55, Roll 2, ATR. Deceased, February 1, 1855, probate file, Pulaski Co., AHC.

Birnie, Charles A., Jr.

"Upholstering & Mattress Manufacturing George S. and Charles A. Birnie." *FSNE* 12–23–70. Secondary Source: "Charles A. Birnie Jr. was a resident of Fort Smith from childhood on. After service (CSA) in the Civil War, he went into the furniture business with his uncle, George S. Birnie. Their business was mainly retail sales, but some small scale manufacturing was done in their furniture shop. When George retired from the business, c. 1876, Charles continued on alone." Bernard Johnson III, "Fort Smith Furniture Manufacturers of The Late 19th Century." Old Fort Museum: Fort Smith, Arkansas. 1982, 13.

Birnie, Cornelius

Mattress Manufacturer, A.20, B.TN: MCR 1860 Sebastian Co., Roll 50, AHC.

Birnie, George S.

See Charles Birnie

Birnie, Nealey

"Mattress Manufactory Nealey Birnie also repairs . . . sofas and chairs . . . Ft. Smith." *FSTWB* 6–24–62.

Bis——?——(smear) & Bris——?——,

Cabinet shop [Cabinetmakers], Sebastian Co., *Products of Industry* 1870, Roll 18, AHC.

Bittle, W. A.

"House Carpenter and furniture Manufacturer. Arkadelphia, Ark. . . . A good cabinet workman can find a permanent situation by applying soon." *OCJ* 7–4–61, ATR.

Blackburn, Sylvanus W.

[Cabinetmaker] Miller, A.41, B.SC: MCR 1850 Washington Co., Roll 31, AHC. Secondary Source: Blackburn lived in Tennessee until he was 21 years old. Then, in 1832, he traveled to the Ozark Mountains in Arkansas. By 1832 he had a blacksmith shop, sawmill, and gristmill. Later he opened a carpenter's shop where all the family's furniture was made. The shop also produced coffins for the family and for neighbors. Blackburn died on March 18, 1890. Vera Key, *The Benton County Pioneer* (Benton County Historical Society, 1955), 2–4.

Blakely, John

[Cabinetmaker] Listed in Washington Co. tax records 1854–55, Roll 62; and 1856, Roll 63, AHC. Cabinet workman, A.28, B.TN: MCR 1860 Washington Co., Roll 52, AHC.

Blaylock, William

Carpenter & Cabinetmaker, A.42, B.NC: MCR 1860 Jefferson Co., Roll 44, AHC. Also listed in JCTR 1858, 1860, Roll 116, 1861–62 and 1865, Roll 117, and 1866 and 1868, Roll 118, AHC.

Blennerhassett, Thomas Spotswood

"Cabinet ware Manufactured By a Regular bred Cabinetmaker . . . inform the citizens of Fayetteville and surrounding country that I have determined to carry on the Cabinet Business. . . ." *SWI* 1–28–54. Also listed in Washington Co. tax records 1854, Roll 62, AHC.

Bochal, Julius

Cabinetmaker, A.28, B.Hungary: MCR 1850 Pulaski Co., Roll 29, AHC.

Bostwick, Miller J.

Cabinetmaker apprentice, A.18, B.MO: MCR 1850 Crawford Co., Roll 25, AHC.

Bowers, Bryant M.

Cabinet workman, A.28, B.TN: MCR 1860 Randolph Co., Roll 49, AHC.

Bowers, Robert

Cabinetmaker, A.28, B.SC: MCR 1860 Benton Co., Roll 37, AHC.

Bowers, William M.

Cabinetmaker, A.33, B.TN: MCR 1850 Washington Co., Roll 31, AHC. Also listed in WCTR 1848–49 and 1851–54, Roll 62, AHC. "Fayetteville Cabinet Shop . . . long successful in the line of cabinet making . . . will manufacture to order . . . bureaus, bedsteads, tables, centre tables, wardrobes, secretaries, safes, wash stands, etc. . . . Bowers and Buie." *SWI* 2–17–55.

Boyd, Green W.

Cabinetmaker, A.25, B.AR: MCR 1850 Johnson Co. (Clarksville), Roll 27, AHC.

Boyd, Thomas J. (A)

Cabinetmaker, A.32, B.NC: MCR 1860 Prairie Co., Roll 48, AHC.

Brackney, John

Cabinetmaker, A.21, B.IN: MCR 1850 Hempstead Co., Roll 26, AHC. Also listed in HCTR 1851–52, Roll 74, and 1858, Roll 75, AHC.

Bradley, Daniel

Chairmaker, A.36, B.AL: MCR 1860 Saline Co., Roll 50, AHC.

Bradshaw, William H.

Cabinetworkman, A.52, B.VA: MCR 1870 Greene Co., Roll 54, AHC.

Bratten, T. G.

Cabinetmaker, A.22, B.TN: MCR 1860 Clark Co., Roll 39, AHC.

Brickell, Nicholas

Cabinetmaker, A.46, B.NC: MCR 1870 Phillips Co., Roll 60, AHC. Secondary Source: In 1870 Brickell moved to Phillips County from Franklin, Georgia. In 1875 he moved his cabinetshop to Poplar Grove, Arkansas. *Goodspeed Eastern Arkansas,* 752–53.

Brooks, William

Cabinetmaker, A.33, B.NC: MCR Benton Co. (Bentonville), Roll 47, AHC.

Brown, Charles

Cabinetmaker, A.40, B.NY: MCR 1870 Benton Co., Roll 47, AHC.

Brown, George H.

Cabinetworkman, A.37, B.NY: MCR 1860 Sevier Co., Roll 51, AHC. Also listed in SCTR 1869–72, Roll 49, AHC.

Brown, H. R.

Cabinetmaker, A.31, B.TN: MCR 1850 Washington Co., Roll 31, AHC.

Brown, William V.

Cabinetmaker, A.25, B.TN: MCR 1860 Madison Co., Roll 45, AHC.

Brunson, J.

Cabinetwork, A.46, B.GA: MCR 1870 Ouachita Co., Roll 59, AHC.

Bryant, David

Cabinetmaker, A.26, B.NC: MCR 1860 Dallas Co., Roll 40, AHC. Also listed in DCTR 1858, 1861–62, and 1867, Roll 45, AHC.

Bryant, Robert

Cabinetmaker, A.45, B.VA: MCR 1860 Randolph Co., Roll 49, AHC.

Buchanan, J. H. (James)

Cabinetmaker, A.29, B.KY: MCR 1850 Pope Co., Roll 29, AHC. Also listed in PCTR 1845, 1847–49, and 1851–52, Roll 65, AHC. James Buchanan and Eleazar Cady made drawers, blinds, and furniture for the state supreme court offices between 1841 and 1851. General Warrant Register Book, Auditor of State.

Bucher, Charles

Cabinet Workman, A.40, B.Germany: MCR 1850 Benton Co., Roll 58, AHC.

Buie, John

Cabinetmaker, A.36, B.TN: MCR 1860 Washington Co., Roll 52, AHC. Buie and Stigowest, Cabinetmakers, Washington Co., Ark., *Products of Industry* 1860, Roll 7, AHC. Also listed in WCTR 1851, 1853 (1854 J. W. Buie listed in Madison Co. tax records, Roll 19), 1855, Roll 62, and 1859 and 1861, Roll 63, AHC. Cabinet workman, A.46, B.TN: MCR 1870 Washington Co., Roll 66, AHC. *See* William Bowers

Bullion, George

Cabinetmaker, A.24, B.TN: MCR 1870 Benton Co., Roll 47, AHC.

Burkett, John

Secondary Source: Burkett moved his family from Mississippi around 1870 and settled on Ballard Creek. The farm is still called "the Burkett place." Besides farming, Burkett had a small furniture factory. Several pieces of his furniture are still used in the community. Zella Cann and Eugene Gibson, *A History of Summers Community* (Summers Community Club: Washington Co., No date) Washington Co., Roll 71, AHC.

Cady, E. (Eleazer)

[Cabinetmaker] Carpenter, A.35, B.RI: MCR 1850 Pulaski Co., Roll 29, AHC. *See* J. Buchanan

Callen, A. G.

Cabinet workman, A.22, B.TN: MCR 1850 Carroll Co., Roll 25, AHC.

Callis, Henry

Cabinetmaker, A.50, B.VA: MCR 1860 Benton Co., Roll 37, AHC. Cabinetmaker, A.60, B.VA: MCR 1870 Benton Co., Roll 47, AHC.

Callis, Samuel

Cabinett, A.23, B.TN: MCR 1860 Benton Co., Roll 37, AHC.

Callis, William

Cabinet Workman, A.50, B.VA: MCR 1860. Benton Co., Roll 37, AHC. Also listed in BCTR 1865(pt.)–67, Roll 40, 1868–73, Roll 41, and 1874–79, Roll 42, AHC.

Campbell, Asa

Chairmaker, A.24, B.TN: MCR 1860 Franklin Co., Roll 41, AHC.

Campbell, Joel R.

Cabinet Workman, A.32, B.TN: MCR 1870 Greene Co., Roll 54, AHC.

Cannon, John

Cabinet Workman, A.27, B.TN: MCR 1860 Sevier Co., Roll 51, AHC. Also listed in SCTR 1857 and 1860–61, Roll 47, 1862–66, Roll 48, and 1870–72, Roll 49, AHC.

Carr, Joshua

Chairmaker, A.45, B.OH: MCR 1870 Crawford Co., Roll 51, AHC.

Carroll, John

"Fort Smith———Mattress Factory." *VBP* 3–2–60.

Carter, Thomas

Cabinet Workman, A.56, B.KY: MCR 1860 Lawrence Co., Roll 45, AHC.

Casey, Aaron

Chairmaker, A.47, B.TN: MCR Hot Spring Co., Roll 42, AHC.

Chamberlain, Richard

Cabinetmaker, A.45, B.SC: MCR 1850 Hempstead Co., Roll 26, AHC. Also listed in HCTR, 1841–42 and 1847–53, Roll 74, AHC.

Chambers, Elijah

Cabinet Workman, A.37, B.NY: MCR 1850 Benton Co., Roll 25, AHC. Wagon-maker, A.40, B.KY: MCR 1860 Benton Co., Roll 37, AHC. Also listed BCTR 1843–44, 1846, 1848–56, and 1859, Roll 39, AHC.

Chandler, Bailey

Cabinetmaker, A.30, B.SC: MCR 1850 Pulaski Co., Roll 29, AHC.

Chandler, John

Chairmaker, A.37, B.IL: MCR 1870 Washington Co., Roll 66, AHC.

Clark, M. C.

Cabinet Workman, A.40, B.AR: MCR 1860 Columbia Co., Roll 39, AHC.

Clayton, W. E.

Cabinetmaker, A.39, B.VA: MCR 1860 White Co., Roll 52, AHC. Also listed as a cabinetmaker in the White Co. census for 1870.

Clemons, James

Cabinetmaker, A.25, B.GA: MCR 1850 Independence Co., Roll 26, AHC. Also listed in ICTR 1850–58(pt.), Roll 59, AHC.

Clendining, John

Furniture Merchant, A.35, B.Ireland: MCR 1870 Phillips Co., Roll 60, AHC. Also listed in PCTR, 1850–

58, Roll 88, AHC. "Southern Furniture House, John Clendining, Manufacturer, Importer and Dealer." *HWC* 2–11–69.

Clingman, Alex M.

Cabinetmaker, A.20, B.TN: MCR 1850 Clark Co., Roll 25, AHC.

Cole, Sam B.

Cabinetmaker, A.24, B.TN: MCR 1860 Marion Co., Roll 46, AHC.

Collins, Josiah T.

[Cabinetmaker] Listed in 1850 Hempstead Co. tax records, Roll 74, AHC. "Cabinet Warehouse, Washington, Arkansas, Josiah T. Collins." *WT* 12–3–51.

Condell, Richard

Cabinetmaker, A.31, B.IN: MCR 1870 Pulaski Co., Roll 62, AHC.

Conditt, Jeduthan Lindley

Secondary Source: Conditt was a cabinet workman and wagon maker from Tennessee. He moved to Bird township in 1856 and purchased a farm. He was active in religious and educational interest and directed the organization of the local school district. He died in 1863. *Goodspeed Northeastern Arkansas*, 850.

Cook, Isaac

Cabinetmaker, A.52, B.VA: MCR 1860 Benton Co., Roll 37, AHC. Farmer, A.62, B.VA: MCR 1870 Benton Co., Roll 47, AHC. Also listed in BCTR 1855–56, 1859, and 1860–61, Roll 39, 1867, Roll 40, and 1869–70 and 1874, Roll 41, AHC.

Cook, James

Cabinetmakers, Ditter and Cook, Pulaski Co. 1870 Industrial Census, Roll 18, AHC. The census indicates that Cook and Ditter had exhausted more than 50,000 ft. of oak, pine, mahogany, walnut, and cypress to construct 35 desks, 40 wardrobes, and 300 coffins.

Cooper, W. V. L.

"Delaney and Cooper, Cabinet and Carpenter's Job Shop." *SS* 3–18–54. Cooper was also listed in Phillips Co. tax records, 1850–58, Roll 88, AHC.

Corsuch, C. L.

"Cabinetmaker. Main and Locust St., Batesville." *NAT* 12–25–69.

Cottrell, William

Cabinetmaker, A.47, B.OH: MCR 1850 Arkansas Co., Roll 62, AHC.

Covey, Welcome Boy

Cabinet Workman, A.37, B.TN: MCR 1850 Benton Co., Roll 25, AHC. Cabinet Workman, A.47, B.TN: MCR 1860 Benton Co., Roll 37, AHC. Farmer, A.57, B.TN: MCR 1870 Benton Co., Roll 47, AHC. Also listed in BCTR 1844, 1846, 1848–54, 1856, and 1859, Roll 39; 1867, Roll 40; 1869–70, Roll 41; and 1874, Roll 42, AHC. Covey died in Benton Co. on June 24, 1880. *Cemeteries of Benton County Arkansas*, Vol. VI, 1975, Northwest Arkansas Genealogical Society, 80. Secondary Source: In addition to being an able preacher of the Christian Church, Welcome Boy was an excellent woodworkman. At the time of his arrival in Benton County, most people's beds were made by nailing boards to the walls in a corner of a room. Covey concieved the idea of making bedsteads detached from the walls, so they could be moved about the room. Letter, Susan LeDuc to Judith Stewart Abernathy (ATR Registrar), dated May 29, 1988, Hermitage, TN.

Cowan, Thomas

Cabinet workman, A.53, B.OH: MCR 1850 Benton Co., Roll 25, AHC. Also listed in BCTR 1844–45 and 1850–55, Role 39, AHC.

Cowden, Albert I.

Cabinetmaker apprentice, A.20, B.AL: MCR 1870 Jackson Co., Roll 56, AHC.

Cowden, James

Chairmaker, A.30, B.TN: MCR 1870 Washington Co., Roll 66, AHC.

Cox, William R.

Casketmaker, A.24, B.PA: MCR 1860 Pulaski Co., Roll 49, AHC.

Curry, William F.

Cabinetmaker, A.37, B.PA: MCR 1850 Independence Co., Roll 26, AHC. Also listed in ICTR 1840, 1848–49, and 1851, Roll 57, AHC.

Curtis, George

Cabinetmaker, A.25, B.MA: MCR 1870 Pulaski Co., Roll 62, AHC.

Curtis, James

Cabinetworkman, A.30, B.IL: MCR 1860 Washington Co., Roll 52, AHC.

Curtis, Nathaniel

Chairmaker, A.36, B.KY: MCR 1850 Carroll Co., Roll 25, AHC.

Dauchirty, Amos

Cabinetworkman, A.29, B.AL: MCR 1860 Phillips Co., Roll 47, AHC.

Daugherty (Dougherty), Samuel

"Furniture-Turning, Repairing and Upholstering. . . . England and Daugherty." *AI* 9–25–47. Cabinetmaker, A.30, B.VA: MCR 1850 Crawford Co., Roll 25, AHC. Also listed in Crawford Co. census as a cabinetmaker 1860–80. Listed in CCTR 1842–46 and 1849–51, Roll 22, 1854–55, 1857–61, and 1866–68, Roll 23, AHC. "Furniture . . . Dougherty & Glass. . . ." *VBP* 12–14–66. Daugherty & Glass; furniture shop [Cabinetmaker]; Crawford Co. (Van Buren) *Products of Industry* 1870, Roll 18, AHC. Daugherty died on September 22, 1883, in Van Buren. Eno Collection, Box 1, Album-Funeral Notices.

Davis, Henry

Joiner/Carpenter, A.25, B.MS: MCR 1870 Phillips Co., Roll 60, AHC.

Davis, Porter A.

Cabinetmaker, A.68, B.GA: MCR 1860 Bradley Co., Roll 38, AHC.

Dawson, Edward

[Cabinetmaker] A.28, B.KY: MCR 1850 Washington Co., Roll 31, AHC. Cabinetworkman, A.43, B.KY: MCR 1860 Washington Co. (Fayetteville), Roll 52, AHC. Also listed in WCTR 1856–67, Roll 63, AHC.

Delaney, Thomas J.

[Cabinetmaker] Trader, A.30, B.KY: MCR 1860 Phillips Co., Roll 47, AHC. Grocer, A.40, B.KY: MCR 1870 Phillips Co. (Helena), Roll 60, AHC. Also listed in PCTR 1854–58, Roll 88, and 1859–61 and 1866–67, Roll 89, AHC. *See* W. V. L. Cooper.

Dennis, Benjamin

Cabinetmaker, A.23, B.Washington, D.C.: MCR 1850 Jefferson Co., Roll 27, AHC.

Devinney, C. B.

"Upholstery . . . Little Rock . . . on Main St. . . where he will attend to the manufacture of mattresses and cushions. . . ." *AG* 4–22–40.

Ditter, Francis

[Cabinetmaker] "Dissolution of Partnership" [with Augustus Ostwald] *AG* 7–23–52. "Furniture Establishment Francis Detter Cabinetmaker and Undertaker." *AG* 7–15–53. "A Fine Assortment of Furniture for Sale." *TD* 3–3–57. Also listed in Pulaski Co. tax records 1850–53, 1855–58, 1861–63, and 1865–68. Ditter, a native of Germany, lived in Little Rock from 1849 until his death in 1870. *AG* 11–6–70. *See* James Cook

Dorman, G. W.

Cabinetmaker, A.30, B.GA: MCR 1850 Dallas Co., Roll 26, AHC. Also listed in DCTR 1850, Roll 45, AHC.

Douglas, Thomas

Chairmaker, A.23, B.DC: MCR 1850 Pulaski Co., Roll 29, AHC.

Drake, William

"Chairs, Chairs, Chairs . . . at Prasch's old stand, Little Rock, Ark." *AG* 4–11–57.

Duffer, R. O.

Cabinetmaker, A.43, B.TN: MCR 1870 Jackson Co., Roll 56, AHC.

Edlin, A. H.

Seller of Furniture, A.29, B.IN: MCR 1870 Crawford Co., Roll 51, AHC.

Edmondson, E.

"Edmondson, E., cabinet-maker, 114 e Markham." LRCD, 1871, 63.

Edmonson, S. B.

"Edmonson, S. B., cabinet-maker, 212 Elm." LRCD, 1871, 63.

Edwards, ?

"Edwards, ———, cabinet-maker, bds 402 e Second." LRCD, 1871, 63.

Elkins, Funbin (Turbin)

Cabinetmaker, A.29, B.VA: MCR 1860 Crawford Co., Roll 40, AHC. Also listed in CCTR 1858–60 and 1866–68, Roll 23, AHC. Farm Laborer, A.40, B.VA: MCR 1870 Crawford Co., Roll 51, AHC.

Elmore, Elijah

Cabinetmaker, A.35, B.AR: MCR 1870 Clark Co., Roll 49, AHC.

Emrich, John

Cabinetmaker, A.30, B.Germany: MCR 1860 Sebastian Co., Roll 50, AHC.

England, W. F.

"Cabinet Wareroom I. J. Howard W. F. England . . . Markham St. Sofas, Mahogany rockers, other chairs, sideboards, bureaus, . . . *ATA* 12–13–41. Cabinet-

maker, A.36, B.Germany: MCR 1860 Pulaski Co., Roll 49, AHC.

England, William F.

"Cabinet Maker, Undertaker, Chair & Sofa Manufacturer." *AI* 7–21–49. Cabinetmaker, A.34, B.SC: MCR 1850 Crawford Co., Roll 25, AHC. Also listed as a cabinetmaker in the 1860 Crawford Co. census. Listed in CCTR 1849–51, Roll 22, and 1854–55, 1857–60, and 1865–68, Roll 23, AHC. *See* S. Daugherty

Enshaw, John

Cabinetmaker, A.22, B.Germany: MCR 1860 Prairie Co., Roll 48, AHC.

Ervin, Wade H.

Cabinetmaker, A.39, B.IN: MCR 1850 Independence Co., Roll 26, AHC.

Estes, N. C.

Cabinetmaker, A.25, B.AL: MCR 1860 Carroll Co., Roll 38, AHC.

Estill, Benjamin G.

Cabinetmaker, A.43, B.TN: MCR 1850 Washington Co., Roll 31, AHC. Also listed as a cabinetmaker in the 1860 Washington Co. census. Secondary Source: Benjamin G. Estill was listed as being one of the postmasters of Washington County in August of 1835. *Goodspeed Northwestern Arkansas*, 319.

Evans, Andrew J.

Cabinetmaker, A.45, B.NC: MCR 1870 Pulaski Co., Roll 62, AHC.

Evans, S.

Cabinetmaker, A.33, B.NC: MCR 1860 Dallas Co., Roll 40, AHC.

Ewing, John

Cabinetmaker, A.38, B.KY: MCR 1850 Pope Co., Roll 29, AHC. Carpenter, A.46, B.KY: MCR 1860, Roll 48, AHC. Also listed in PCTR 1849, 1851–54, 1856–59, Roll 65, and 1860, Roll 66, AHC.

Falkner, Dickeson

Cabinetmaker, A.62, B.NC: MCR 1860 Craighead Co., Roll 40, AHC.

Farrell, Jimmy

Matrass Maker, A.45, B.Ireland: MCR 1860 Phillips Co., Roll 47, AHC.

Faught, J. C.

Cabinetwork, A.48, B.AL: MCR 1870 Montgomery Co., Roll 59, AHC.

Faulkner, Louis R.

Chairmaker, A.34, B.AL: MCR 1870 Craighead Co., Roll 51, AHC.

Fenter, David

Chairmaker, A.55, B.NC: MCR 1850 Hot Spring Co., Roll 26, AHC.

Fields, Green B.

Cabinetmaker, A.29, B.TN: MCR 1860 Sebastian Co., Roll 50, AHC.

Floyd, Richard

[Cabinetmaker] A.16, B.AL: MCR 1850 Johnson Co., Roll 27, AHC. Cabinetmaker, A.27, B.AL: MCR 1860 Johnson Co. (War Eagle), Roll 44, AHC. Also listed as a cabinetmaker in the Johnson Co. census for 1870.

Foles, Wiley

Chairmaker, A.35, B.TN: MCR 1850 Clark Co., Roll 25, AHC.

Forkner, L. R.

Woodworkman, A.27, B.AL: MCR 1860 Craighead Co., Roll 40, AHC.

Forrest, Frank

Cabinet workman, A.30, B.OH: MCR 1870 Van Buren Co., Roll 51, AHC.

Fraiser, David

Cabinetmaker, A.63, B.NC: MCR 1860 Newton Co., Roll 46, AHC.

Franklin, William

Cabinetmaker, A.47, B.VA: MCR 1870 Yell Co., Roll 67, AHC.

Franks, F. A.

"New Cabinet & Carpenter's Shop . . . in West Helena on Porter Street . . . furnishing doors, blinds, sashes, . . . coffins . . . at reasonable, 'live and let live prices.' George W. and F. A. Franks." *SS* 6–27–57.

Franks, G. W.

[Cabinetmaker] Master Carpenter, A.31, B.AR: MCR 1860 Phillips Co. (Helena), Roll 47, AHC. Also listed in PCTR 1855–56 and 1858, Roll 88, and 1859–60, Roll 89, AHC. "Cabinet & Carpenter Shop George W. Franks." *SS* 1–28–60. *See* F. A. Franks

Freeman, Joseph

Cabinet Maker, A.42, B.KY: MCR 1860 Pope Co., Roll 48, AHC. Also listed in PCTR 1858, Roll 65, and 1860–61, Roll 66, AHC.

French, Samuel G.

While an officer stationed at Ft. Smith, Samuel Gibbs French made the table illustrated in figure F–44, according to a label fixed to the underside of the table's top.

Fritts, William H.

Cabinet Maker, A.30, B.VA: MCR 1860 Madison Co., Roll 45, AHC. Also listed in MCTR 1852–54, Roll 19, and 1861 and 1865, Roll 20, AHC.

Gary, ?

"Cabinet & Chair Manufactory—Young & Gary. . . . Helena . . . are informed that our boat is now lying at the landing, where we keep . . . a general assortment of cabinet and chair work. . . . Bedsteads, Bureaus, Tables, Safes, Stands & C., together with an assortment of windsor, splitbottom, and walnut cane—seat chairs. Also rocking chairs, settees, childrens chairs

. . . all of which we are now manufacturing on our boat. . . ." *SS* 2–22–51.

Gaskill, D. L. (S.)

Cabinet Maker, A.38, B.NC: MCR 1860 Madison Co. (Huntsville), Roll 45, AHC. Listed in MCTR 1856, Roll 19, AHC. Also listed as a cabinetmaker in the Madison Co. 1870 census.

Gaskill, Elias

Cabinetmaker, A.22, B.NC: MCR 1870 Madison Co., Roll 58, AHC.

Gillstrap, Thomas P.

Cabinetmaker, A.23, B.TN: MCR 1860 Crawford Co., Roll 40, AHC.

Gilson, ?

Rutherford & Gilson, cabinet [makers]: Benton County, Ark., *Products of Industry* 1870, Roll 16, AHC.

Glass, Henry

Cabinetmaker, A.29, B.Germany: MCR 1860 Crawford Co. (Van Buren), Roll 40, AHC. Listed in CCTR 1858, 1860, and 1866–67, Roll 23, AHC. Also listed as a cabinetmaker in the Crawford Co. 1880 census. *See* S. Daugherty

Glass, John

Apprentice Cabinetmaker, A.19, B.Germany: MCR 1860 Crawford Co., Roll 40, AHC. Cabinetmaker, A.30, B.Hesse Darm: MCR 1870 Sebastian Co., Roll 64, AHC. Also listed in SCTR 1875, Roll 23, AHC.

Glass, M.

M. Glass & Co., Cabinet shop [Cabinetmaker], Sebastian Co., *Products of Industry* 1870, Roll 18, AHC.

Glover, William

Matrass Maker, A.25, B.MS: MCR 1860 Phillips Co., Roll 47, AHC.

Godwin, Alexander

Cabinetmaker, A.40, B.KY: MCR 1850 Hot Spring Co., Roll 26, AHC.

Good, Eli W.

Cabinetmaker, A.38, B.VA: MCR 1860 Drew Co. (Monticello), Roll 41, AHC. Also listed in DCTR 1859, 1861–65, and 1865, Roll 74, AHC. B. C. Hyatt and Good, Cabinetmakers, Drew Co., Ark., *Products of Industry* 1860, Roll 8, AHC.

Gorsuch, C. C.

Cabinetmaker, A.40, B.MD: MCR 1870 Independence Co. (Batesville), Roll 55, AHC.

Gortney, Joseph

Chairmaker, A.46, B.SC: MCR 1870 Lafayette Co., Roll 57, AHC.

Gottchalk, William (Frederick W.)

Cabinetmaker, A.Unknown, B.Unknown: MCR 1860 Jefferson Co., Roll 44, AHC.

Gould, W. B.

Cabinetmaker, A.33, B.KY: MCR 1850 Pike Co., Roll 29, AHC. Secondary Source: Gould served as a representative from Pike County in 1854–55. He resided for several years in Hempstead County before moving to Pike County. *Goodspeed Southern Arkansas*, 308 and 327.

Grave, Herman

Cabinetmaker, A.34, B.Prussia: MCR 1870 Sebastian Co., Roll 64, AHC.

Green, Frederick

Cabinetworkman, A.36, B.Germany: MCR 1850 Benton Co., Roll 50, AHC. Listed in BCTR 1843–44, with Sager 1852–54, 1856, 1859–61, and 1865, Roll 39, and in 1867 with Sager, Roll 40, AHC. Farmer, A.46, B.Prussia: MCR 1860 Benton Co., Roll 37, AHC. Also listed in Benton Co. probate court records Book "C," 1871–84(pt.), AHC.

Green, Jordan

Cabinet Workman, A.35, B.TN: MCR 1860 Washington Co., Roll 52, AHC.

Gridstaff, J. T.

Molder, A.40, B.TN: MCR 1870 Ouachita Co., Roll 59, AHC.

Griffin, John

Cabinetmaker, A.25, B.Washington, D.C.: MCR 1850 Pulaski Co., Roll 29, AHC.

Griffin, Phinas

Cabinet Workman, A.18, B.OH: MCR 1850 Pulaski Co., Roll 29, AHC.

Griggs, James

Cabinet Workman, A.25, B.MO: MCR 1860 Sevier Co., Roll 51, AHC.

Griggs, Lorenzo D.

Cabinetmaker, A.25, B.AR: MCR 1860 Sevier Co., Roll 51, AHC.

Grimes, ?

"Cabinet Furniture Manufactory. At Washington, Hempstead Co. . . . Spence & Grimes. . . ." *WT* 11–3–41.

Grisham, W.

Cabinetmaker, A.21, B.MS: MCR 1870 Drew Co., Roll 52, AHC. "Grisham, William Edwin, (b.16 Oct. 1848; d.Tillar, Drew County) m. Eugenia Prewitt (b.14 Oct. 1853; d.18 Sept. 1895, Drew County)." Rebecca DeArmond, *Old Times Not Forgotten: A History of Drew County* (Little Rock: Rose Publishing Co., 1980), 375.

Gritts, W. H.

Cabinetworkman, A.40, B.VA: MCR 1870 Madison Co., Roll 58, AHC.

Gross, Henry

Cabinet Workman, A.40, B.OH: MCR 1870 Crawford Co., Roll 51, AHC.

Grubb, Jacob C.

"Furniture . . . the citizens of Little Rock . . . he has opened a chair and cabinet furniture commission warehouse on Markham St. . . ." *AG* 11–10–41. Also advertised in *AG* 7–6–42 and *AG* 7–24–43.

Grubbs, John B.

Woodworkman, A.46, B.VA: MCR 1850 Dallas Co., Roll 26, AHC.

Guibor, H.

"T. E. Watkins-late of St. Louis, H. Guibor-late of C.S. Army. Furniture for parlors, bedrooms, libraries, dining room and kitchen. Chairs & rockers, etc. Repairs, varnishers, upholsters, coffins made, undertakers. . . ." *AG* 10–23–66.

Gutton, John

"To the Public . . . a certain John Gutton, son-in-law of Raney P. Brown, living on Little Red River, has asserted, that he held a note on me . . . for services rendered in the carpenter's and cabinetmaker's line . . . it is a base forgery . . . Hewes Scull, Post of Arkansas." *AG* 12–2–28.

Hamilton, Alexander

Cabinetmaker, A.29, B.TN: MCR 1860 Poinsett Co., Roll 48, AHC.

Hamith, Hansin A.

Cabinetmaker, A.42, B.PA: MCR 1860 Crawford Co., Roll 40, AHC.

Hancock, J. L.

"Upholstery in all its branches . . . Little Rock . . . receives orders for Feather Beds, Moss, Shuck, Cotton & Straw Mattresses; Bolsters, Pillows, Cushions, Ottomans, etc. . . ." *AG* 7–15–40.

Haney (Haynie), William C.

Enumerated as a carpenter in the Pulaski County Censuses of 1850 and 1860. Haney made desks for the school in Pulaski County in 1858. He was paid $42.19 by G. D. Sizer, school commissioner. Report on a 16th Section School, Pulaski Co. records, Book "B", AHC.

Harris, Adolphus

[Cabinetmaker] Carpenter, A.37, B.NC: MCR 1860 Randolph Co., Roll 49, AHC. Secondary Source: Adolphus Harris emigrated from North Carolina to Pope County in 1851. He purchased eighty acres of land and carried on agricultural pursuits in connection with cabinetmaking. *Goodspeed Western Arkansas,* 231.

Hastings, Henry C.

Cabinet Workman, A.57, B.NC: MCR 1850 Benton Co., Roll 25, AHC. Listed as a farmer in the Benton Co. census for 1860 and 1870. Also listed in BCTR 1837–46, 1848–54, 1856, and 1859–60, Roll 59; 1867, Roll 40; and 1870 and 1873–74, Roll 41, AHC. Secondary Source: Hastings was one of the organizers of Benton County and served as the county's first sheriff. *Goodspeed Northwestern Arkansas,* 36.

Hawkins, Thomas

Cabinetmaker, A.23, B.TN: MCR 1860 Franklin Co., Roll 41, AHC.

Hawks, D. H.

[Cabinetmaker] Listed in Hempstead Co. tax records 1854, Roll 74, AHC. "Furniture Cabinet Manufactory." WT 1–2–56.

Hayton, W. M.

Cabinetmaker, A.38, B.TN: MCR 1860 Carroll Co., Roll 38, AHC.

Head, Joseph

Secondary Source: Head came to Washington County, Arkansas, from North Carolina in January 1855. He worked as a millwright, carpenter, and cabinetmaker. In 1862 he was taken prisoner by U.S. forces and sent to Springfield, where he died less than a year later. *Goodspeed Northwestern Arkansas,* 845.

Henkins and Son

Henkins and Son, Chair manufactory, Sebastian Co., *Products of Industry* 1870, Roll 18, AHC.

Herst, William M.

Cabinetmaker, A.27, B.PA: MCR 1860 Pulaski Co., Roll 49, AHC.

Hitt, John S.

Chairmaker, A.35, B.GA: MCR 1850 Ashley Co., Roll 25, AHC.

Hobbs, Jacob G.

Chairmaker, A.48, B.NC: MCR 1860 Pope Co., Roll 48, AHC.

Holaday, John W.

Chairmaker, A.67, B.GA: MCR 1860 Lafayette Co., Roll 45, AHC.

Holt, David

David was listed along with his father, Edward Holt, as a woodworkman in *The History of Craighead County, Arkansas,* Indexed by Harry Lee Williams, 1977, Reprint of the 1930 edition with index by the Craighead County Historical Society, 321.

Holt, Edward

Woodworkman, A.51, B.VA: MCR 1860 Craighead Co., Roll 40, AHC. *See* David Holt

Hornberg, C. F.

Cabinetworkman, A.30, B.Sweden: MCR 1870 Washington Co., Roll 66, AHC.

Hotchkiss, H. K.

[Cabinetmaker] Listed in the Izard Co. 1840 census. Cabinetmaker, A.52, B.VA: MCR 1850 Independence Co., Roll 26, AHC. Also listed in ICTR 1839–49, Roll 56, 1851, Roll 57, and 1852, Roll 58, AHC.

Hotchkiss, Hesekiah

Cabinetmaker, A.26, B.TN: MCR 1850 Independence Co., Roll 26, AHC.

Howard, Isaac J.

"New Cabinet Wareroom." *AG* 8–11–41. Cabinetmaker, A.41, B.KY: MCR 1850 Pulaski Co., Roll 29, AHC. Also listed in PCTR 1843 and 1845–48, Roll 1, and 1850, Roll 2, ATR. *See* W. F. England

Howard, J. J.

Cabinetmaker, A.35, B.OH: MCR 1850 Pulaski Co., Roll 29, AHC.

Huckabey, Daniel F.

Secondary Source: Huckabey moved to Arkansas in 1839 and worked initially as a cabinetmaker, later combining this trade with farming. He went on to attend medical school in South Carolina. *Goodspeed Western Arkansas,* 158.

Huddleston, John G.

Cabinetmaker, A.36, B.TN: MCR 1860 Lawrence Co., Roll 45, AHC.

Hyatt, Benjamin C.

Secondary Source: Hyatt immigrated to Arkansas in 1846 with his wife and children. He was first a mechanic and then a Baptist minister until his death in 1887. *Goodspeed Southern Arkansas,* 956. *See* Eli Good

Hybart (Hygarth), Charles

Hygarth, Charles, Mattressmaker, Pulaski Co., Ark., *Products of Industry* 1870, Roll 18, AHC.

Jackson, O. T.

Matrass Maker, A.35, B.Unknown: MCR 1860 Phillips Co., Roll 47, AHC.

Jacobs, Learcus

Cabinetmaker, A.28, B.NC: MCR 1850 Dallas Co., Roll 26, AHC. Also listed in DCTR 1850–51, Roll 45, AHC.

Jamison, David A.

Cabinetmaker, A.24, B.MO: MCR 1850 Johnson Co., Roll 27, AHC. Also listed in JCTR 1850, Roll 32, AHC.

Jamison, George

Cabinetmaker, A.32, B.MO: MCR 1850 Pope Co., Roll 29, AHC. Carpenter, A.42, B.MO: MCR 1860 Pope Co., Roll 48, AHC. Also listed in PCTR 1852–54 and 1856–59, Roll 65, 1860–61 and 1865–67, Roll 66, AHC. Jamison died in Pope County October 21, 1868. *AG* 10–22–68.

Jefferson, George

Secondary Source: Jefferson was born in Virginia in 1802 and came to Washington County, Arkansas, in 1835 from Tennessee. In 1841 he moved to Benton County, where he ran a hotel in connection with a cabinet-shop until his death in 1846. *Goodspeed Northwestern Arkansas,* 853.

Johns, Francis M.

Cabinetmaker, A.27, B.TN: MCR 1860 Van Buren Co., Roll 51, AHC.

Johnson, Henry J.

Cabinetmaker, A.34, B.TN: MCR 1850 Pope Co., Roll 29, AHC. Also listed in PCTR 1845–49 and 1851, Roll 65, AHC.

Johnson, William R.

Chairmaker, A.20, B.TN: MCR 1860 Independence Co., Roll 43, AHC.

Jones, John

Jones, John; furniture [maker], Hempstead Co. (Greenville), *Products of Industry* 1870, Roll 16, AHC.

Jones, Thomas

Cabinetmaker, A.29, B.MD: MCR 1860 Bradley Co., Roll 38, AHC.

Justice, Stephen

Chairmaker, A.70, B.SC: MCR 1860 Lawrence Co., Roll 45, AHC.

Khors (Khors-Jek), Engel

Cabinetmaker, A.33, B.Germany: MCR 1860 Pulaski Co., Roll 49, AHC.

King, Elonzo D.

Cabinetmaker, A.33, B.KY: MCR 1850 Independence Co., Roll 26, AHC. Also listed in ICTR 1851, Roll 59, AHC.

King, J. D.

Cabinetmaker, A.38, B.SC: MCR 1860 Pike Co., Roll 47, AHC.

Kingwell, John W.

"J. W. Kingwell . . . is prepared to execute all orders, both in the Cabinet and Upholstery line. Moss, Shuck, Hair & Spring Matresses . . . Camden . . . ." *OH* 7–29–58. Also listed in Ouachita Co. tax records, 1858–62, Roll 36, AHC.

Lacy, John W.

[Turner] "Died—[Little Rock] on Sunday last, Mr. John W. Lacy, Turner, aged about 30 years." *AG* 6–23–35.

Lamb, William

Woodworkman, A.36, B.TN: MCR 1860 Craighead Co., Roll 40, AHC.

Lamberson, Elijah

Cabinetmaker, A.42, B.NC: MCR 1860 Independence Co., Roll 43, AHC. Also listed in ICTR 1858 and 1861, Roll 60, AHC.

Lamberson, James

Cabinet workman, A.31, B.NC: MCR 1860 Independence Co., Roll 43, AHC. Also listed in ICTR 1858, Roll 60, 1860, Roll 61, and 1870, Roll 64, AHC.

Lamberson, Thomas

Cabinetmaker, A.27, B.NC: MCR 1860 Independence Co., Roll 43, AHC. Also listed in ICTR 1857–60, Roll 61, AHC.

Lambert, William

Cabinetmaker, A.55, B.NC: MCR 1870 Independence Co., Roll 55, AHC. Also listed in ICTR 1867–72, Roll 64, AHC.

Lancaster, John

According to family tradition, John Lancaster made furniture in Izard County, including the clothes press illustrated in figure F–54.

Land, James

Cabinetmaker, A.34, B.France: MCR 1870 Drew Co., Roll 52, AHC.

Langston, Singleton

C. Workman, A.52, B.SC: MCR 1850 Benton Co., Roll 25, AHC. Also listed as a farmer in the Benton Co. census for 1860 and 1870. Langston's will is dated Dec. 13, 1873, Benton Co. will records, Book "B", 1837–1900, Roll 8, AHC.

Laude, Joseph

Secondary Source: Laude was born in France in 1835, and in 1852 he immigrated to Ft. Wayne, Indiana, where he learned cabinetmaking and undertaking. In 1858 he went to Monticello and opened a shop which he ran until the outbreak of the Civil War. In 1867 he attempted to reopen his shop in Monticello, but his furniture and tools had disappeared during his absence. He then began to make and patent a corn and cotton planter. *Goodspeed Southern Arkansas*, 960.

Lavaseur, Charles

Cabinetmaker, A.36, B.France: MCR 1860 Crittenden Co., Roll 40, AHC.

Lee, Charles

Chairmaker, A.19, B.OH: MCR 1850 Arkansas Co., Roll 25, AHC.

Lewis, Anthony

"Cabinet Business." *ATA* 10–7–39. Cabinetmaker, A.42, B.NC: MCR 1850 Johnson Co., Roll 37, AHC. Cabinetmaker, A.52, B.NC: MCR 1860 Johnson Co., Roll 37, AHC. Also listed in JCTR 1849–51, 1853, and 1855–57, Roll 32, and 1860–62, Roll 33, AHC.

Lewis, J. Robert

Cabinetmaker, A.37, B.MO: MCR 1870 Pulaski Co., Roll 62, AHC.

Lick, John

Chairmaker, A.31, B.AR: MCR 1850 Hempstead Co., Roll 26, AHC.

Lightfoot, John S.

"Chair Manufactory." *AG* 1–16–39. Listed in Pulaski Co. tax records 1845, Roll 1, ATR.

Liles, Elie

Cabinetmaker, A.31, B.NC: MCR 1850 Washington Co., Roll 31, AHC. Cabinet workman, A.42, B.NC: MCR 1860 Washington Co., Roll 52, AHC. Also listed in WCTR 1849, 1851, and 1853–55, Roll 62, and 1859–61 and 1867, Roll 63, AHC.

Lindsley (Linsley), Darwin

[Turner of Iron, Brass, Ivory, Wood, etc., with Moffatt.] *See* Gunsmiths

Livi, John F.

Cabinetmaker, A.29, B.IL: MCR 1870 Madison Co., Roll 58, AHC.

Lonebridge, James

Cabinetmaker, A.56, B.PA: MCR 1860 Madison Co., Roll 45, AHC. Also listed in MCTR 1852–56, Roll 19, and 1858–60, Roll 20, AHC.

Lorreison (?), Josiah M.

Cabinetmaker, A.33, B.TN: MCR 1860 Crawford Co., Roll 40, AHC.

Lowe, B. B.

"Sunk and Rising Again . . . Little Rock . . . will continue the CABINET BUSINESS . . . will keep constantly on hand a stock of ready made furniture, consisting in part of sideboards, sofas, common and mahogany chairs, bureaus, tables, Bedsteads, mattresses . . . as well as turning of all kinds handsomely executed. . . . The business wil be attended to . . . by Mr. B. B. Lowe, during the next few weeks absence of S. S. Sanger." *AG* 1–9–47. Listed in Pulaski Co. tax records 1847–48(pt.), Roll 1, and 1848(pt.)–49, Roll 2, ATR.

Loyd, John

Cabinetmaker, A.24, B.TN: MCR 1870 Boone Co., Roll 48, AHC.

Mackbee, Henry

Cabinetmaker, A.28, B.TN: MCR 1860 Arkansas Co., Roll 37, AHC.

Mallicoat, James

Cabinetworkman, A.28, B.IN: MCR 1860 Washington Co., Roll 52, AHC.

Manning, I. M.

"Chair Factory. Fancy, Windsor, and Common Chair Making . . . in Batesville, Ark. . . ." *BN* 8–2–38.

Manning, W.

Cabinetworkman, A.45, B.NC: MCR 1860 Jackson Co., Roll 44, AHC.

Manor, W. W.

Cabinetworkman, A.26, B.TN: MCR 1860 Izard Co., Roll 43, AHC.

Markham, Orson

Cabinetmaker, A.22, B.NY: MCR 1850 Montgomery Co., Roll 28, AHC.

Maxey, George M.

CabinettMaker, A.26, B.KY: MCR 1860 Lawrence Co., Roll 45, AHC.

Mayo, Nathan

Furniture Merchant, A.36, B.NC: MCR 1870 Phillips Co. (Helena), Roll 60, AHC.

McAllister, W. H.

MatrassMaker, A.30, B.NY: MCR 1860 Phillips Co., Roll 47, AHC.

McClamrock, D. B.

Cabinetmaker, A.29, B.TN: MCR 1860 Greene Co., Roll 42, AHC.

McClung, Charles

Cabinetmaker, A.22, B.GA: MCR 1850 Dallas Co., Roll 26, AHC.

McClung, Josiah

Cabinetmaker, A.45, B.SC: MCR 1850 Dallas Co., Roll 26, AHC. Also listed in DCTR 1847–48 and 1850, Roll 45, AHC.

McCollum, Alexander

Cabinetmaker, A.49, B.Scotland: MCR 1860 Madison Co., Roll 45, AHC.

McCord, Isaac

Cabinetmaker, A.23, B.MO: MCR 1860 Independence Co., Roll 43, AHC.

McCord, John

Cabinetworkman, A.50, B.NJ: MCR 1860 Washington Co., Roll 52, AHC.

McCord, Samuel

Cabinetworkman, A.20, B.PA: MCR 1860 Washington Co., Roll 52, AHC.

McCoy, J. W. R.

Cabinetmaker, A.50, B.TN: MCR 1870 Ouachita Co., Roll 59, AHC.

McCullan, John

Cabinetmaker, A.45, B.TN: MCR 1860 Madison Co., Roll 45, AHC.

McDonald, Milton

"Cabinet Warehouse. W. W. Weldon and Milton McDonald. Old Furniture repaired—coffins made. . . ." *WT* 11–14–55.

McGarity, John

Chairmaker, A.45, B.SC: MCR 1850 Chicot Co., Roll 25, AHC.

McKnett, Robert H.

Cabinetmaker, A.20, B.MD: MCR 1850 Crawford Co., Roll 25, AHC.

McNeil, John

Cabinetmaker, A.31, B.Unknown: MCR 1850 Yell Co., Roll 31, AHC.

Megehee, John

Cabinet Shop Apprentice, A.25, B.MO: MCR 1870 Benton Co., Roll 47, AHC.

Mendenhall, George W.

Cabinetmaker, A.31, B.AL: MCR 1870 Ouachita Co., Roll 59, AHC. Also listed in OCTR 1867, Roll 36, AHC.

Merit, William H.

Cabinetmaker, A.35, B.MO: MCR 1850 Randolph Co., Roll 30, AHC.

Merk, John

Apprentice Cabinetmaker, A.15, B.Württemberg: MCR 1860 Sebastian Co., Roll 50, AHC.

Meyers (Meier) (Meir), Frederick W.

Cabinetmaker, A.27, B.Prussia: MCR 1870 Sebastian Co., Roll 64, AHC. "Upholstering & Mattress Manufacturing." *FSNE* 12–23–70. Secondary Source: "Furniture manufacturing in Fort Smith begins with the arrival of Fred Meier. He came to Sebastian Co. in 1867. His first partnership was with C. Erhart. He continued to work with various partners until 1891, he then worked alone in his own cabinet shop. Meier died in Ft. Smith on May 2, 1922." Bernard Johnson III, "Fort Smith Furniture Manufacturers of the late 19th Century." Unpublished Typescript, Old Fort Museum: Fort Smith, Arkansas, September 10, 1982.

Mickle, August

Cabinet Maker, A.45, B.Hesse-Darmstadt: MCR 1870 Sebastian Co., Roll 64, AHC.

Miller, John

Cabinetmaker, A.88, B.Germany: MCR 1870 Columbia Co., Roll 50, AHC.

Mitchell, Thomas P.

Cabinetmaker, A.28, B.TN: MCR 1860 Madison Co., Roll 45, AHC.

Moffett,

See Lindsley

Moore, Archibald

Cabinetmaker, A.26, B.NC: MCR 1860 Benton Co., Roll 37, AHC. Also listed in BCTR 1865(pt.)–67, Roll 40, AHC.

Moore, Hannible

Cabinet Workman, A.27, B.TN: MCR 1860 Washington Co., Roll 52, AHC.

Moore, Hugh

Cabinetmaker, A.17, B.AR: MCR 1870 Pulaski Co., Roll 62, AHC.

Moore, W. Henry

Cabinetmaker, A.16, B.AR: MCR 1870 Pulaski Co., Roll 62, AHC. Moore died Dec. 31, 1879, Pulaski Co. Probate Records, Box 82, AHC.

Morell, C. A.

"Upholsterer, C. A. Morell . . . paper hanging . . . Higlis Hotel . . . ." *WT* 4–16–51.

Morrison, Jenny

Morrison, Jenny; furniture [maker], Hempstead Co. (Washington), Ark., *Products of Industry* 1870, Roll 18, AHC.

Morrison, John

Woodworkman, A.30, B.AR: MCR 1860 Craighead Co., Roll 40, AHC.

Mortimer, Isaac

"Cabinet Maker . . . in the rear of the Arkansas Hotel is prepared to do all work in his line . . . Bureaus, wardrobes, wash stands, Dining and Breakfast tables & C. . . . Helena. . . ." *ASD* 1–8–41.

Mosley, D. P.

[Cabinetmaker] Worked in White Co. (Searcy) and exhibited a bedstead at the White County Agricultural and Mechanical Fair. *AG* 10–30–58.

Mosley, E.

Cabinetmaker, A.21, B.KY: MCR 1860 White Co., Roll 52, AHC.

Mouldin, John

Cabinetworkman, A.33, B.TN: MCR 1870 Greene Co., Roll 54, AHC.

Mulder, William

Chairmaker, A.70, B.NC: MCR 1860 Hot Spring Co., Roll 42, AHC.

Mullins, Leland

Cabinetmaker, A.45, B.KY: MCR 1860 Madison Co., Roll 45, AHC. Also listed in MCTR 1858–67, Roll 20, AHC.

Murphy, Isaac

Cabinetmaker, A.30, B.KY: MCR 1850 Clark Co., Roll 29, AHC.

Murphy, Isaac

Cabinetmaker, A.32, B.KY: MCR 1850 Prairie Co., Roll 50, AHC.

Mury, Bodo

Cabinetworkman, A.30, B.TN: MCR 1870 Greene Co., Roll 54, AHC.

Musgraves, Anderson

[Cabinetmaker] Farmer, A.41, B.TN: MCR 1850 Sevier Co., Roll 30, AHC. Cabinetmaker, A.51, B.TN:

MCR 1860 Sevier Co., Roll 51, AHC. Blacksmith, A.61, B.TN: MCR 1870 Sevier Co., Roll 51, AHC. Also listed in SCTR 1846, 1849–57, and 1859–61, Roll 47; 1862–63, Roll 48; and 1869–72, Roll 49, AHC.

Myers, William

Cabinetwork, A.35, B.Germany: MCR 1870 Ouachita Co., Roll 59, AHC.

Neal, George

Cabinetmaker, A.19, B.MO: MCR 1860 Crawford Co., Roll 40, AHC. Also listed in CCTR 1868, Roll 23, AHC.

Neal, W. T.

Cabinetmaker, A.41, B.SC: MCR 1860 Johnson Co., Roll 44, AHC.

Neesmith, J. C.

Woodworkman, A.59, B.AL: MCR 1870 Greene Co., Roll 54, AHC.

Omer, Francis

Cabinetmaker, A.55, B.France: MCR 1870 Independence Co., Roll 55, AHC. Also listed in ICTR 1861, 1865–66, and 1869–72, Roll 64; 1873–77, Roll 65; and 1878–83, Roll 66, AHC.

Onstot, John W.

"Carver and Cabinet Maker . . . has opened a shop at the Post of Arkansas. . . . He has brought with him a considerable quantity of unfinished work. . . . He is sending a part of his work to Little Rock. . . ." *AG* 1–16–27. Also listed in Pulaski Co. tax records 1828 and 1835, Roll 1, ATR. "Cheap House of Entertainment" (Fayetteville) *AG* 2–19–40. Innkeeper, A.60, B.PA: MCR 1850 Washington Co., Roll 31, AHC. Also listed in WCTR Hotel Keeper, A.71, B.KY: MCR 1860 Washington Co., Roll 52, AHC.

Ostwald, Augustus

"Furniture Manufactory. Ostwald & Stellfox Cabinet and Chair Makers. . . . at the warehouse on . . . E. Main St. . . . one door south of Mr. Stelfox's store. . . .

Little Rock. . . ." *AG* 10–18–50. "Dissolution of Partnership A. Ostwald J. Stellfox." *AG* 11–14–51. Also listed in Pulaski Co. tax records 1849–53 and 1855, Roll 2, ATR, and Washington Co. tax records 1837 and 1841–45, Roll 61; 1847–49 and 1851–54, Roll 62; and 1856, Roll 63, AHC. *See* F. Ditter and George Berryman

Pate, Sarah

Cabinetworkman, A.64, B.SC: MCR 1860 Hempstead Co., Roll 42, AHC. Sarah Pate was the first documented female cabinetmaker working in Arkansas.

Patterson, Alfred H.

Cabinetmaker, A.60, B.PA: MCR 1870 Ouachita Co., Roll 59, AHC. Patterson & White, Cabinetmakers; Ouachita Co.(Caney), *Products of Industry* 1870, Roll 18, AHC.

Paulk, Jacob

Secondary Source: Born in South Carolina, Paulk came with his wife, Elizabeth, to Lafayette County, Arkansas. He worked as a cabinetmaker, then moved to Mississippi shortly before his death in 1863. *Goodspeed Southern Arkansas,* 202–03.

Pears (Peers), J. M.

"J. M. Pears, Cabinet Workman and Dealer in Furniture, Camden, Arkansas. . . ." *OH* 7–29–58. Also listed in Ouachita Co. tax records 1858–60, Roll 36, AHC.

Pearson (Pierson), Albert

Cabinetmaker, A.40, B.NY: MCR 1870 Madison Co., Roll 58, AHC.

Phenise, Preston

Cabinetmaker, A.21, B.IL: MCR 1870 Benton Co., Roll 47, AHC.

Pierson, John H.

Cabinetmaker, A.25, B.NC: MCR 1850 Dallas Co., Roll 26, AHC. Also listed in DCTR 1850, Roll 45, AHC.

Pinkston, John

Chairmaker, A.50, B.TN: MCR 1870 St. Francis Co., Roll 65, AHC.

Plouf, Michael J.

[Cabinetmaker] Carpenter, A.36, B.Canada: MCR 1870 Pulaski Co., Roll 62, AHC. "Cabinet Maker, Upholsterer, and Manufacturer of Mattresses, etc., 715 Main Street. . . . Mr. M. J. Plouf, is by birth a French Canadian, coming here in 1864, and started business as above described. He will be found a genial, courteous gentleman, honorable, liberal and fair in all transactions, and well deserving of the success he has achieved," *Little Rock: The City of Roses, and Argenta, Ark. with Rambles in the Path of Industrial and Commercial Circles: Descriptive Review* (Memphis: Historical and Descriptive Publishing Co., 1888), 68.

Poore, P. M.

Cabinetmaker, A.30, B.MS: MCR 1870 Drew Co., Roll 52, AHC.

Pope, I.

Chairmaker, A.50, B.TN: MCR 1860 Crawford Co., Roll 40, AHC.

Putman, A. V.

Cabinetmaker, A.20, B.GA: MCR 1860 Drew Co., Roll 41, AHC.

Pyeatt (Pyatt), John Rankin

[Cabinetmaker] Carpenter, A.44, B.KY: MCR 1850 Washington Co., Roll 31, AHC. Wagonmaker, A.55, B.KY: 1860 Washington Co., Roll 52, AHC. Miller, A.64, B.KY: MCR 1870 Washington Co., Roll 66, AHC. Also listed in WCTR 1847, 1849, 1852, and 1878–80, Roll 65, AHC. Deceased, 1897, Washington Co. Probate Books "A–K" 1837–1901, 122, AHC. Secondary source: Between 1850 and 1870, Pyeatt made several pieces of furniture, including a blanket chest, now in the collection of the Arkansas Territorial Restoration. Conversation with Conrad Russell of Cane Hill, 1981.

Ramsey, Joseph

Cabinetmaker, A.31, B.PA: MCR 1860 Clark Co., Roll 39, AHC.

Ramsey, William

Cabinetmaker, A.50, B.TN: MCR 1860 Washington Co., Roll 52, AHC. Also listed in WCTR 1861 and 1867, Roll 63, AHC.

Ratcliff, Reuben

Chairmaker, A.69, B.NC: MCR 1860 Pope Co., Roll 48, AHC.

Ray, William

Chairmaker, A.52, B.TN: MCR 1860 Washington Co., Roll 52, AHC.

Reed, Albert R.

"Upholsterer . . . Hot Springs. . . ." *HSC* 7–22–69.

Reffly, Martin

Cabinetmaker, A.20, B.Prussia; MCR 1870 Sebastian Co. (Ft. Smith), Roll 64, AHC.

Regard, J. T.

Cabinetworkman, A.38, B.MO: MCR 1870 Crawford Co., Roll 51, AHC.

Rehkopf, Henry

Cabinetworkman, A.35, B.Prussia: MCR 1870 Woodruff Co., Roll 67, AHC.

Reichenbacher, ?

"New Cabinet Shop, Mr. Reichenbacher Maker of all types furniture, ample experience in Spring Mattress Making Upholstering, Varnishing, Polishing, completely renovates and refits old furniture fast to make it appear like new. Main St. L.R." *TD* 1–18–60.

Reynolds, Walter

Cabinetmaker, A.62, B.NC: MCR 1860 Arkansas Co., Roll 37, AHC.

Reynolds, William H.

Cabinetmaker, A.22, B.NC: MCR 1860 Arkansas Co., Roll 37, AHC.

Rich, Josiah

Cabinetmaker, A.28, B.NC: MCR 1850 Union Co., Roll 30, AHC.

Robertson, Silas K.

Cabinetmaker, A.24, B.OH: MCR 1870 Scott Co., Roll 63, AHC.

Roe, Erla (Earla) (Early)

Cabinetmaker, A.36, B.GA: MCR 1850 Ouachita Co. (Camden), Roll 28, AHC. Also listed in OCTR 1851–53 and 1855, Roll 35, AHC.

Ruder, Rene

Cabinetmaker, A.44, B.France: MCR 1860 Crittenden Co., Roll 40, AHC.

Runnel, Silas

Cabinetmaker, A.48, B.KY: MCR 1860 Phillips Co., Roll 47, AHC.

Russell, Elisha

Cabinetworkman, A.30, B.NC: MCR 1860 Benton Co., Roll 37, AHC.

Rutherford, ?

See Gilson, ?

Saffell, S. P.

Wagonmaker, A.29, B.TN: MCR 1850 Pope Co., Roll 29, AHC. Cabinetmaker, A.49, B.TN: MCR 1870 Boone Co., Roll 48, AHC.

Saffell, Samuel A.

Cabinetmaker, A.19, B.AR: MCR 1870 Boone Co., Roll 48, AHC.

Sager (Seager), Christian C.

Cabinetmaker, A.35, B.Germany: MCR 1850 Benton Co., Roll 25, AHC. Also listed in BCTR 1839–40 and 1843, Roll 39, 1869, Roll 41, AHC, and in the 1870 Benton Co. census.

Sager (Sagur), Simon (Simeon)

Cabinetmaker, A.64[46], B.Germany: MCR 1850 Benton Co., Roll 25, AHC. Lumber, A.56, B.Germany: MCR 1860 Benton Co., Roll 37, AHC. Also listed in BCTR 1840–46, 1848–56, 1860–61, and 1865. Sager died in 1866. *Benton County Arkansas Census Index 1850–60*, 91. *See* Green, Frederick

Sanger, Stephen S.

Cabinetmaker, A.39, B.DC: MCR 1850 Pulaski Co. (Little Rock), Roll 29, AHC. "Removal. Ho! every one that wants Furniture Cheap, without credit, and for Cash, call on, S. S. Sanger at his new and commodious Furniture Ware-rooms, on the East Side of E. Main St. . . . The CABINET BUSINESS will be continued . . . also of his own manufacture. . . . Funerals will be attended to in a proper manner . . . Little Rock . . . ." *AG* 2–8–50. *See* Lowe, B. B.

Sciafe, Thomas (B.)

Joiner/Carpenter, A.34, B.SC: MCR 1870 Phillips Co., Roll 60, AHC.

Shark, M.

Cabinetmaker, A.Unknown, B.Unknown: MCR 1860 Jefferson Co., Roll 44, AHC.

Sharp, Urban

Cabinetmaker, A.24, B.TN: MCR 1850 Sevier Co., Roll 30, AHC.

Short, Josiah

Chairmaker, A.84, B.NC: MCR 1860 Polk Co., Roll 48, AHC.

Sikes, Andrew

[Cabinetmaker] Blacksmith, A.34, B.NY: MCR 1850 Madison Co., Roll 27, AHC. Cabinetmaker,

A.46, B.NY: MCR 1860 Madison Co., Roll 19, AHC. Also listed in MCTR 1858–61, Roll 20, AHC.

Simmons, Fredrick

Cabinetmaker, A.42, B.Ireland: MCR 1860 Benton Co., Roll 37, AHC.

Simmons & Co.,

"Furniture! . . . Wholesale and Retail dealers in furniture, matrasses, chairs . . . Fashionable furniture . . . at Lafferty and Co.'s Building, Markham St. Little Rock." *VBP* 10–12–66–2–5. Simmons & Co., Upholstery, Pulaski Co., Ark., *Products of Industry 1870*, Roll 18, AHC.

Simon, Joseph

Cabinetmaker, A.Unknown, B.Unknown: MCR 1860 Jefferson Co., Roll 44, AHC.

Skinner, J. S.

[Cabinetmaker] Merchant, A.25, B.MS: 1860 Hempstead Co., Roll 42, AHC. Also listed in HCTR 1858–61, Roll 75, AHC. *See* J. Arnett

Smith, K. F.

Smith, K. F. Cabinet [maker]: Sharp Co., Ark., *Products of Industry 1870*, Roll 18, AHC.

Smith, Richard

Chairmaker, A.33, B.NC: MCR 1860 Van Buren Co., Roll 51, AHC.

Smith, Thomas

Chairmaker, A.59, B.TN: MCR 1860 Scott Co., Roll 30, AHC.

Sparks, Hardy

Cabinetworkman, A.67, B.NC: MCR 1850 Scott Co., Roll 30, AHC.

Spence, John S.

"Look Here! Old Furniture made to look almost equal to new. John S. Spence is establishing himself ten miles from here, on the Fort Gibson road, for the purpose of manufacturing CABINET FURNITURE, of every description . . . ." *AG* 10–10–38. "Cabinet Ware-House At Washington." *WT* 8–23–48. "Chairs! . . . As I receive them in pieces, and put them up here, and save on freight. I can sell them low. I can afford a good article of Windsor Chair for $1.25; large Rocking Chairs for $3.50, and other kinds in proportion . . . ." *WT* 4–18–59. "Furniture Manufactory." *WT* 4–18–49. Also listed in Pulaski Co. tax records 1835 and 1837–40, Roll 1, ATR, and Hempstead Co. tax records 1839, 1841–42, and 1847–50, Roll 74, AHC. *See* Grimes

Spicer, Joseph

Woodworkman, A.23, B.AL: MCR 1860 Ouachita Co., Roll 47, AHC.

Stags (Staggs), Samuel S.

Cabinetmaker, A.45, B.SC: MCR 1860 Dallas Co., Roll 26, AHC. Also listed in DCTR 1848 and 1850–51, Roll 45, AHC.

Stellfox, John

[Cabinetmaker] Merchant, A.34, B.England: MCR 1850 Pulaski Co., Roll 29, AHC. Also listed in PCTR 1848(pt.)–56, Roll 2, ATR. *See* Ostwald

Stern, Calvin

Cabinetworkman, A.51, B.VT: MCR 1850 Benton Co., Roll 25, AHC.

Stigowest, Edward

Cabinetmaker, A.26, B.Prussia: MCR 1860 Washington Co. (Fayetteville), Roll 52, AHC. *See* J. Buie

Strawn, Fieling

Cabinetmaker, A.46, B.NC: MCR 1850 Montgomery Co., Roll 28, AHC.

Strother, William

Cabinetmaker, A.26, B.TN: MCR 1860 Izard Co., Roll 43, AHC.

Tarwater, James

Chairmaker, A.23, B.MO: MCR 1870 Sebastian Co., Roll 64, AHC.

Teeter, Peter

Wheelwright, A.62, B.NC: MCR 1850 Pope Co., Roll 29, AHC. Chairmaker, A.75, B.NC: MCR 1860 Pope Co., Roll 48, AHC.

Temple, William B.

Cabinetworkman, A.39, B.VA: MCR 1850 Carroll Co., Roll 25, AHC.

Terry, Alonzo

Cabinetmaker, Apprentice, A.21, B.CT: MCR 1870 Ashley Co., Roll 47, AHC.

Terry, Robert Y. H.

Cabinetmaker, A.33, B.SC: MCR 1870 Ashley Co., Roll 47, AHC. Secondary Source: Terry arrived in Arkansas in 1859 and opened a woodland farm in Ashley County on the Ouachita River. In 1867 he moved to Hamburg and opened a furniture store and Cabinet Shop. *Goodspeed Southern Arkansas*, 921.

Thendal, Joseph

Cabinetmaker, A.33, B.NC: MCR 1850 Poinsett Co., Roll 29, AHC.

Thomas, Joseph

Cabinetmaker, A.44, B.Prussia: MCR 1860 Independence Co., Roll 43, AHC. Also listed in ICTR 1853–54 and 1858, Roll 59, 1859 and 1861, Roll 60, and 1860, Roll 61, AHC.

Thomas, Lafayette

Woodworkman, A.25, B.MO: MCR 1870 Washington Co., Roll 66, AHC.

Thomas, T.

See F. Baer

Thompson, Lawrence

[Cabinetmaker] Farmer, A.31, B.KY: MCR 1850 Greene Co., Roll 26, AHC. Secondary Source: Thompson came to Arkansas in 1821 and settled in a part of Greene County that later became Craighead County. He died there in 1856. Thompson made a chest of drawers that now belongs to the Arkansas Territorial Restoration. Sue Thweatt, Unpublished Family Typescript.

Thompson, Moses R.

Thompson, Moses R., Cabinetmaker, Saline Co., Ark., *Products of Industry* 1860, Roll 8, AHC.

Tilson, Joseph

Cabinetmaker, A.30, B.TN: MCR 1870 Benton Co., Roll 47, AHC.

Timbs, John

Chairmaker, A.25, B.SC: MCR 1860 Washington Co., Roll 52, AHC.

Timms, John

Woodworkman, A.45, B.SC: MCR 1870 Washington Co., Roll 66, AHC.

Titsworth, William P.

Chairmaker, A.36, B.KY: MCR 1860 Madison Co., Roll 45, AHC.

Toland, T. L.

Cabinetmaker, A.33, B.SC: MCR 1860 Pike Co., Roll 47, AHC. Secondary Source: Toland came to Arkansas in 1856 and settled near the Pike County line. After farming for a few years, he participated in the Civil War, running a wagon factory. He returned home and opened a wagon shop. From 1886 to 1888 he taught school in Lafayette and Pike counties and then went on to medical school at Vanderbilt University, graduating as an M.D. in 1890. He later became a successful surgeon in Pike County. *Goodspeed Southern Arkansas*, 297–98.

Towers, Abram

Cabinetmaker, A.23, B.SC: MCR 1870 Phillips Co. (Helena), Roll 60, AHC.

Trulove, James

Moulder and Finishes F., A.47, B.NY: MCR 1870 Searcy Co., Roll 64, AHC.

Tucker, Calvin M.

Cabinetmaker, A.32, B.TN: MCR 1850 Fulton Co., Roll 26, AHC.

Tucker, Hiram (Nivan)

Cabinetworkman, A.30, B.AL: MCR 1860 Lawrence Co., Roll 45, AHC.

Tucker, James

Cabinetmaker, A.35, B.NC: MCR 1850 Clark Co., Roll 25, AHC.

Tuckness, Jordan

Cabinetmaker, A.55, B.TN: MCR 1860 Craighead Co., Roll 40, AHC.

Tunnah, James

[Marble Dealer] "James Tunnah, Marble Dealer, Little Rock, Ark. Has just received and will constantly keep on hand a full assortment of Italian and American Marble, and will furnish Monuments, Grave Stones and Tomb Slabs of every description on the most reasonable terms and in good style. He will also make bureau tops, table tops, and do every kind of work in his line—his yard is on Markham Street." *TD* 3-3-57.

Turkies, C.

See F. Baer

Turner, George F.

Cabinetmaker, A.27, B.SC: MCR 1860 Bradley Co., Roll 38, AHC.

Turner, William

Chairmaker, A.45, B.NC: MCR 1860 Dallas Co., Roll 40, AHC.

Tutewiler, Jacob

"Cabinetmaking." *ATA* 7-24-43. Carpenter, A.50, B.VA: MCR 1850 Pulaski Co. (Little Rock), Roll 29, AHC. Also listed in PCTR 1837, 1839, and 1846-48(pt.), Roll 1, 1848(pt.)-49 and 1852-53, Roll 2, ATR.

Vansickle, B. Franklin

Cabinetworkman, A.31, B.VA: MCR 1860 Columbia Co., Roll 39, AHC.

Walker, L. F.

"Cabinet & Carpenter Shop. . . . He will keep constantly on hand, ready made, or make, at the shortest notice, COFFINS of any size or quality, out of Walnut, cypress, poplar, or pine. Old Furniture repaired or Varnished on reasonable terms. Shop 4 miles from Helena, on the place formerly owned by Dory Ashen. L. F. Walker." *SS* 9-27-51. Also listed in Phillips Co. tax records 1854, Roll 88, AHC.

Wallace (Wallis), Mortimer R.

Cabinet Maker, A.41, B.NC: MCR 1850 Independence Co., Roll 26, AHC. Cabinetmaker, A.53, B.TN: MCR 1860 Independence Co., Roll 43, AHC. Also listed in ICTR 1850-56, Roll 59, and 1861, Roll 60, AHC.

Ware, James

Cabinetmaker, A.29, B.Ireland: MCR 1850 Washington Co., Roll 31, AHC.

Watkins, Thomas E.

Furniture Dealer, A.49, B.VA: MCR 1870 Pulaski Co., Roll 62, AHC. *See* H. Guibor

Watson, Thomas Anderson

Secondary Source: "Thomas Anderson Watson, with his wife and four daughters moved to Bentonville in 1869. . . . The battle of Pea Ridge had been fought in 1862 and Bentonville was almost reduced to ashes, either by bushwackers or northern soldiers. [Watson], a carpenter, wagon maker, and cabinet maker, purchased about two blocks of land where the downtown Wal-Mart now stands just west of the old court house. . . . Watson helped rebuild Bentonville . . . made furniture for himself and his friends. . . . Watson learned dentistry as an apprentice under Dr. A. C. Armstrong in 1873 and continued that profession until his death in 1911" *New Traditions* (a supplement to the Benton County *Daily Democrat,* 10 January 1982, 8.

Waynisek (Waymack), Frederick

Waynisek worked at a saddle shop and was "one of the best harness and furniture hands in the state." *TD* 3–3–57.

Webb, Wesley

Chairmaker, A.23, B.TN: MCR 1860 Yell Co., Roll 52, AHC.

Weber, Henry

Cabinetmaker, A.23, B.GA: MCR 1860 Drew Co. (Monticello), Roll 41, AHC.

Weitzel, Theodore (Thomas)

Cabinetmaker, A.23, B.Germany: MCR 1850 Pulaski Co., Roll 29, AHC.

Weldon, W. W.

Cabinetmaker, A.29, B.NC: MCR 1860 Hempstead Co., Roll 42, AHC. Also listed in HCTR 1858–61, Roll 75, AHC. *See* M. McDonald

Wells, Samuel

Cabinetmaker, A.21, B.AR: MCR 1850 Hot Spring Co., Roll 26, AHC.

Wettick, Christian

Cabinetmaker, A.31, B.Prussia: MCR 1860 Sebastian Co., Roll 50, AHC.

Wheeler, Benjamin

Cabinetmaker, A.25, B.GA: MCR 1860 Sevier Co., Roll 51, AHC.

White, Jesse

Cabinetmaker, A.53, B.SC: MCR 1860 Jefferson Co., Roll 44, AHC. Also listed in JCTR 1855–60(pt.), Roll 116, and 1865–68, Roll 118, AHC.

White, John W.

Cabinetmaker, A.21, B.TN: MCR 1850 Dallas Co., Roll 26, AHC. Also listed in DCTR 1850–51, 1857–59, and 1861, Roll 45, AHC.

White, William T.

[Cabinetmaker] Machinist, A.45, B.TN: MCR 1870 Ouachita Co., Roll 59, AHC. Also listed OCTR 1887, Roll 36, AHC. See A. H. Patterson

Whitson, Jacob

Chairmaker, A.40, B.IL: MCR 1860 Conway Co., Roll 39, AHC.

Wickersham, John

Cabinetmaker, A.31, B.KY: MCR 1850 Marion Co., Roll 28, AHC. Wickersham and Bros., Cabinetmakers, Marion Co., *Products of Industry* 1850, Roll 17, AHC.

Wiley, Newton A. (M.)

Cabinetmaker, A.27, B.TN: MCR 1860 Craighead Co., Roll 40, AHC. Cabinetmaker, A.37, B.TN: MCR 1870 Craighead Co., Roll 51, AHC.

Wilkins, Bishop

Chairmaker, A.48, B.GA: MCR 1850 Polk Co., Roll 29, AHC.

Wilkinson, Moses N.

Cabinetmaker, A.40, B.KY: MCR 1850 Independence Co., Roll 26, AHC. Also listed in ICTR 1857–60, Roll 61, AHC.

Williams, Bill E.

Cabinetmaker, A.34, B.AR: MCR 1860 Lawrence Co., Roll 45, AHC.

Williams, James

Cabinetmaker, A.35, B.TN: MCR 1860 Independence Co., Roll 43, AHC. Also listed in ICTR 1858–61, Rolls 60 and 61, AHC.

Williams, James

Cabinetmaker, A.35, B.MI: MCR 1870 Benton Co., Roll 47, AHC.

Williams, Moses B.

Joiner/Carpenter, A.59, B.VA: MCR 1870 Phillips Co., Roll 60, AHC.

Willis, William

Cabinetmaker, A.35, B.AL: MCR 1850 Hempstead Co., Roll 26, AHC.

Wills, Samuel

Cabinetworkman, A.32, B.AL: MCR 1860 Izard Co., Roll 43, AHC.

Wilson, Hue B.

Chairmaker, A.35, B.SC: MCR 1860 Pulaski Co., Roll 49, AHC.

Winkler, Frederic

Cabinetmaker, A.35, B.TN: MCR 1850 Mississippi Co., Roll 28, AHC.

Wood, A. J.

Cabinetworkman, A.33, B.TN: MCR 1870 Greene Co., Roll 54, AHC. Secondary Source: An Alex Wood is listed as a Treasurer for Greene Co. from 1866–68. *Goodspeed Northwestern Arkansas,* 118.

Wood, Eli N.

Chairmaker, A.29, B.TN: MCR 1860 Hempstead Co., Roll 42, AHC.

Wood, G. W.

Chairmaker, A.26, B.TN: MCR 1860 Hempstead Co., Roll 42, AHC.

Wood, George W.

Cabinetmaker, A.55, B.MA: MCR 1850 Pope Co., Roll 29, AHC. Also listed in the 1840 Marion Co. census.

Wood, John M.

Chairmaker, A.29, B.OH: MCR 1850 Jefferson Co., Roll 27, AHC.

Wood, William

Chairmaker, A.48, B.TN: MCR 1860 Hempstead Co., Roll 42, AHC.

Woodruff, George H.

Chairmaker, A.25, B.AR: MCR 1860 Pulaski Co., Roll 49, AHC. Also listed in PCTR 1855–56, Roll 2, ATR.

Wright, Anderson W.

Cabinetworkman, A.41, B.AL: MCR 1870 Searcy Co., Roll 64, AHC.

Wright, James P.

Cabinetworkman, A.26, B.TN: MCR 1870 Greene Co., Roll 54, AHC.

Wright, John

Cabinetmaker, A.33, B.VA: MCR 1860 Johnson Co., Roll 44, AHC. Also listed in JCTR 1856–58, Roll 32, and 1860–61 and 1865, Roll 33, AHC.

Yandel, Pickney C.

Cabinetworkman, A.45, B.KY: MCR 1870 Jackson Co., Roll 56, AHC.

Yater, Julius

"Yater, Julius, cabinet maker, 101 Scott." LRCD, 1871, 117.

Yong (Young), William A.

Cabinetmaker, A.54, B.TN: MCR 1860 Dallas Co., Roll 40, AHC. Also listed in DCTR 1859, 1861–62, and 1867, Roll 45, AHC.

Young, ?

See ? Gary

Zelner (Zellner), Emiel (Emil)

Cabinetmaker, A.27, B.Berlin: MCR 1860 Washington Co., Roll 52, AHC. Also listed in WCTR 1861, Roll 63, AHC. Cabinetworkman, A.37, B.Prussia: MCR 1870 Washington Co., Roll 66, AHC. Secondary Source: A William E. Zellner is listed as postmaster of Viney Grove in August of 1870. *Goodspeed Northwestern Arkansas,* 322.

Ziegel, Andrew

". . . Furniture Maker. . . . Manufactures All Descriptions of Household Furniture. Turning Lathe Aids In Making Billiard & Alley Balls . . . ." *TD* 12–2–56. Also listed in Pulaski Co. tax records 1857, Roll 3, ATR.

An Illustrated Catalog of Arkansas Furniture

F–1. Bureau, c. 1840–50, Hempstead County. H: 47¼″, W: 43⅝″, D: 22⅛″. Primary: walnut. Secondary: pine. Maker unknown. *Courtesy of Old Washington State Park.*

One of the most commonly occurring bureau forms, having a projecting upper drawer supported by a combination of plain- and ring-turned full columns and ball-turned feet. The original stain and varnish, although much worn, are still intact.

F–2.   Crib, c. 1850–70, Hempstead County. H: 41" (at posts), W: 22½", L: 43". Primary: pine. Maker unknown. *Courtesy of Old Washington State Park.*

Description: The flattened, ring-turned posts surmounted by inverted pear-shaped finials are combined with spool- and ball-turned spindles to furnish the only ornament for this simple but patently functional crib. The lower end rails are fitted with slots for slats to support the bedding. Casters were added later.

F–3.   Bedstead, c. 1845–60, Hempstead County. H: 58", W: 56½", L: 76". Walnut throughout. Maker unknown. *Courtesy of the Pioneer Washington Foundation.*

Description: A shaped and scrolled headboard is flanked by bold ring- and cup-turned posts, with top chamfered blocks where the rails join. The elongate taper of the turned, peg-shaped feet is quite similar to those of simple ladderback chairs for the period. The rear posts are spanned by a medial ring-turned stretcher, which at some undocumented point in time received the cognomen "blanket roll."

F–4.   Bedstead, c. 1850–70, Pike County. H: 52⅞", W: 58", L: 78¾". Walnut throughout. Maker unknown. *Courtesy of Parker and Lucille Westbrook.*

Description: Another bedstead with considerable turning, again in familiar ring and ball or spool variations common throughout the third quarter of the century. Taller front posts with cone-shaped finials frame a plainly shaped headboard with applied ring- and ball- or vase-turned crest over turned spindles, which mirror the larger turnings of the posts. Similar turnings are seen at the footboard. Possible replacement side rails are fitted to receive slats to support bedding. Purchased from the estate of long-time Pike County resident Charles "Buck" Jones, whose family settled in the area prior to the Civil War.

F–5.   Bedstead, c. 1850–60, Benton County. H: 49⅝", W: 54¼" L: 79½". Walnut throughout. Made by Simon or Christian Sager. *Courtesy of the Siloam Springs Museum.*

Description: Taller turned and block front posts support an S-scrolled headboard with turned spindles. The turned foot posts are joined by a top stretcher, which begins at either edge with vase and ring turnings evolving into a long hexagonal span. The side rails, fitted for slats, are joined to the posts by cast-iron fittings.

Brothers Simon and Christian Sager, natives of Germany, arrived in Benton County from Missouri by 1839 and are the earliest of the more than thirty documented furnituremakers in that county for the period.

By 1850 the Sagers were operating a water-powered combination cabinetmaking and sawmill business in Benton County, employing four men. According to the 1850 *Products of Industry* schedules, they used considerable amounts of walnut, cherry, and pine lumber to produce an unspecified number of sideboards, tables, bedsteads, bureaus, and chairs. While brother Christian lived well into the last quarter of the century, the elder Simon was murdered in 1864 by unknown assailants. ("The Tragic Story of Simon Sager, Founder of Siloam Springs," Benton County *Pioneer*, September 1960, 12–14.) Although no signed pieces by either Sager have come to light, there are several pieces in the Siloam Springs vicinity attributed to the brothers Sager (*see* figure F–13).

F–6.   Bedstead, c. 1868, Little Rock, Pulaski County. H: 75¼", W: 55¾", L: 79¼". Walnut and an unidentified wood for recessed headboard panels. Michael J. Plouf maker. *Courtesy of Mrs. James D. Reed.*

Description: Little Rock cabinetmaker Michael Plouf's freewheeling interpretation of at least two important American furniture revival styles, the Renaissance and rococo, are evident in this bedstead. Part of a suite of bedroom furniture which included a wardrobe and bureau, this bedstead's overall rectilinear form, flat veneered or inset surfaces, applied plaque (at footboard), columnar-like turned front posts (the style's rather stiff neoclassic influence), and replicated factory-sawn framing and moldings all point to the Renaissance revival forms made popular c. 1850–80. Yet, the one element which vigorously promotes another influence, the rococo, is overwhelmingly present in the exuberantly handcarved crest and serpentine top of the headboard. Plouf and others would normally have referred to this piece as a "French" or "Antique" bedstead, the term rococo not being commonly used. The handsome ring-, block-, and baluster-

turned front posts are subordinate to this impressive headboard. Shaped rails for slats extend to a much truncated serpentine version of the headboard less the applied carving. The rounded rear posts are matching half sections of a solid-turned column. The footboard with its imitative central plaque or medallion has tenons which are mortised into the foot posts, while the side rails have cast-iron fittings which lock into those of the rear posts.

The back side of the headboard is signed "M. J. Plouf—Little Rock, Ark." Both the bureau and wardrobe are similarly inscribed by the maker.

The pieces have descended in the William Henry Harrison Brown family to the present owner, Brown's great-granddaughter, Mrs. James D. Reed. Brown and his family came to Little Rock c. 1857 from Maryland. The bedstead, according to family tradition, was made by Plouf for William H. H. Brown prior to the birth of his son Alonzo on November 1, 1868. Alonzo himself worked as a cabinetmaker in Ft. Smith and then Galveston. He returned to Little Rock following the disastrous Galveston hurricane of 1900.

F—7. Blanket Chest, c. 1870, Van Buren County. H: 34⅝", W: 47⅝", D: 17⅛". Walnut throughout. Maker unknown. *Courtesy of Mrs. E. C. Witham.*

An original lead-based red paint covers this walnut blanket chest. Painting was often reserved for less attractive woods rather than the rich grain and high quality finish walnut afforded local makers. Its straightforward simplicity and equally economical matter-of-fact construction may be the by-product of the local carpenter rather than a trained cabinetmaker. The entire case has been butt jointed and face nailed together with cut nails, while the sides of the case are extended, each having a cut-in single arch to form feet. The top consists of a narrower nailed board to which two butt hinges are attached which in turn allow a second wider board to serve as the lid.

F—8. Blanket Chest, c. 1860, Cane Hill Community, Washington County. H: 24⅞", W: 38¹¹⁄₁₆", D: 20¹¹⁄₁₆". Pine throughout. Attributed to J. R. Pyeatt. *From the collection of the Arkansas Territorial Restoration.*

Description: Function before form best describes this simple blanket box used for the storage of household textiles. The chest's plain two-board lid has mitered cleats attached with cut nails. The case is constructed in an exposed frame and panel fashion, consisting of upper and lower stretcher rail members joined to square stiles, with traditional mortise and tenon joints, secured with exposed wooden pegs. The recessed panels are dadoed (grooved) loosely into the frame, to allow for the expansion and contraction of the panels and framing, so as to avoid splitting and warping. The case stiles extend to become feet. The one-piece skirt and bracket foot is applied to front and sides as decoration. As may be noted, the lower halves of the skirts, which once were scalloped, along with the bracket feet, are now missing. The Japanned, stamped metal keyhole escutcheon may or may not be the original. The lock is missing. The blanket chest descended in the Pyeatt family who settled in the Cane Hill community as early as 1828. It was purchased in 1979 at the estate sale of a Pyeatt descendant.

F—9. Blanket Chest, nineteenth century, purchased in Carroll County. H: 16⅞″, W: 37″, D: 16¼″. Cherry throughout. Maker unknown. *From the collection of the Arkansas Territorial Restoration.*

Description: Much of the original surface stain and varnish remains despite the obvious hard use the chest has received. The lid's applied edge molding is missing. The back edge of the lid has been trimmed, due possibly to damage, and a one-inch strip face nailed to it to receive the small cast-iron butt hinges. Original lid edge molding is missing. Stiles terminate in turned ring- and inverted pear-shaped feet. The lower edge of case front and sides is decorated with shallow horizontal reeding, while the bottom edges of front and sides have face-nailed, split-ringed moldings.

F—10a. Blanket Chest, c. 1840. Either Batesville, Independence County, or Aldie, Virginia. Primary: walnut. Secondary: pine (back and bottom). H: 24½″, W: 43½″, D: 20″. Maker unknown. *From the collection of the Arkansas Territorial Restoration.*

Description: A simple applied edge molding frames the rectangular two-board lid attached to the case by handwrought strap garnet hinges. These large decoratively molded hinges are the only examples documented on any form of Arkansas furniture. The case is joined by exposed dovetailing to the bottom of the case frame. The bracket feet are in turn mitered at the front corners and nailed to the case bottom using large L-shaped cut brads. Both the lock and keyhole escutcheon are missing.

The chest once belonged to Charles Fenton Mercer Noland (1810–58), a native of Aldie, Virginia, who moved to Batesville, Arkansas, in 1825 with his father, William Noland, who had been sent there as receiver of monies in the federal land office. Young Noland went on to become Arkansas's, and one of the South's, best known antebellum literary humorists. Using the pen name "Pete Whetstone," after a legendary local rustic, he used a good deal of ink throughout his adult life portraying Arkansas frontier characters and the environment in which they lived. Noland died suddenly in Little Rock in 1858. Following the death of his widow, many of his personal belongings were returned to family members in Aldie, Virginia. Fortunately, recent descendants decided to return some of these possessions, including the chest, to his beloved Arkansas.

F–10b. Detail of figure F–10a, showing one of the wrought-iron strap hinges and the undulating marks of the cabinetmaker's jack plane, which was used to smooth the surface.

F–11. Bureau, c. 1840–50, Hempstead County. H: 47¾", W: 41¾", D: 20⅝". Primary: walnut and cherry. Secondary: pine. Maker unknown. *Courtesy of Old Washington State Park.*

Description: The scrolled, classically inspired uprights supporting the large projecting upper drawer hark to the published drawings of Baltimore cabinetmaker John Hall who published his *Cabinetmaker's Assistant* in 1840. The *Assistant* was a graphic harbinger of a whimsical design for furniture vaguely interpreted and referred to as "Grecian." Literally thousands of similar bureaus were sold as such during the first half of the past century.

It would be more logical to ascribe a precedent for such designs upon the local furnituremaker's exposure to pieces arriving from other cabinetmaking centers such as Cincinnati and New Orleans.

The method of construction for the graduated drawers of the bureau was a combination of sliding and locking joints with distinctive regional or shop variations. This method was popular throughout the United States. The drawer fronts, sides, and backs are connected by locking dovetail joints. The length of the lower inside edges of the front and sides has been dadoed to receive the chamfered edges of the drawer bottoms which were slid into the dadoes or grooves from the rear of the drawer and nailed to the back. The framed panel back has been cut nailed to the base of the case frame and the rabbets along the inside edges of the frame and paneled sides. The ornamental scrolled front and plain rear case stiles are extended to form feet. Cherry drawer blades and pine runners cut nailed to the inside edges of the stiles support each drawer. The raised splashboard and the modern cast brass knobs are recent additions.

F–12.   Dressing or Toilet Bureau, c. 1868, Little Rock, Pulaski County. H: 75 ½", W: 41 ¼", D: 18⁵⁄₁₆". Primary: walnut. Secondary: unidentified. Michael J. Plouf maker. *Courtesy of Mrs. James D. Reed.*

Description: Without its strongly angular moldings and outlines, this bureau is quite plain. The second quarter of the century saw the term "bureau" begin to replace the more common eighteenth-century term "chest-of-drawers." References in advertisements and inventories to toilet or dressing bureaus referred to forms such as this one, having attached looking glasses often flanked by small cased drawers for toiletry articles. This toilet bureau was part of a suite of bedroom furniture made by Little Rock cabinetmaker Michael J. Plouf which included a bedstead, shown figure F–6, and a wardrobe.

The angularly molded, scrolled supports hold a framed looking glass that is entirely similar in form and ornament. The complete fixture is set into a ring-turned, flattened, cone-shaped base which swivels. A small rectangular marble plate is flanked by the cased drawers and a walnut base which supports the swivel dressing glass. Chamfered case corners have applied split ring- and ball-turned ornaments somewhat resembling drop finials. The solid case sides extend and join with the front stiles to form bracket feet. Tenoned drawer blades or dividers are morticed into front stiles, while pine runners are nailed to the case frame. The graduated drawers of the case are dovetail joined, with interior dadoed edges to receive fitted drawer bottoms. Drawer fronts are two part, consisting of recessed panels with "mushroom" shaped knobs (pulls) attached to the back of the molded drawer front frames with screws.

For a history of the piece see Plouf bedstead figure F–6.

F—13a.   Bureau, c. 1845–60, Benton County. H: 70″, W: 43⅞″, D: 20¾″. Primary: walnut. Secondary: pine. Made by Christian or Simon Sager. *Courtesy of the Siloam Springs Museum.*

Description: The looking glass with its ogee molded frame is held by lyre or "dolphin-tail" shaped supports that are nailed and blocked to step-backed upper-cased drawers. The bureau top is partially nailed to the case with countersunk cut nails which have been puttied over and stained. The top has been secured at the back with screws inset into diagonally gouged alcoves (*see* figure F—13b). The graduated drawers of the main case all retain their brass keyhole surrounds, mushroom knobs, and fitted cabinet locks. Wide horizontal molded bands (wider at bottom) have been glued to the top and bottom of the case, causing the medial portion of the case to appear recessed. Figure F—13b clearly shows the applied profile of each molded band. The simple bracket feet are formed of a series of built-up wooden blocks that, as one unit, are nailed to the base of the case. The darkened finish caused by the oxidation of the piece's original varnish conceals highly figured walnut.

F—13b.   Verso of Sager Bureau. Wide, vertical tongue and grooved back boards are cut nailed to case frame. Two diagonally gouged alcoves near the upper edge of the back boards have screws which secure the top to the case frame. Also evident are the profiled ends of the raised molded panels applied to the front and sides of the bureau.

F–14. Bureau, c. 1860, Greene County. H: 41", W: 43½", D: 17". Primary: cherry, with unidentified inlaid woods. Secondary: tulip poplar. Attributed to Lawrence Thompson (1799–c. 1856). *From the collection of the Arkansas Territorial Restoration.*

Description: An unmolded two-board top rests above two small drawers and four slightly graduated full drawers that are of lap-jointed and cut-nailed construction. The fronts of the smaller drawers are inlaid only while the larger drawers have line and spandrel or quarter-fan inlays. The mushroom drawer knobs are recent replacements. Double recessed, framed panel sides are tenoned and pegged to square stiles which terminate in turned, inverted pear-shaped feet (replacements).

The case back is framed with vertically lap-jointed boards, leveled and cut nailed to the case.

The use of the deciduous tulip poplar as a cabinet-making wood was highly favored by makers east of the Mississippi River where it grew widely and abundantly. However, in Arkansas its indigenous range was limited to a narrow chain of hills running southeast from Greene County, where this piece was made, down into Phillips County, and continuing on to their terminus in northeast Mississippi.

The maker, Lawrence Thompson, arrived in Arkansas as early as 1821 and settled in the northeast portion of Lawrence County, which became Greene County in 1833. The only reference to his occupation occurred in the 1850 Census for Greene County, which listed Thompson's occupation as that of farmer. However, there was a strong tradition of dual occupations among artisans in rural areas. Often a potter, cabinetmaker, or gunsmith would abandon his profession altogether to take up farming.

F–15. Bureau, c. 1840–60, found near Bingen, Hempstead County. H: 52", W: 46½", D: 23". Primary: cherry. Secondary: pine. Maker unknown. *Courtesy of Parker Westbrook.*

Description: Rectangular two-board top is secured with screws set in gouged alcoves in the upper rails of the back case frame. Two small drawers surmount four graduated full drawers with modern replacement pulls. The original cabinet locks for drawers are intact. Brass keyhole surrounds remain on the small upper drawers. The dovetailed drawers have sliding bottom boards dadoed into drawer sides. Pine runners are tenoned into drawer blades and nailed to back stiles. The faint struck beading around the edge of each drawer rather than an applied cockbeading was a utilitarian way of adding decoration. The frame and panel sides tenoned to square stiles terminate in turned generically tapered ball feet. A separate dustboard is fitted below the bottom drawer only, with drawer blades above.

F–16. Bureau, c. 1870, found in Washington County. H: 46¾", W: 41", D: 18½". Walnut throughout. Maker unknown. *From the collection of the Arkansas Territorial Restoration.*

Description: Rectangular case, with double beaded edge, two-board top, and beveled edge splashboard, all nailed to the case. The mortised, tenoned, and pegged case framing has paneled sides. Two small upper drawers top three graduated drawers. Their original knobs are missing. Rather than dovetailed, the rabbeted inside edges of the drawer fronts are lap jointed and cut nailed to the drawer sides. The case back is framed into the square stiles which extend to form lengthy tapered legs with a pronounced inward rake. The shaped skirt is tenoned and pegged to stiles.

F–17.   Bureau, c. 1850–60, Batesville, Independence County. H: 42¼", W: 41⅞", D: 21⅝". Primary: walnut, mahogany veneer (drawer fronts), and maple veneer (drawer fronts). Secondary: pine (banding). Attributed to Francis Omer. *Courtesy of Dr. Roberta Brown.*

Description: The visual plane of the bureau's square front is boldly broken by highly figured mahogany veneers and brightly contrasted mitered maple crossbanding surrounding each drawer edge. The projecting top drawer, lacking knobs, is drawn out by grasping the rounded corners of the drawer, which when closed fit flush with the stiles. Below are three graduated drawers having elliptical stamped brass pulls with threaded posts and curved bails, which appear to be original. The pulls are somewhat dated and would have better suited furniture constructed thirty or forty years earlier. The piece's rather low, solidly square profile, bracket feet, and mahogany veneers hark back to earlier "Federal" period chests so popular at the turn of the century. The graduated drawers are completely framed by an applied compound molding in walnut and string inlay. Each of the top four drawers has its original interior cabinet lock and accompanying round stamped-brass keyhole escutcheon, inlet and nailed to the drawer. Each drawer is joined by dovetailing, while the bottoms are seated into sliding dadoed joints and nailed at the back. The covers are of a much

later vintage, stylistically much better suited for Grecian, transitional, and early Renaissance revival pieces of the third quarter of the period. There is a narrower fifth and final drawer fitted into the base of the case which lacks pulls, but is similar to the others with its mahogany veneer and maple crossbanding. In fact it almost doubles as a skirt and projects farther forward than the drawers above. The separate bracket feet are pegged to square stiles, as are the bottom and top rails of the paneled sides. The back of the case has a top, medial, and bottom rail with two dadoed inside beveled pine panels. The tenoned rails are mortised into the rear case stiles.

In addition to this bureau, the desk shown in figure F–35 is the second of two strongly related pieces attributed to Omer.

Francis Omer (1818–1888), a native of France, arrived in America during September, 1853, settling and working in New Orleans. He had moved to Batesville, Independence County, Arkansas, by March, 1855, where he lived and worked the remainder of his life. Both the 1860 and 1870 census schedules for population list Omer as a cabinetmaker. Yet, by 1880 his occupation, as was the case for many rural artisans, was given as farmer.

F–18. Bureau, c. 1850–60, Fayetteville, Washington County. H: 41″, W: 41″, D: 20″. Primary: cherry. Secondary: pine. Inscribed in pencil on back "Made by J. W. Buie." *Courtesy of Frances Philip.*

Description: This bureau has a rectangular case with framed panel sides. The front stiles terminate in bracket feet with an inside curve that meets and continues the curvilinear shape of the skirt. The case back has top and bottom rails dadoed to receive three horizontal tongue and groove panels which are set into the rabbeted edges of the rear stiles. A large top drawer surmounts three graduated drawers, all with replacement knobs. Pine drawer runners are tenoned to the front and rear stiles, while the drawer blade is mortised and tenoned to the front stiles.

John W. Buie's presence in Fayetteville is first noted in the 1850 census for the county of Washington. The twenty-six-year-old Buie, a native of Tennessee, was living in the household of another local cabinetmaker, William M. Bowers, with whom he joined in a partnership. In one of their many local advertisements, they offered potential patrons: "Bureaus, bedsteads, tables, center tables, wardrobes, secretaries, safes, wash stands, etc. . . . of (the) newest and most approved patterns . . . also coffins of every style, size and finish" (*Southwest Independent*, 10 February 1855, 4–6). The partnership abruptly ended upon the death of Bowers later that year. Buie continued his thriving business, and by 1860 was in business with Edward Stigowest. They used 10,000 feet of lumber to construct "Bedsteads, Bureaus, Tables and no doubt, coffins" (*1860 United States Census Products of Industry for Washington County, Arkansas*, Microfilm Role 7, AHC).

The absence of descriptions makes it virtually impossible, except for when a signed piece surfaces, to ascertain the style and method of construction. Buie remained in the business well after 1870.

F–19. Child's High Chair, c. 1850–70, Howard County. H: 36¼″, W: 18¼″, D: 13½″. Hickory turnings, unidentified wood for slats, oak splints for seats. Maker unknown. *Courtesy of Mary Sue Williams.*

Description: Except for the two angular back slats, this attractive child's chair with white oak splint seat is entirely turned. The spool- and elongate conical-shaped finials top graduated backposts, each with a single ring turning just above the seat rails, while the bun-like feet may have once been ball turned like the front feet. Shallow scoring marks indicate where the top and lower edges of the slat tenons are mortised and pegged to the rear posts, or stiles as they are often called. Elongate undulating turned arms extend forward from just above the bottom slat of the back posts. Both are doweled into front posts which extend slightly above the arms. The front posts just below the hand rests have been cut away and turned to resemble the bamboo-like profiles of many "stick" Windsors of an earlier period. The posts are graduated and terminate in sharply cut ball feet. The top plain tapering stretcher between the top front legs is considerably worn from having been used as a foot rest. A bright red paint has been applied to the chair in recent years.

F–20.   Ladderback chairs, c. 1860, Hempstead or Sevier County. H: 34⅛″, W: 19″, D: 14¾″. Unidentified hardwoods. Maker unknown. *Courtesy of the Pioneer Washington Foundation.*

Description: Successive layers of lead-based, flat-white paint have been applied to these matching "common" or "split bottom" (referring to the woven oak seating) chairs. Both terms are found often in advertisements and inventories to describe what has become known as the slat, ladderback, or "mule ear" chair.

Except for the slats, all of the members have been turned. The plain-turned posts with their flattened or shaved fronts have been bent to splay outward. Just above the seat rails, the posts are ring turned, continuing as plain turning to the slightly tapered feet. Only the uppermost of the stepped or angular slats has been pegged to the back stiles or posts. Plain-turned front posts with tapered feet connect with plain doweled boxed stretchers, which are glued and cut nailed in

place. Nineteenth-century chairmakers normally referred to these stretchers as "rounds," while the stiles were called "posts." The chairs are so closely allied stylistically that they are very likely from the same shop. However, each chair was acquired from unacquainted families from separate, but adjoining, counties.

F–21.   Rocking Chair, before 1865, Pulaski or Hot Spring County. H: 39″, W: 27¾″, D: 18″. Hickory turnings, wood unidentified for slats and rockers. Maker unknown. *Courtesy of Mr. and Mrs. George Toney.*

Description: It is an understatement to say that this chair has wide proportions. It was supposedly made for Little Rock (Pulaski County) and Rockport (Hot Spring County) physician Lorenzo P. Gibson (1804–1866) by one of his artisan slaves. The chair seems to corroborate a family tradition which held that Dr. Gibson was a man of prodigious height and girth.

Except for the four bent and tapered slats of the rockers, all of the chair members are turned. The ball and ring finials project above graduated back posts. Each post has four sets of ringed scoring marks to indicate the placement of mortises to receive each of the four back slats, which were pegged in place. The arms are attached to the front posts by doweling beneath each ball- and ring-turned hand rest. The front post below each hand rest is turned in an elongated, bulbous shape, with a medial flattened ring, followed by graduated plain turning with interspersed flat rings. These rings appear positioned like scoring marks to indicate seat rail and stretcher placement.

F–22.   Rocking Chair, c. 1850–80, Brownstone, Sevier County. H: 35¾″, W: 17⅛″, D: 14¼″. Unidentified hardwoods. Maker unknown. *Courtesy of the Pioneer Washington Foundation.*

Description: Except for the rockers, slats, and seat rails, every element of this utilitarian and truly generic form of American chair has been plain turned. No finials grace the flattened or shaved fronts of the slightly bent back posts. Two plain, slightly bent slats frame a medial angular slat. The upper slat has been morticed and cut nailed to the posts. The twill woven "split" seat is a possible replacement. The seat rails are hand shaped and doweled to the posts. Box-turned stretchers are doweled and glued to the posts. Both the front and back posts are plain turned to the rockers.

F–23.   Ladderback Armchair, c. 1840–60, found in Hempstead County. H: 37″, W: 24″, D: 17⅜″. Unidentified woods. Maker unknown. *Courtesy of the Pioneer Washington Foundation.*

Description: Cone-shaped finials surmount graduating plain-turned posts, which have been rabbeted at the base (as are the front posts) to receive rockers which are missing, but were likely not original to the piece. A simple narrow, bent slat tops two angular-shaped and bent slats, all of which have been set into back post mortises. Only the top slat has been pegged to the posts. Curve-shaped arm rests are doweled at the back posts and set into doweled front posts. Shaped seat rails have twill-woven oak "splits" (splints). Stretchers have been shaped to imitate elongated sausage-like turnings.

F-24.   Side Chair (one of a set of four), c. 1840–60, Washington County. H: 32½", W: 16", D: 16". Unidentified hardwoods. Maker unknown. *Courtesy of Prairie Grove Battlefield Park.*

Description: Many cabinetmakers would have referred to this style of chair as Grecian. Much of the inspiration for Grecian furniture came from the genre scenes which decorated many of the ceramics that were retrieved in European archeological excavations during the eighteenth and early nineteenth centuries. People would often be depicted reclining upon couches or sitting on various forms of chairs at tables all normally sparse of ornament and crisp of line.

This "Klismos" or Grecian chair represents the small-town cabinetmaker's translation of the high style forms shown in design books or of pieces with which he had direct experience.

To accommodate the sitter's back, the rounded top or crest rail is slightly bowed on either side of the sawn arched splat; the undersides of the top have also been sawn to create pointed arches. The solid splat has been mortised into both the underside of the crest and the top of the seat rail. The upper portion of the stiles gracefully curve to meet the seat rail before continuing to form concave or "saber" shaped legs. The side seat rails, which taper slightly inward from front to back, complement the rake of the back legs. The

original removable slip seats are missing on all four chairs.

The side seat rails are mortised into and pegged to the back stiles and front legs. While the front and back rails are "through-tenoned" and pegged to the chair legs.

F-25.   Chair, c. 1850–1900, purchased in Madison County. H: 30¾", W: 17⅜", D: 13⅞". Posts possibly ash, slats and stretchers are hickory. Maker unknown. *From the collection of the Arkansas Territorial Restoration.*

Description: Pointed finials with pinched necks and flattened ring turnings cap the plain-turned, graduated rear posts or stiles that, like the front posts, end in sharply tapered feet. Only the upper three arched and bent slats have been pinned to the posts. Plain-turned, boxed stretchers or "rounds" are doweled to the chair legs.

F–26. "Fancy" Chair (one of a pair), c. 1850, Benton County. H: 30⅛", W: 17⅝", D: 14⅞". Unidentified hardwoods. Attributed to Christian or Simon Sager. *Courtesy of the Siloam Springs Museum.*

Description: The chair's entire surface has been painted and grained to imitate rosewood, an expensive and popular furniture hardwood. In addition to the fancy graining, there are remnants of stenciled gilding on the shaped crest rail.

The Benton County fancy painted chair shown here may very well represent the efforts of cabinetmakers such as the Sagers to compete with local merchants who were importing this style of furniture from larger furniture manufacturing centers such as Cincinnati and Boston. Fancy, a popular term at the time, refers to a wide variety of furniture forms often cheaply made, with brightly painted, stenciled and/or grained surfaces in imitation of more expensive cabinet woods such as mahogany or rosewood. Its popularity remained constant throughout much of the first half of the nineteenth century. Although the Sagers did not publicize their services in the fancy furniture line, numerous other Arkansas cabinet- and chairmakers did. I. M. Manning, a Batesville chairmaker, informed local patrons in the August 2, 1838, *Batesville News* that at his "Chair Factory," they might buy from present stock or order "FANCY, WINDSOR AND COMMON" chairs. While on the next page of the paper,

Manning offered additional services as a "House, Sign and Ornamental [imitation graining and marbleizing of architectural woodwork] painter." It was not uncommon for ornamental or fancy chairmakers to practice a trade which was in numerous ways closely allied to the other in methodology and materials. In truth, many of these men took up the manufacture of painted furniture as a new avenue of income only after having just taken up the profession of ornamental or sign painting. So too was this a practice among many of the non-academically trained portrait painters of the period, such as Horace Harding, who worked in Arkansas.

The arched top rail is ring and ball turned except for a flattened central panel which may have been decorated at one time. The flattened and bent back stiles or posts flare slightly outward. Multiple ring turnings decorate the graduated stiles above the seat rail. The slightly flared square seat rails are tenoned to the back posts, while the flared front ring-turned legs are doweled into the bottom of the side seat rails. Numerous cut-brad (nail) holes along the sides of the seat rail indicate that there may have once been facing panels of wood applied and doweled to the tapering legs to decorate and conceal the exposed edges of the rail.

F–27. Chair, nineteenth century, St. James, Stone County. H: 36½", W: 19", D: 14". Possibly elm posts, unidentified wood for slats and seat. Maker unknown. *Courtesy of Mrs. James Ford.*

Description: The back posts have pointed finials with short pinched or spool necks. Plain-turned, graduated rear and front posts terminate in tapered feet. The plain-turned boxed stretchers have been glued into doweled holes.

The lower case has paneled sides and square stiles terminating in turned feet. The eighteen small drawers used to hold medical apparatus and apothecary supplies are all fitted with individual runners joined to the drawer dividers and interior rear stiles installed especially for the multiple drawer construction. Each drawer face has "thumbnail" edge molding and is dovetailed to the drawer sides which are in turn dovetailed to the drawer backs. Beveled bottom boards are set into dadoes and nailed at the back. The drawer fronts are purposely made larger than the individual openings for each, so as to serve as drawer stops.

The case once belonged to James Purdom, M.D., a well-known antebellum Hempstead County physician.

F—28. Medical Cabinet, c. 1850–60, Washington, Hempstead County. H: 91½″, W: 38″, D: 17½″. Primary: walnut. Secondary: pine. Maker unknown. *Courtesy of Old Washington State Park.*

Description: Two-part case. Plain rectangular top overhanging two-paneled upper case doors. Applied moldings and struck beading are evident on the upper case door frames and the case itself.

F—29. Corner Cupboard, c. 1850–60, found in Lawrence County. H: 93″, W: 49″, D: 4½″ (at chamfered corners). Primary: walnut. Secondary: pine. Maker unknown. *Courtesy of Sarah Brown. In the collection of the Arkansas Territorial Restoration.*

Description: This corner cupboard has a cavetto cornice, with plain frieze struck beading along the lower edge (as are all of the inside case frame edges). Chamfered case sides extend to the bracket feet. The upper cupboard section has four storage shelves and is missing its original paneled door. The lower cupboard is separated by a narrow waist molding. Its double paneled door conceals two shelves, the lower of which serves additionally as a dustboard. A projecting base molding tops the bracket feet and shaped skirt. The white porcelain knob is a replacement. The back consists of vertical tongue and groove pine boards that from the back edge of the chamfered corners converge diagonally to meet two central backboards which parallel the case front.

molding (partly missing). The case has chamfered corners which continue to the simple bracket feet. The upper case section has two paneled upper cupboard doors. Each door contains two recessed, framed panels divided and framed into a medial rail. The turnbuckle and hand-grip pull are replacements. A waist molding (partly missing) separates the upper doors from the two lower paneled cupboard doors. Each cupboard area contains multiple shelving for the storage of dinnerware. Original cast-iron butt hinges are still present. Original cabinet locks are missing. Only a single span of the base molding located on one of the chamfered corners has survived the many years of hard use.

This cupboard was purchased from a descendant of William Bohannon (1823–1890), the original owner of the piece and an early settler of Madison County.

F–30.   Corner Cupboard, c. 1840–60, found in Madison County. H: 76½″, W: 43″, D: 19¼″. Primary: cherry. Secondary: pine. Maker unknown. *From the collection of the Arkansas Territorial Restoration.*

Description: This cupboard has a rather diminutive applied cavetto (partly missing) and compound molded cornice, with a simple narrow frieze having dentil

F–31.   Corner Cupboard, c. 1855, Woodruff County (at that time Jackson County). H: 72″, W: 41″, D: 22″ (at chamfered corners). Primary: walnut. Secondary: pine. Maker unknown. *Courtesy of Mike Angelo.*

Description: This cupboard has simple cavetto cornice molding, with a narrow plain frieze, chamfered case sides, double paneled upper doors, no midmolding, paneled lower doors, scallop-shaped skirt, and high bracket feet. The cupboard doors have original cast-iron butt hinges and cabinet locks. Back construction is almost identical to the previous "three cornered" cupboard. Inventories for the period refer to them as such.

According to family history, the cupboard was constructed by an artisan slave belonging to the Alexander Miller family. Miller arrived in Arkansas from South Carolina in 1852 or early 1853. He settled on a farm and operated a sawmill located between Augusta and Cotton Plant, Arkansas, in what was then part of Jackson County (Lucille Miller, "The Alexander Miller Home," *Rivers and Roads and Points in Between*, Vol. 1 [Augusta: Woodruff County Historical Society, Summer 1973] 4–7).

F–32. Corner Cupboard, c. 1843, Conway County. Primary: cherry. Secondary: pine. Maker unknown. *Courtesy of the Arkansas Museum of Science and History.*

According to the reminiscences of Effie Harrison Hobbs, "The cherrywood corner cupboard was made in the 1850s for Narcissa Willbanks Harrison, the mother of Robert Weaver Harrison [Mrs. Hobbs' father]. . . . It was made in the Hill Creek community of Conway County, Arkansas, by a journeyman in payment of his board. He had served an apprenticeship for three years in a workman's guild in England. . . ."

The cavetto-molded cornice face is cut nailed to the top of the case, and the chamfered edges of the case are mitered to the front of the case frame. The two upper cupboard doors are an unusual combination of wood-framed panels and glazing. The interior of the upper case portion contains three shelves for the storage of dinnerware. Door frame stiles and rails (stretchers) are struck beaded along their edges. A continuous waist molding divides the upper doors from the lower solid struck-beaded panel doors, which conceal additional shelving for storage.

Plain bracket feet are chamfered to match the angle of the case corners. The back consists of lap-jointed, vertical pine boards set into rabbets at the case edges and cut nailed at the top and bottom and into the bottom shelf of the upper (just below level of waist molding) case. Early reciprocating or sash saw marks are clearly present on these boards.

F–33. Desk, c. 1850–70, used by the General Assembly in the State House, Little Rock, Pulaski County. H: 38", W: 30", D: 18". Primary: pine and unidentified woods (for legs). Secondary: pine. Possibly made by Francis J. Ditter. *Courtesy of the University of Arkansas Museum, Fayetteville.*

Descripton: This desk has a fixed slant top with rectangular splash board and a single drawer with round wooden escutcheon and mushroom-shaped knob. The original cabinet lock is missing. The upper block sections of the legs serve as stiles to frame (with mortise and tenon joints) the back, sides, and front. Below the blocking, the legs continue in a ring, baluster, and plain, slightly tapered, turning, ending in inverted pear-shaped tapered feet.

According to museum records, the desk was used either by the Senate or House of Representatives in Arkansas's first State Capitol (completed 1841) in Little Rock.

There are numerous extant state auditor's warrant records for several local artisans who were contracted to make and repair Capitol furnishings. Among the most active was Francis J. Ditter.

Ditter garnered $35.00 for "making desk for general assembly" late in 1868. (State Auditor's Office, Warrant Record Book, Warrant (check) number 644, dated July 7, 1868.)

F–34. Desk, c. 1853–60, Independence County. H: 57¾″, W: 40¼″, D: 21¾″. Primary: walnut. Secondary: pine. Attributed to Francis Omer (1818–1888) of Batesville. *Courtesy of Robert Stroud.*

Description: This desk has a flat, molded cornice with projecting half-round canted corners. A cove molded drawer the width of the case is situated directly beneath the cornice and serves almost as a frieze. Its molded profile is extended along the sides with two bands of molding having coved upper edges to match those of the drawer. The coved molded corners of the case at the height of the drawer are round and flare in similar fashion to the drawer and sides, giving a visual impression of highly stylized foliate blossoms such as those of the lotus. The lotus was a classically inspired ornament both in France, Omer's country of origin, and in high style American pieces of three decades earlier. The entire piece has an almost architectural quality with the stylized lotuses serving as capitals for the slender, turned, canted colonettes. The cabinet lock, oval brass escutcheon, and mushroom-shaped knob appear original. The paneled, fall-front writing lid is fitted at the sides with folding brass strap hinges.

The lower half of the case has two deep storage drawers with mushroom knobs and oval stamped brass escutcheons. The wide baseboard molding across the front is mortised and tenoned into the stiles which are lathe turned and canted at the corners to serve as the plinth block for the colonettes. The vacant space directly beneath the base molding is to allow for the projection of a person's feet when sitting at the desk.

The interior of the writing compartment contains an upper drawer extending the entire width of the interior. An open document storage area is directly beneath the drawer. The lower portion of the compartment contains a deep central drawer with smaller stacked drawers to either side. All have their original turned brass knobs.

The simple rectilinear lines of this chastely ornamented desk mirror the tastes of Americans for a popularized and much honed-down vocabulary of design and ornament for furniture in the French neoclassic style. All of which was based vaguely upon an adaptation of extant architectural motifs, frescoes, and genre decorated vases of the ancient Greek, French, and English furnishings from the late eleventh to the early nineteenth centuries. Designers such as the brothers Adams, Thomas Sheraton, George Hepplewhite, Thomas Hope, and George Smith, along with the Frenchmen Percier and Fontaine, had a field day producing illustrated texts and drawings on the proper way in which to interpret this much adulterated vocabulary of design.

It is difficult, if not impossible at this juncture, to know how much Omer was aware of popular furniture styles either in Europe or America. However, this desk does reflect awareness of the popularized and much simplified designs of neoclassic interpretations of antique forms in architecture and furnishings.

For a brief history of Omer's presence in Batesville, see figure F–17.

F—35.   Desk and Bookcase, c. 1840—50, Little Rock, Pulaski County. H: 84½", W: 43½", D: 22¼". Primary: mahogany veneers. Secondary: pine. Maker unknown. *Courtesy of Mr. and Mrs. Sterling Cockrill.*

Description: A removable one-piece ogee cornice and frieze surmounts the upper section of this mahogany-veneered desk and bookcase. The upper section has plain sides and rounded front edges which frame two arched and paneled cupboard doors. A continuous line of bead molding has been applied to the inside edges of the door frames. The upper doors enclose two fixed bookshelves over a writing compartment or cabinet. This compartment contains four large document compartments and several pigeonholes that frame a central open mirrored prospect, all of which tops three drawers with small turned brass knobs.

The lower case consists of a two-board folded double writing lid that is hinged at the sides with long brass strap hinges. Inside is a single large cupboard; rectangular, beaded panel doors conceal a large cupboard with two shelves, the bottom of which serves as a dustboard. Bold ogee feet flank the scalloped skirt of the base.

This piece is quite similar in design to the large, rectilinear, almost architectural quality, furniture advertised by the New York cabinetmaking firm of Joseph Meeks and Sons in an 1833 broadside. The broadside contained 44 lithographed illustrations of case and seating furniture known as scrolled or Grecian. This advertisement by the well-known firm appears to have introduced a definite new American style (Celia Jackson Otto, *American Furniture of the Nineteenth Century* [New York: Viking Press, 1965] 114).

This style is extremely plain and often bulky and is characterized by the rectilinear shapes of the case furniture with their wide expanses of mahogany veneer, in lieu of ornamental or more sophisticated turnings and carvings. Turned elements are at a minimum, being substituted for square or rectangular in-section pilasters and scrolled supports for large case pieces such as wardrobes, bureaus, and desks.

The popularity of the style was further cemented with the appearance of an 1840 Baltimore publication authored by architect John Hall and entitled *The Cabinet-Maker's Assistant*. "As far as possible the style of the United States is blended with European taste, and a graceful outline and a simplicity of parts are depicted. . . . Throughout the whole of the designs . . . , particular attention has been bestowed in an economical arrangement to save labor" (John Hall, *The Cabinet-Maker's Assistant, Embracing the Most Modern Style of Cabinet Furniture* [Baltimore: John Murphy, 1840] 3—4).

Hall included almost 200 illustrations pertaining to drafting perspectives and designing and using individual furniture elements. Illustrations of finished pieces completed the book.

rectangular case stiles continue below the cupboard section to form plain rectangular legs.

A considerable amount of the original flat, dark-green paint remains on this simple utilitarian piece which most likely was relegated to the kitchen or porch for use in the storage of foodstuffs and kitchen and dinnerware.

F–36.   Safe, c. 1860–80, found in Washington County. H: 68½″, W: 39¾″, D: 20¼″. Pine throughout. Maker unknown. *From the collection of the Arkansas Territorial Restoration.*

Description: A narrow cavetto-molded cornice and smaller compound-molded band are cut nailed to the case top. Like the case, the framed cupboard doors are of mortise and tenon construction and contain three punched-tin panels each, as do the case sides. The twelve tin panels have identical geometric, punched decorations. A template was invariably used to create a pattern which consists of three lines of punching forming a framed rectangle with punched, quartered spandrels at their inside corners and a central concentric ring motif. Each recessed panel (including each side panel) is held in place by strips of molding applied to the inside edges of the door frames. The pronounced vertical struck bead and rabbeted inside edge of the right door overlap the reverse rabbet of the left door when closed to serve as a stop. The cupboard contains fixed storage shelves, with the bottom board serving as a dustboard. The bottom drawer sits atop a drawer blade which serves also as a baseboard. The drawer face, sides, and back are dovetailed, with a beveled bottom attached through dadoes in the sides, and the drawer is nailed together at the back. The straight,

F–37.   Safe, c. 1860, found in Washington County. H: 55⅝″, W: 44″, D: 16½″. Primary: walnut. Secondary: pine. Maker unknown. *From the collection of the Arkansas Territorial Restoration.*

Description: A rectangular two-board top with molded edges sits over a single drawer. The drawer has dovetailed construction with the beveled bottom being dadoed into the drawer sides and nailed at the back. Each of the cupboard doors, like the sides, contains three punched tin panels. All of the panels are cut nailed to the doors and case frames. The cupboard interior contains three fixed shelves, the bottom of which serves as a dustboard. There is thumbnail base molding, and the stiles continue below the case to form feet which in the front have been sawn on their inside in an angular scroll profile. The back feet are simply square-in-section tapered on their inside edges.

The tin panels have been painted at least twice. There is a light base coat beneath flat white. The case retains an old, flat, dark-red paint, which may or may not be original.

F–38.   Press, c. 1850, found in Washington County. H: 55¾″, W: 43″, D: 19½″. Primary: cherry and walnut (top board). Secondary: pine. Maker unknown. *From the collection of the Arkansas Territorial Restoration.*

A three-board rectangular top, possibly replaced, sits above two drawers with mushroom knobs. The mortise and tenon constructed case has paneled sides with a two-door storage cupboard below the drawers. Each is mortise and tenon framed with recessed panels. A wide top panel is separated by a stretcher or rail from three narrow vertical panels divided by stiles. The upper drawers project beyond the lower cupboard section and are supported by half-columns attached to recessed stiles which have been cut out to receive them. The columns are primarily a combination of ring and plain turning. The feet, which are part of the stiles, are spool, vase, and ring turned.

Multiple vertical backboards have been tongue and grooved together and set into a dado on the underside of the back top rail of the case, while the bottoms of the boards are cut nailed to the bottom structural cupboard shelf. Located beneath the drawer divider, or drawer blade, is a draw-board (sliding) work shelf with mushroom knobs matching those of the drawer and doors.

F–39.   Press or Sideboard, c. 1850, Madison County. H: 46¾″, W: 43¾″, D: 21″. Primary: cherry. Secondary: pine. Maker unknown. *Courtesy of Mr. and Mrs. Bunn Bell.*

This sideboard has a rectangular top above double drawers with ogee or cyma molded fronts. Drawer front, sides, and back are dovetailed while the beveled bottom board is fitted in dadoes in drawer sides. The two paneled cupboard doors have struck-beaded trim and retain their original brass keyhole surround over an iron cabinet lock. The doors are flanked by applied angular-turned half columns supporting the projecting drawers. The stiles have been recessed to receive the columns. Narrow plinths are supported by sawn scrolled feet. It also has covered base molding.

F–40.   Sideboard, c. 1850, Washington County. H: 45″, W: 76″, D: 20″. Primary: walnut and walnut veneer (for concave top drawer front). Secondary: pine. Maker unknown. *Courtesy of Mr. and Mrs. Ewing Jackson.*

This sideboard has a separate stepped case with three cutlery drawers above. The central drawer of the upper recessed case is deeply concave. Its drawer front is walnut veneered with replacement escutcheons and old knobs. Beneath the stepped drawers are two wide projecting ogee-molded front drawers. Scroll square-in-section pillars or columns serve as supports and

flank three paneled cupboard doors. The central cupboard door is boldly convex in shape. Each cupboard is compartmentalized by solid dividing boards. The scrolled support columns sit upon small plinth blocks that at one time were supported by scrolled feet that were removed many years ago.

Note: All of the door and drawer escutcheons are twentieth-century replacements; however, the knobs are old, if not original.

This piece has descended in the family of James Mitchell, to whom it once belonged. Mitchell was a prominent antebellum settler in Washington County.

F–41.   Sideboard, c. 1845–60, Fayetteville, Washington County. H: 44¾″, W: 42½″, D: 22″. Primary: walnut. Secondary: pine and unidentified wood. Maker unknown. *From the collection of the Arkansas Territorial Restoration.*

Description: This sideboard has a rectangular top with splashboard over two projecting cutlery drawers. These drawers are above a single large drawer with a deep well for the possible storage of linens. Applied S-scrolled supports for the projecting upper section flank the single large drawer. Each of the drawers has dovetail construction, with the bottom board being beveled and dadoed into drawer sides. The knobs, brass key-hole surrounds, and mortised cabinet locks are original. The paneled sides are mortised and tenoned to the stiles, which below the case form the legs. The legs are a combination of spool, ring, and block (square section), culminating in tapered, arrow-shaped feet. The stiles are recessed to receive the scrolled supports of the upper two case projecting drawers.

F–42.   Sideboard, c. 1840, Cane Hill, Washington County, H: 47″, W: 69″, D: 20″. Primary: walnut and mahogany veneer (on drawer fronts, top, and frieze area around drawers). Secondary: pine. Maker unknown. This piece was once the property of Wharton Rector (1800–1842) of Fort Smith in whose family it has descended. *Courtesy of Mr. and Mrs. Fadjo Cravens, Jr.*

Description: Both of the double torus-molded cutlery drawers and the rectangular top are veneered in mahogany. There are three separate cupboards below with recessed panel doors. The widest central cupboard has double doors with the right door having an applied bead edge molding which serves as a stop for the other door when closed. The turned walnut knobs on the two single flanking cupboard doors are original, while the brass escutcheon for the central cupboard doors may have been replaced. Two large scroll pillars support the projecting upper-drawer frieze. The square-in-section scroll feet continue the line by the upper pillars.

F–43.   Table, c. 1850–60, Hempstead County. H: 28¼″, W: 25½″, D: 22¾″. Primary: walnut. Secondary: pine. Maker unknown. *Courtesy of Parker Westbrook.*

Description: The functional, almost square, two-board top has a single butt-jointed drawer below. Square, tapering legs are mortised and tenoned to the skirts or sides.

F—44a.   Round Center Table, dated 1854, Ft. Smith, Sebastian County. H: 31½″, D (top): 33½″. Woods unidentified. Maker: Samuel French. *From the collection of the Arkansas Territorial Restoration.*

Description: This elaborately inlaid table has applied edge molding and sits atop four ring-turned legs. An abacus (scrolled platform) base with a flat section at the scrolled feet supports the top and legs.

The bold centralized design motif for the top consists of colorfully contrasting woods geometrically inlaid in the form of an eight-pointed star. The star is encircled by an extravagant sawtooth pattern inlay border radiating outward to the table's edge, while the abacus style base or platform has a smaller contrasting block and diamond inlay in the center.

Both the eight-pointed star and sawtooth border motifs are quite commonly used as ornaments for Arkansas pieced quilts of the period.

Samuel Gibbs French was born in New Jersey, November 12, 1818, graduated from West Point in 1843, and won two brevets in the Mexican War (1846–48) as an artillery officer. He acquired, through marriage, a plantation in Mississippi and resigned from the army in 1856 to operate the farm. He served throughout the War Between the States as an officer in the Confederate army, attaining the rank of major general. He died a planter in Florala, Florida, on April 20, 1901. French cannot be documented as having worked as a professional cabinetmaker.

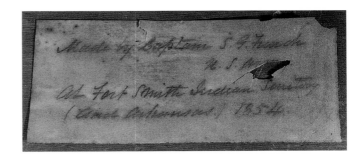

F—44b.   Detail of the signed label beneath the top of the table made by S. G. French.

F–45. Table, c. 1860, Hempstead County. H: 28½″, W (top): 35¾″, W (frame): 20⅞″. Pine throughout. Maker unknown. *Courtesy of Old Washington State Park.*

Description: The wide top overhangs one drawer. The drawer sides are butted and cut nailed together. The drawer front has chamfered edges, and the legs are spool and plain taper, with ring-turned feet.

F–46. Communion Table, c. 1856, Washington, Hempstead County. H: 30⅜″, W: 34¼″, D: 21⅝″. Walnut throughout. Maker unknown. *Courtesy of the First Methodist Church, Washington, Arkansas.*

Description: This table has a rectangular top with clipped corners and square-tapered legs. Tradition among church members holds that this table was built to hold the collection or tithing baskets during

services and is original to the church, which was built in 1856.

F–47a. Table, c. 1850, Independence County. H: 28½″, W: 23″, D: 21″. Primary: walnut. Secondary: pine. Attributed to Independence County cabinetmaker William Curry. *See* Biographical Appendix. *Courtesy of Robert Stroud.*

Description: The rectangular three-board top sits over one drawer with string inlay in a cut-corner pattern. The drawer has a diamond-inlaid wood escutcheon. The drawer sides have been dovetailed, with the beveled drawer bottom set into dadoes in the drawer sides, and cut nailed at the back. The pulls are replacements. The table has square-tapered legs.

F–47b. Detail of the drawer dovetailing on figure F–47a.

F–48.   Table, c. 1860, Dardanelle, Pope County. H: 28⅞", D (top): 34⅜". Pine throughout. Maker unknown. *From the collection of the Arkansas Territorial Restoration.*

Description: The round top is cut nailed to the table frame. The table has square-tapered legs. Old paint and varnish residue is still visible.

This table was purchased at an auction held in a pre–Civil War building in Dardanelle, a town situated on the Arkansas River, in the northwest part of the state. The table was supposedly one of the original furnishings of the building when it was being operated as a tavern before 1870.

F–49.   Table, c. 1819, probably Little Rock, Pulaski County. H: 29½", W: 48", D: 29⅝". Cypress throughout. Maker unknown. *From the collection of the Arkansas Territorial Restoration.*

Description: This table has a large, rectangular top over two drawers (dovetail construction), with square-tapered legs.

This table has descended directly in the family of William E. Woodruff, Sr. (1795–1885), who founded the *Arkansas Gazette* in 1819. The table was, according to his great-granddaughter, used in his printing office, either at Arkansas Post (Arkansas County), where the paper was first printed between 1819–21, or in Little Rock where Woodruff moved his presses late in 1821.

F–50.   Table, c. 1850–70, found in Madison County. H: 28⅜″, W: 24″, D: 20″. Primary: walnut. Secondary: pine. Maker unknown. *From the collection of the Arkansas Territorial Restoration.*

Description: The single board top sits over one drawer with dovetail construction (bottom board beveled and fitted into dadoes in drawer sides). It has square-tapered legs. Remnants of an old, if not original, stain and varnished finish are still visible.

F–51.   Table, c. 1860, Washington or Carroll County. H: 28⅞″, W: 49¾″, D: 36½″. Pine throughout. Maker unknown. *From the collection of the Arkansas Territorial Restoration.*

Description: The long rectangular top no doubt made this table an excellent surface on which to work in the nineteenth-century kitchen. It has square-tapered legs.

F–52a.   Clothes Press, c. 1845–50, Round Bottom, Izard County. H: 72″, W: 49⅜″, D: 18½″. Primary: walnut. Secondary: pine. Made by John Lancaster (1801–1855). *Courtesy of Mae Lancaster Dobbins.*

Description: This clothes press has a flaring cavetto-molded cornice over an applied keyhole-dentil molding situated against the base of the cornice on all three sides. The upper case contains two large cupboard doors on original cast-iron butt hinges (pre-1845 type, *see* figure F–52b). Each cupboard door has three chamfered edged, fielded (raised central portion) panels dadoed into mortise and tenon door frames that are wooden pinned. The inside edges of the door frames have a small, diagonally stepped double bead. The old, well-worn turnbuckle and knob may be original. The press has the original diamond-shaped, inlaid escutcheon and mortised cabinet lock. The cupboard interior contains four shelves to store clothing.

The lower case section is separated by a projecting shelf. It has two cupboard doors constructed the same as the upper ones. The enlarged escutcheon and mortised cabinet lock are original. Knobs and turnbuckles are missing. The cupboard contains only a bottom shelf which serves as a dustboard.

The flat case stiles have short, turned half columns flanking both upper cupboard doors. These columns sit upon the projecting shelf which separates the two sections. Similarly, block and turned half columns flank the lower cupboard doors. The large, projecting case base also projects to support both tiers of columns and has bun feet.

The back consists of five vertically-arranged pine boards, tongue and grooved together and fitted into the rabbeted edges of the plain sideboards, and then cut nailed to the case frame.

The large, imposing press was made, according to the present owner, by John Lancaster, her great-grandfather, on his farm at Round Bottom in Izard County. Lancaster, who had moved from Tennessee to Arkansas c. 1844, was married twice and fathered ten children, whose many descendants still live in the area. John died in Izard County in June, 1855.

F–52b.   Detail view of one of the original cast-iron butt hinges on the doors of the John Lancaster clothes press (figure F–52a). The hinge is case marked "BALDWIN," on one leaf, and "PATENT" on the other, measure: 3″ × 2½″.

The replacement of handwrought hinges with those of cast iron reflects a major change in the production of house and furniture hardware. Cast-iron butt hinges, along with a variety of cast door latches (Norfork and Suffolk varieties) and shutter accessories, were patented in England during the last quarter of the eighteenth century. Soon, American foundries would follow suit. By 1815, in Pittsburgh, America's Birmingham, cast-iron hardware, including butt hinges, was being offered to the public.

Donald Streeter, an authority on early American hardware, described the process for making these hinges.

First, the male part was cast [in a sand mold], perhaps with a core for the pin [pintle] hole, to center it and keep it straight for reaming and drilling, and with the countersunk screw holes in the pattern. Then, once the male part was cast, its parts were cleaned, and wire pins [pintles] inserted. . . . Then in a mold prepared for it and its mate, with pin in place, it was ready for casting. Molten iron flowed in, up to the male half hinge, and around the pin, shrinking tight upon it, and, at the same time, shrinking away from the male part allowing proper movement. A little filing finished the hinge. (Donald Streeter, "Early American Wrought Iron Hardware: H and H L Hinges, Together with Mention of Dovetails and Cast Iron Butt Hinges," *The Bulletin*

of the Association for Preservation Technology, Vol. V, 1, 1973, 47–49).

Cast-iron butts with fixed pins of this kind remained popular even after patents for removable pins began to appear during the 1840s.

F–53. Wardrobe, c. 1860–70, Fayetteville, Washington County. H: 84½", W: 48⅞", D: 22¾". Primary: cherry. Secondary: pine. Maker unknown. *From the collection of the Arkansas Territorial Restoration.*

Description: The case's broad vibrant surfaces of solid cherry suffice well as its only ornament.

The flaring beveled cornice and plain frieze are cut nailed to the case top. Two long, paneled cupboard doors retain their original cast-iron butt hinges and mortised cabinet lock. A single raised bead is attached to the length of the right door to serve as a stop when the doors are closed.

The single storage drawer has dovetailed joined sides and a beveled bottom board dadoed in the drawer sides. The drawer knobs appear original.

The wardrobe was found in a home built c. 1870 in Fayetteville. Recent owners, descendants of the builder, stated that the piece was original to the house.

The case feet are extensions of the square stiles. Each of the sides of the individual feet has been sawn in a vertical cyma curve, which gives the feet an undulating form.

F–54.   Wardrobe, c. 1850–60, Tulip, Dallas County. H: 86″, W: 49″, D: 21″. Pine throughout. Maker unknown. *Courtesy of Miss Glenn Mallett.*

Description: This wardrobe has a flaring beveled cornice over paneled cupboard doors and two storage drawers. It has simple bracket feet. The case sides are cut out to form the feet.

The turnbuckle is a replacement. The doors' cast-iron butt hinges are original. The wardrobe has been painted white in recent years.

According to the owner, this piece is one of a pair of wardrobes that remain as part of the original furnishings of the George Mallett (1825–1877) home built c. 1860.

F–55.   Wardrobe, c. 1868, Little Rock, Pulaski County. H: 84″, W: 39¼″, D: 16½″. Primary: walnut. Secondary: unidentified hardwood. Made by M. J. Plouf. *Courtesy of Mrs. James D. Reed.*

Inscribed "M. P. Little Rock, Ark." on the back panel of the right door and one side of the right drawer. Part of a suite of bedroom furniture, which included a bedstead (figure F–6) and a bureau (figure F–12), all of which were made for William Henry Harrison Brown, prior to the birth of his first child in November, 1868. See figure F–6 for more history on this furniture, and the cabinetmaker, M. J. Plouf, who is also listed in the biographical appendix.

Description: The flat, upright cornice board with angularly shaped molded upper edges was typical for a popular furniture style of the late third quarter of the century. Collectors and curators alike have come to refer to these vertically rectilinear forms with angular moldings and incised line ornament as Renaissance in style.

The plain case contains two long cupboard doors with a single drawer directly above bracketed front feet. The recessed panels of the cupboard doors appear shaped by the angular or scalloped inside edge moldings of the frames. The molding theme is continued in the drawer with its three-piece paneled front. The primary recessed panel, which is screwed to the back of the drawer-front frame, has a second long, narrow raised panel glued to it. Both the drawer front frame and the inset, raised panel have been given edge moldings that, like the door moldings, are quite rectilinear and angular in profile.

Very little pre-1870 furniture made in Arkansas in Renaissance style has surfaced to date. Future research may very well uncover a considerable amount of this furniture in both the Little Rock and Fort Smith areas where several small furniture factories sprang up following the Civil War.

Thomas Anderson Watson (1830–1911). *Courtesy of Kathy Sewell Worthen and Ruth Wharton.*

Description: Although Thomas Anderson Watson was not a professional cabinetmaker, his obvious skills as woodworker are apparent in this well-proportioned round-top table. The single drawer is of lap-joint construction, secured by cut nails. The simple turned legs terminate in what appear to be original cast-iron casters.

F–57.   Table, c. 1870, found in Washington County. H: 30″, W: 24″, D: 23⅞″. Unidentified wood. Maker unknown. *From the collection of the Arkansas Territorial Restoration.*

Description: This almost square topped table has a single drawer with scalloped skirts. The square section-tapered legs are unusually chamfered at their corners to create an undulating or ripple effect.

The drawer sides are butted into the rabbeted back corners of the front and cut nailed, while back edges of the drawer sides are butted to the back drawer board and cut nailed. The drawer bottom is nailed directly to the bottom of all of the drawer sides. The pull has been replaced.

F–56.   Table, c. 1870, Benton County. H: 29¼″, D (top): 32⅜″. Primary: walnut. Secondary: pine. Maker

F–58.   Stand, c. 1850–60, Hempstead County. H: 20½", D (top): 16⅜". Walnut throughout. Maker unknown. *Courtesy of Old Washington State Park.*

Description: A stationary top covers the ring- and vase-turned pedestal or shaft. Three cabriole legs are mortised into the pedestal base.

F–59.   Stand, c. 1860, Hempstead County. H: 29¼", D (top): 14¾". Walnut throughout. Maker unknown. *Courtesy of Old Washington State Park.*

Round stationary top above combination ring- and slightly tapered plain-turned pedestal, shaft, or "pillar," as it was referred to by some cabinetmakers of the period. Three S-shaped, flat-sectioned legs are mortised and tenoned to the plain-turned shaft base.

ARKANSAS
QUILTS

Quiltmaking in Arkansas

Whether pieced, stuffed, or appliquéd, the quilts created out of necessity by Arkansas women constitute the largest body of decorative and functional art that has survived to the present time. Unfortunately, throughout the nineteenth century the individual artists were not enumerated within the census pages or touted in the commercial advertisements of the local newspapers. Only an occasional diary or letter or a newspaper list of premium winners at county fairs chronicled the quiltmaker's creative presence. As a result, these artists in fabrics have been all but forgotten by modern historians. Thankfully, many of the descendants of these neglected craftswomen have preserved untold numbers of their forebears' beautifully planned and executed quilt documents which enrich our cultural heritage.

Although there are in existence some Arkansas-made quilts that pre-date 1850, by far the greatest number of surviving quilts were produced during the third quarter of the nineteenth century, primarily because of the increased availability of inexpensive, mass-produced fabrics and a substantial increase in population during the 1850s.

A majority of the newly arrived immigrants that contributed to this population increase came from Southern states east of the Mississippi River, especially from Tennessee and North Carolina, where the textile arts had flourished as early as the late eighteenth century. Consequently, the immigrants to Arkansas brought with them not only an appreciation for the art of quilting, but also the quilting skills that had been passed down from generation to generation.

Through the Needle's Eye—The Quiltmakers

Almost every young Arkansas woman was taught by her mother or older sisters a considerable amount of plain and fancy or ornamental needlework, which she would perform throughout the remainder of her life. In her reminiscences of her childhood on a nineteenth-century farm, Marion Rawson described her early efforts at learning the art and mysteries of needlework.

> Before I was three years old, I started at piecing a quilt. Patchwork you know. My stint was at first only two blocks a day, but these were sewn together with the greatest care or they were unraveled and done over.[1]

Along with instruction from family members, quilting was offered in many of the early private academies. The Pine Bluff Female Academy was typical in its inclusion of "Plain and Ornamental

Needlework" as part of a traditional curriculum for the spring semester of 1838 which also included botany, chemistry, arithmetic, painting, and music lessons.[2]

Plain work consisted of utilitarian needlework, the making of clothing, bed coverings, towels, and curtains, while ornamental or "fancy" needlework was applicable to the making of intricately designed quilts and multipurpose counted cross-stitch samplers, as well as embroidery of garments, kerchiefs, purses, and upholstery, with a variety of stitching techniques. If a family could afford it, these services were performed by professional needleworkers, seamstresses and milliners, who worked in most towns in the state. In eastern Helena in Arkansas, Mrs. M. Burnett "Milliner and Dress Maker" maintained an advertisement over a period of years prior to the Civil War which reminded potential patrons that she was constantly available at moderate prices to make dresses, cloaks, and children's clothing and would perform at the shortest notice fancy needlework and embroidery.[3] As in the case of Mrs. Burnett, the milliner was most often an experienced needlewoman who, in addition to fashioning fancy ladies' headgear and clothing, kept on hand a variety of fabrics, ribbons and trims, soaps, perfume, jewelry—in fact, almost any article used for needlework or the personal toilet.

These artistic immigrants continued a long-standing tradition in the textile arts, which had flourished in America for over three centuries. "The remarkable persistence of the craft," quilt historian Jonathan Holstein wrote, "indicated two things about quilts: their practicality and our sentimental attachment to them . . . no other thing Americans have made has been so universally loved."[4]

The Arkansas quiltmaker of the nineteenth century was usually a farm woman who was required to do far more than practice her art. She was often required to plow the fields, chop and pick cotton, cook, clean, maintain a garden, and raise the children. These farm families were generally from the yeoman class—small, nearly self-sufficient, non-slaveholding landowners, who were dependent on their own labor. One survey has noted that as early as 1840 only nineteen of every hundred taxpayers in the state owned even a single slave.[5]

Despite the demands of day to day life, many Arkansas women found the time to create some of the most exquisitely crafted quilts in the entire country. Like woven coverlets, the quilt often served as a part of the necessary bedcovering required in a household which could not afford "store bought" blankets and bedding, and, although producing a quilt may seem a laborious task to many modern observers, the many nineteenth-century accounts contained in letters and diaries which refer to competitions at local fairs or the completion of a special creation attest to the love and joy that went into the making of a quilt. Quiltmaking also furnished a needed relief from the drudgery of frontier life.

The routine drudgery of the farm woman or small-town merchant's wife improved in 1857 when several local agricultural and mechanical societies from around the state began sponsoring fairs and competitions within their respective counties. The fairs were ostensibly organized to promote and improve agricultural technology and manufactured goods, as well as the domestic accomplishments of the ladies.[6] For the first time local farmers and artisans alike were brought together to display products from their fields and workbenches. In deference to the women, separate ladies' departments were created so they too might competitively exhibit everything from foodstuffs to their most prized embroideries, woven coverlets, or quilts. Cash premiums and printed certificates of merit were awarded to the winners in each of several categories.

At the first annual Prairie and White counties "Agricultural and Industrial Fair" of 1857, *The Des Arc Citizen* reported that of the one thousand to fifteen hundred visitors attending the exhibits, not a single report of dissatisfaction could be documented.[7] Never before had the participants had their prized quilts inspected outside of their own immediate family and circle of friends. And, certainly, never before had they been offered the opportunity to win cash premiums for their own handiwork—handiwork routinely expected of them. It must have been a difficult experience for many of these women to enter and then submit their prized creations to the scrutiny of judges and strangers alike. Yet, when the decisions were rendered and printed in the local newspaper, the victorious quiltmakers emerged as local celebrities.

> Best Cotton Patch [work] Quilt, Mrs. Harshaw—$2. Second Best Cotton Patch Quilt, Mrs. D. Harshaw—Certificate. Best Cotton, Cotton Counterpane [woven coverlet], Mrs. Hannah Ford—$2.50. Best Wool Counterpane [coverlet], Mrs. Simeron—$2.[8]

Results like the one above, printed in a local paper, gave the winners a new status and a considerable amount of deserved recognition.

In 1849, young Everard Dickinson, a recent arrival on the Arkansas frontier, reported in a letter home to his parents in Massachusetts that he had "been to several reapings . . . and quiltings lately—It is customary here for the Neighbors to take turns in helping each other harvest. They all go with their Wives and Daughters and Babies."[9]

But Dickinson did not attend to admire wheat shocks or the acumen of the quilters, rather he reveals his real intentions, as he continues: "The men gather the wheat, while the Women quilt—and have a good dinner . . . and the young men (if they are popular), can get a chance—maybe to hug and kiss the Galls [girls] a little."[10]

The quilting frolic or bee was, in many rural areas, the only form of social contact available. Actually there was a wide variety of occasions when neighbors assembled to enjoy one another's company, celebrate with a dance and /or supper, and cooperatively assist a neighbor with a specific task. There were barn- and house-raising frolics, log-rolling frolics, and quilting frolics. Dr. J. G. M. Ramsey, an early settler in western Tennessee, reminiscing about his antebellum experiences noted that "failure to ask a neighbor to a raising, clearing, . . . or his family to a quilting, was considered a high indignity; . . . to be explained or atoned for at the next [militia] muster or County Court. Each settler was not only willing but desirous to contribute . . . [to the] general comfort and . . . improvement [of the community], and felt aggrieved and insulted if the opportunity to do so was withheld."[11]

The German visitor, Friedrich Gerstäcker, a well-known wanderer through the interior of frontier Arkansas during the 1830s and 1840s, especially enjoyed his memories of such gatherings. "Frolics" he wrote

> generally take place in spring. When a farmer calls his neighbors together to collect and burn all the wood he has cut down, it is called a "log rolling frolic," and when the women assemble to sew together a number of difficult colored patches, it is called a "quilting frolic," and in the evening, there is generally a dance, or a game of forfeits.[12]

At other times quiltings were apparently exclusively for women as Van Buren County resident Fanny Love recorded in her diary for the month of December, 1861.

> [Dec. 12] Mrs. Garner asked us to a quilting this evening . . . [Dec.13] I went down to Mrs. Garners this morning we like to froze. . . . When we got there I found all the girls. There was twenty four of us and not the first boy, never saw girls enjoy them selves better in my life. . . . We quilted all day, but did not get the quilt rolled [finished and taken off the frame], it was quilted in flowers.[13]

It is interesting to note Miss Love's allusion to the absence of "boys" having little or no affect on the apparent success of the quilting party. There existed in the nineteenth century a separate and distinct society inhabited by women only. It was a world to which they had been relegated as a conservative male reaction to the emergence of a more highly urban and industrialized American society, a society which many felt was causing the breakdown of the more traditional, rural, tight-knit family unit. This unique sisterhood—although considered by the male population at the time to be intellectually inferior—was at the same time felt to be purer, more devout, and by an almost divine nature domestically and maternally superior.[14] The traditional all-female quilting party, bee, or frolic was an important element of this unique sisterhood from the past century. Generally, before the event, the quilt top had been pieced or appliquéd with the appropriate pattern and awaited only the nimble needles of the attendants to the frolic to carry out the background quilting. The quilting served both to decorate and bind the three layers (backing, batting, and quilt top) fairly together.

There were also several customs in Arkansas attendant to the "christening" of a completed quilt. One of the most persistent was recorded by the noted Arkansas folklorist Vance Randolph. He wrote: "Groups of unmarried women at quilting bees used to shake up a cat in the newly completed quilt and then stand around [holding the quilt] in a big circle as the animal was suddenly released. The theory was that the girl toward whom the cat jumped would be the first . . . to catch a husband."[15]

However, one male eyewitness to this practice in the Ouachita mountains humorously recalled that when the unmarried girls began tossing the cat in the quilt at a local frolic, "the cat got so scared it ran out by all of them—like jumping on a horse and riding off in all directions—because within a very short time they were all married."[16]

A somewhat macabre bit of quilt lore held that once a quilt top was stretched onto its frame it was never to be turned until finished. If it did happen to be turned, at least one of the quilters would lose her skills, her eyesight might fail, or "her hands became paralyzed."[17]

Patterns

Despite a widespread proliferation of fanciful names given to American quilt patterns over the past century and a half, there is precious little historical data (i.e., letters, diaries, wills, etc.) to establish their provenance. Arkansas quilters were not the exception in this practice. When they did make note of their quilting activities, such as the following reference made in 1849 by Saline County resident Sarah A. Nelson, no mention of a specific pattern is given. "We have been envited," she wrote "to one quilting but did not go as we had not got acquainted . . . [but] we have quilted our spreads since we got here. . . ."[18]

Although, upon rare occasion, an Arkansas quilter such as Fanny Love would entice future quilt enthusiasts with an elusive reference to pattern. Miss Fanny Love's diary entry for January 28, 1862, reads, " . . . came home this morning and went to work spinning . . . sewing thread [and] to piece my quilt [called] the Russian Battery. . . ."[19]

Miss Love makes no further mention of her "Russian Battery" spread. Nor have any other Arkansas references or quilt examples of this pattern come to light. Added to the local deficiency of data is the shortage of any graphic or written account of this pattern in any of the standard American quilt reference books.

A number of theories about the origin of pattern names have been posited by contemporary quilt historians. Obviously, pattern names were passed down from generation to generation and from friend to friend at gatherings such as the quilting frolic. And, by the mid-decades, fashion and design journals with nationwide circulation in tandem with other female oriented periodicals such as *Godey's Lady's Book and Magazine* were proffering a variety of illustrated quilt patterns from which to select. "What little girl does not recollect her first piece of patchwork," an 1856 *Godey's* article begins, in conjunction with the inclusion of several unidentified illustrated patterns. Since the author does not ascribe specific names to any of the quilt designs, it may be that aspiring quilters would infuse their own names in colloquial fashion for those they wished to recreate.[20]

An incalculable number of whimsical names may have been coined by subscribing needleworkers throughout the nation.

The careful savings in a ragbag of hundreds or even thousands of scraps of fabric marked the beginning of this uniquely creative outlet for American women.[21] Within the parameters of the quilting frames and the needle's eye a woman could express her creativity in regard to ornament (patterns, colors, or background quilting), harmony, and overall design. In addition, to produce a successful quilt, the quiltmaker had to be concerned with the quality of line and surface unity in a particular pattern.

Arkansas quilters used their art to respond to the world around them, whether their interest was in politics, religion, nature, or current events. In this regard, the pattern names of their quilts often reflected their concerns. As Americans moved west and the nation evolved both politically and socially, the introduction of new pattern names and designs, as well as name and design variations for existing patterns, became common. Patterns ranged from high stylization and complete abstraction to closely realistic or representational appliquéd foliate patterns.

The "Star of Bethlehem's" biblical name serves well this distinctively American quilt. The numerous kinds of factory roller-printed bits of fabric used are, as one quilt historian phrased it, "an enviable encyclopedia of the styles and types available to the quiltmaker even in the newly settled areas of antebellum America."[22]

Two of the most often documented quilt patterns found in Arkansas serve well to illustrate the impact migration and the politically volatile climate had on choices for pattern names. Nancy Buckley's c. 1860 asymmetrically pieced masterwork from Washington County (figure Q–5) was known variously as "New York Beauty," "Indian Summer," "Road to Jericho," and as Americans migrated westward "Rocky Mountain Road." It is a significant example of how quilt names were constantly being amended to fit new experiences and lifestyles into antebellum America. Somewhat surprisingly, each of these colloquial names has remained in popular use.

If the frontier spirit of westward migration and political ferment was a prerequisite, then nineteenth-century Arkansas was an ideal setting for the continuation and creation of new quilt patterns. Although mostly anonymous, there can be little doubt that many of these early artists who substituted needle and thread for pen and ink would have readily agreed with the reminiscences of one early settler from Ohio:

> It took me more than twenty years, . . . I reckon, in the evening after supper when the children were all put to bed. My whole life is in that quilt. It scares me sometimes when I look at it. All my joys and all my sorrows are stitched into those little pieces. When I was proud of the boys and when I was downright provoked and angry with them. When the girls annoyed me or when they gave me a warm feeling around my heart. And John too. He was stitched into that quilt and all the thirty years we were married. Sometimes I loved him and sometimes I sat there hating him as I pieced the patches together, so they are all in that quilt, my hopes, and fears, my joys and sorrows my loves and hates. I tremble sometimes when I remember what that quilt knows about me.[23]

The author and members of the artists and artisans project are in hopes that our documentary and artifactual findings, which in no way should be considered definitive, will instigate further and much needed research into the textile arts of nineteenth-century Arkansas.

Much more field work is needed to locate and document the nineteenth-century quilts which remain secluded in private collections throughout the state. At the same time scholarly attention must be levelled at a variety of aesthetic questions dealing with approaches to the iconology of quilt patterns, as well as the significance of style, form, and ornament in the elemental production of a creative palette. Of no less importance is a need to uncover additional documentary evidence which may furnish answers to many unanswered questions relating to the creative mind of nineteenth-century Arkansas quilters.

Quilting—The Techniques of Construction

The often realistically composed appliqué, along with the geometrically stylized pieced quilts, were the two most popular forms of quilted textiles produced a century or more ago in Arkansas. Literally, all but one of the quilts, a "white worked" spread included in the illustrations at the end of this chapter, are either appliquéd, pieced, or a combination of both techniques.

Before defining the differences between appliqué and pieced work it first should be noted how they are alike. That is, each is made of three distinct layers: the top, an interlining of cotton batting (upon rare occasions omitted), and a backing fabric. The three layers are ultimately joined by stitching the appliquéd or pieced top to the filling and backing fabric. The completed creation might then be referred to as a quilt.

Pieced Quilting

Most surviving American quilts from the nineteenth century were constructed using a technique known as piecing or pieced work. That is, hundreds or even thousands of geometrically cut bits of decorative fabrics were sewn together, edge to edge, to create an overall preplanned block or repeat design that became the quilt top. The strikingly colorful explosion of colors and pattern in the c. 1870 "Star of Bethlehem" quilt, shown in figure Q–1, is a perfect example of pieced work. The attention to detail, the almost invisibly minute stitches, and the exact fitting of the thousands of pieces mirror the skill and artistry of the maker of this quilt from Hempstead County.

Appliqué—A Realistic Approach to Ornament

It is difficult to ascertain which method came first—the appliqué or pieced quilt. Both forms were certainly being made by American women during the latter half of the eighteenth century.

Appliqué, a French word meaning to lay on, was created by stitching small pieces of fabric or units of fabric sewn together in a specific motif onto a larger background piece. In effect, the background fabric would serve as the quilt top when it came time to sew all three layers (top, filling, and backing) together.

Often the background fabric on which the design was to be applied would be the size of the requisite finished top. In this case, the quilter might mark (with pencil, chalk, or charcoal) her design freehand, and/or with a template for often-repeated motifs. At other times she might appliqué a motif onto many smaller pieces of background which ultimately would be sewn together to form an entire top.[24]

Even though appliquéd spreads or "set on" quilts, as they were known at the time, could be intricately abstract with a geometric orientation similar to most pieced work, they were, in the main, realistically naturalistic in effect. Figure Q–18, is an appliquéd "Rose of Sharon" quilt which represents the quilter's exuberant attempt to imitate the vibrant qualities of roses and of natural foliage as accurately and realistically as possible. Outline or relief quilting, a trademark of nineteenth-century appliqué, serves to enhance and integrate the two techniques.

Prior to 1850, Mrs. William Maloney of Drew County created what has become this project's earliest found example of the "broderie perse" variation of the appliqué technique. Well known in England and America during the eighteenth century, the term means Persian, to imitate Persian embroidery; in this country it came to mean something entirely different.

Basically, broderie perse is an appliqué in which whole motifs such as flowers, animals, and even human figures were precisely cut from block and/or roller printed cottons and sewn to a foundation fabric. Once completed, it became in effect the quilt top to be decoratively sewn to the filling and backing fabrics similar to any other quilt.

The more free form method of appliqué and the realistic nature of the motifs figured prominently in its widespread popularity among needlewomen. Rather than the regimented tedium of exactly fitting straight edged bits of fabric together in pieced quilt fashion, the lay-on quilt allowed for a sinuous, more curvilinear, form of creative design perspective. Although never as numerous as pieced varieties, appliqué quilts remained a constant favorite in Arkansas.

It appeared to be not only a favorite of the quilters but of many of the judges where the pride and competitive nature of these textile artists surfaced—and where three of the eight first prize premiums were awarded to "set on" quilts.[25]

Stuffed Work

Stuffed work was an ornamental technique used separately or in combination with all-white, pieced and appliquéd quilting. Mrs. Green Mc-Phearson's patriotic pieced quilt with its stuffed-work stars (figure Q–19a) and Mary Jane Berthurum Stroud's floral all-white bridal quilt (figure Q–13) both illustrate the marvelous effects of this technique and its high relief method of giving quilts a three-dimensional quality.

Quilts were normally stuffed after the quilting was completed. It was carried out from the back side of the quilt by actually separating the woven threads of the backing with needle or bodkin. Bits of cotton batting were then carefully forced through the openings, until the desired padded effect for the quilting was attained. Then the separated warp and weft threads were realigned, closing the hole.[26]

A second method of making a small slit in the backing is evident on Mrs. McPhearson's quilt (figure Q–19b), detail. After it was stuffed, the cut opening would be stitched back together, as in this case.

NOTES

1. Patsy and Myron Orlofsky, *Quilts in America* (New York: McGraw-Hill Co., 1974) 26–27.

2. *Arkansas Gazette*, 14 February 1838, 3–5.

3. *Southern Shield*, 13 March 1858, 2–6.

4. The Kentucky Quilt Project, *Kentucky Quilts: 1800–1900* (New York: Pantheon Books, 1982) 7.

5. Charles Bolton, "Inequality and Social Change in the Arkansas Territory." An unpublished paper presented to the annual meeting of the Southern Historical Association, November 13, 1981.

6. *Arkansas Gazette*, 7 November 1857, 2–5.

7. *Des Arc Citizen*, 7 November 1857.

8. Ibid.

9. Letter, Everard Dickinson to Philo Dickinson, 22 June 1849. University of Arkansas, Little Rock, Collections.

10. Ibid.

11. The reminiscences of Dr. J. G. M. Ramsey, c. 1853, of west Tennessee, quoted in Orlofsky, 45.

12. Friedrich Gerstäcker, *Wild Sports in the Far West: The Narrative of a German Wanderer Beyond the Mississippi, 1837–1843*, eds. E. L. Steeves and H. R. Steeves (Durham: Duke University Press, 1968) 220.

13. Diary of Miss Fanny Love, 1861–63, Love's Hill, Arkansas. Collection of the Arkansas Territorial Restoration.

14. Pat Ferrero, Elaine Hodges, and Julie Silber, *Hearts and Hands: The Influence of Women and Quilts on American Society* (San Francisco: Quilt Digest Press, 1987) 22–24.

15. Vance Randolph, *Ozark Magic and Folklore* (New York: Dover Publications, 1964) 185.

16. Nancy McDonough, *Garden Sass: A Catalog of Arkansas Folkways* (New York: Coward, McCann and Geoghegan, 1975) 173.

17. Randolph, 70.

18. Letter, Sarah A. Nelson (Benton, Saline County) to Miss Mence Wilson (Hawfields, Orange County, North Carolina) 22 February 1849.

19. Fanny Love diary.

20. Sarah J. Hale and Louis A. Godey, *Godey's Lady's Book and Magazine*, Vol. LV (Philadelphia: Louis A. Godey, 1856) 166–169.

21. Renwick Gallery Exhibit Catalog, *American Pieced Quilts* (Washington, D.C.: Smithsonian Institution Traveling Exhibition Service, 1972) 12.

22. Edwin Binney, III, and Gail Binney Winslow, *Homage to Amanda: Two Hundred Years of American Quilting* (San Francisco: R. K. Press, 1984) 40.

23. Carleton L. Safford and Robert Bishop, *America's Quilts and Coverlets* (New York: Weathervane Books, 1974) 88.

24. Orlofsky, 78–86.

25. *Arkansas Gazette*, 26 November 1867, 2.

26. Orlofsky, 186.

An Illustrated Catalog of Arkansas Quilts

Q–1. Star of Bethlehem. Pieced quilt. Fan-shaped background stitching. Made by a member of the John J. Thomas family. Washington, Hempstead County, Arkansas, c. 1870. 96″ × 95 ¼″. *Courtesy of the Pioneer Washington Foundation, Washington, Arkansas.*

Q–2. Star of Bethlehem. Pieced quilt. Maker unknown. Westfork, Washington County, Arkansas, c. 1870. 85″ × 79″. Possibly a memorial to assuage the loss of a deceased family member, this macabre "mourning quilt" is a reminder of the immediacy of death. Death-related textiles in a variety of media were not uncommon during the last century. *Courtesy of Peg Newton Smith.*

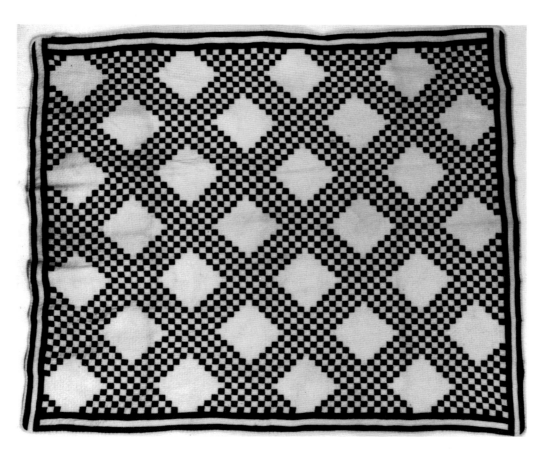

Q–3. Irish Chain. Pieced quilt. Diapered background quilting. Maker unknown. Washington County vicinity, third quarter of the nineteenth century. 79½″ × 72⅛″. *Courtesy of the University of Arkansas, Fayetteville, Collection.*

Q–4.   Whigs' Defeat. Unquilted, pieced top. Descended in the Silas Toncray family of Little Rock, c. 1845–60. Overall measurements of top, 79¼″ × 82¼″. *From the collection of the Arkansas Territorial Restoration.*

Q–5.   Rocky Mountain Road. Known variously as Indian Summer, New York Beauty, and the Road to Jericho. Pieced quilt. Closely and evenly stitched floral background. Made by Nancy Buckley. Washington County, Arkansas, c. 1865. 78″ × 75″. *Courtesy of Bo and De De Long.*

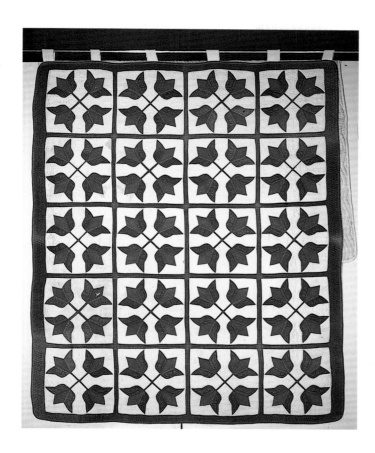

Q–6. Variation of Tulip or Virginia Lily. Appliquéd and pieced quilt. Made by Mrs. Fleming Burk (neé Mary Jane Sharman, 1841–1936) of (Frog Level Plantation) Magnolia, Columbia County, Arkansas, c. 1866. 88″ × 74″. *Courtesy of Harold and Billy Stockton.*

Q–7. Magnolia. Appliqué quilt. Made by Mrs. William Maloney. Monticello, Drew County, Arkansas, c. 1840. 70″ × 88″. *Courtesy of the Drew County Museum, Monticello, Arkansas.*

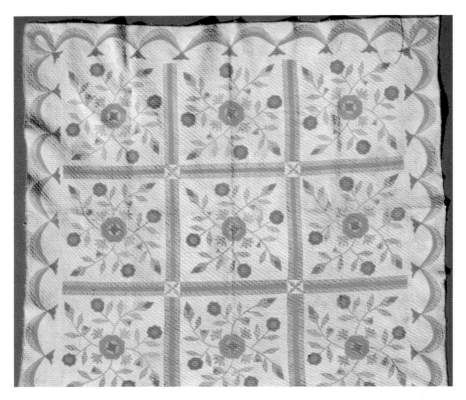

Q–8. Ohio Rose. Appliqué quilt. Maker unknown. Dallas County, Arkansas, c. 1870. 94″ × 84″.

Courtesy of the Hot Spring County Museum, Malvern, Arkansas.

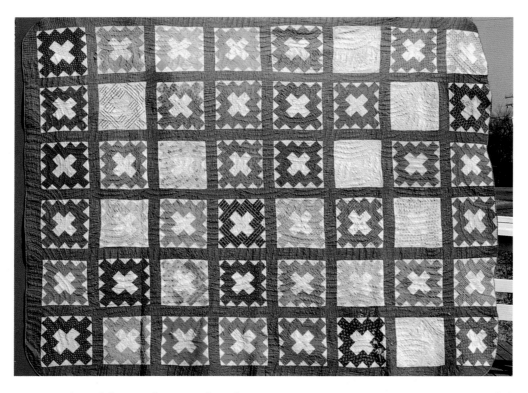

Q–9. Chimney Sweep, friendship quilt. Pieced quilt. One of the many signed and dated blocks is inscribed "Mary L. Wylie/Dallas Co./Ark./Nov. 17th 1868,"

1868–69. 86½″ × 69¾″. *Courtesy of the Hot Spring County Museum.*

Q–10. Rose Wreath. Appliquéd and stuffed work quilt. Made by Mrs. W. D. Rogers. Monticello, Drew County, Arkansas, c. 1870. 102″ × 104″. *Courtesy of the Drew County Museum.*

Q–11. Peony. Pieced and appliquéd quilt. Made by Nancy Stroud Cheek. Pleasant Plains, Independence County, Arkansas, c. 1850–60. 97½″ × 87″. *From the collection of the Arkansas Territorial Restoration.*

Q-12.   Unknown pattern. Broderie perse technique.
Made by Emily Beckham Protho. Pulaski County,
Arkansas.

Third quarter of the nineteenth century. 87″ × 76″.
Courtesy of Mr. and Mrs. Carl Olsson.

Q–13. White work quilt. Stuffed and background quilting. Made by Mary Jane Berthurum Stroud, who later gave the quilt to her son, George (b. 1870), when it was time for his marriage. Pea Ridge, Benton County, Arkansas, c. 1870. 64″ × 80″. *Courtesy of Pat Simpson.*

Q–14. Rattlesnake. Pieced quilt. Maker unknown. Independence County, Arkansas.

Third quarter of the nineteenth century. 71″ × 66″. *Courtesy of Elmer and Virginia Kirk.*

Q–15a.   Princess Feather or Feathered Star. Appliquéd and pieced quilt. Made by Mary E. Johnson Anderson, Izard County, Arkansas, c. 1874.

80¼" × 69¼". *Courtesy of the Old State House Museum.*

Q–15b.   Detail of the inscription on the backing fabric of figure Q–15a. "Feathered Star" quilt. Mary Johnson has hand-printed the following at one corner on the back of her quilt:

1874
MODESA
FEATHERED
STAR

However, this is a pattern that almost all quilt historians have come to call "Princess Feather," and most reflect the personal whims and colloquial nature of quiltnaming among American needlewomen. Dr. Robert Bishop, director of the Museum of American Folk Art and co-author with Carleton Stafford of *American Quilts and Coverlets* (Weathervane Books: New York, 1974), has remarked that it is the only documented period reference to the pattern name of which he is aware.

Q–16. Ocean Waves. Appliqué quilt. Made by Susan Boone. Colony Community, Van Buren County, Arkansas, c. 1861–65. 79″ × 62½″. Due to looting by soldiers and bushwhackers, the quilt and other family possessions were buried in a wooden box. The quilt was damaged, and the lighter shades of the fabric were used to mend it after the war. *Courtesy of Louise Hall and Dollie Hall Jackson.*

Q–17. Eight Pointed Variable Star. Pieced quilt. Made and signed in corner by Juliana Steinkampf. Hempstead County, Arkansas, 1840–60. 72″ × 91″.

From the collection of the Arkansas Territorial Restoration.

Q–18.   Rose of Sharon. Appliqué quilt. Made by Mary Sammons. Magness, Independence County, Arkansas, c. 1860. 81½″ × 66½″. *Courtesy of Jewell Daugherty, the great-granddaughter of the quiltmaker.*

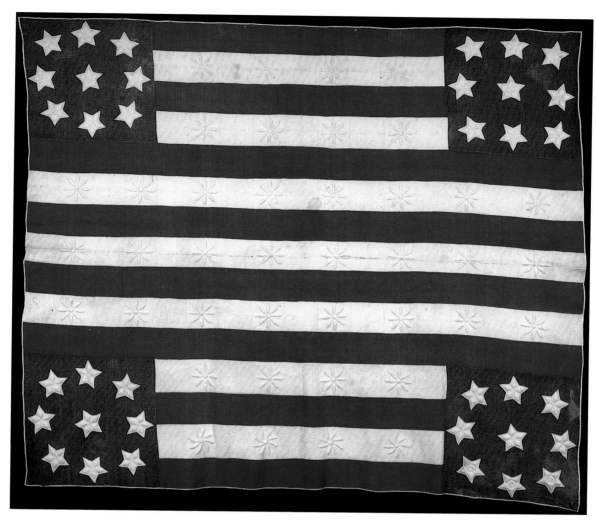

Q–19a.   Secession Quilt. Pieced quilt. Circular pattern of nine stars in each corner represent Arkansas as the ninth state to secede from the Union. Made by Mrs. Green McPhearson. West Point, White County, Arkansas, c. 1861. 85½" × 97". *From the collection of the Arkansas Territorial Restoration, Gift of Mrs. Kenneth Spore.*

Q–19b.   Detail of the backing fabric showing a sewn-over slit of one of the stuffed worked stars in the McPhearson patriotic quilt (figure Q–19a).

Q–20.   Broderie Perse. Appliqué quilt. Made by Mrs. Stephen Gaster. Drew County, Arkansas, c. 1840.   78″ × 96″. *Courtesy of the Drew County Museum.*

Q–21. Rocky Mountain Road. Pieced quilt. Made by Jeanette (Paden) Moffatt. Salem, Pike County, Arkansas, third quarter of the nineteenth century. 81″ × 82″. *Courtesy of Marsha Moffatt Daniels.*

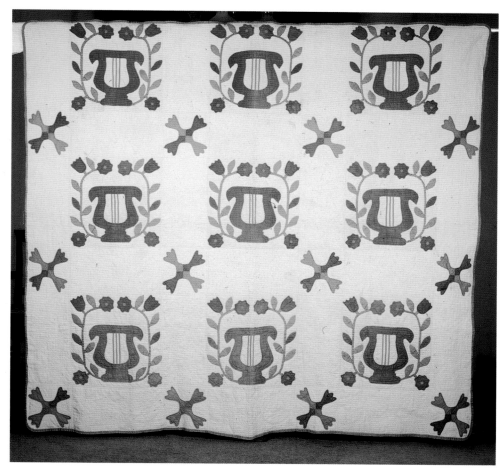

Q–22. Unidentified lyre-shaped pattern. Appliquéd and pieced quilt. Made by Elizabeth Anne Washington Rogers. Arkadelphia, Clark County, Arkansas, third quarter of the nineteenth century. 77″ × 83½″. *Courtesy of Elizabeth Wright.*

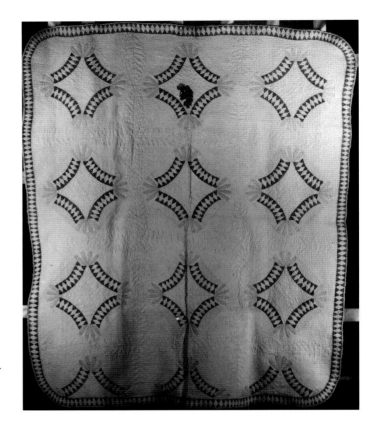

Q-23.   Whigs' Defeat. Known also as Democratic Victory. Pieced quilt. Made by Mariah Aikman Trayler (1799–1858). Izard County, Arkansas, c. 1839. 67½″ × 79¼″. *Courtesy of Mrs. V. A. Hook.*

Q-24.   Rocky Mountain Road. Pieced quilt. Made by Artemece Wardlaw (1810–1891) for her daughter's wedding. This pattern is frequently referred to as New York Beauty or Crown of Thorns. Cleveland County, Arkansas, c. 1850–60. 90″ × 69″. *Courtesy of Mary Glover Formby.*

Q–25.   Unknown Confederate patriotic pattern. Pieced, appliquéd, and embroidered quilt. Made by Susan Robb, Arkansas, c. 1861. 81″ × 77″. Susan Robb's pro-Southern sentiments are commemorated in this quilt depicting Confederate troops on parade early in the Civil War. The two flags represent the first two Confederate national banners adopted by the Con- federacy in 1861. The appliquéd pelican toppling an eagle symbolizes the Southern defeat of their North- ern foe. According to the Robb family history, the yellow calico dog represents the family pet which followed the maker's son off to war. *Courtesy of the Texas Tech University Museum, Lubbock, Texas.*

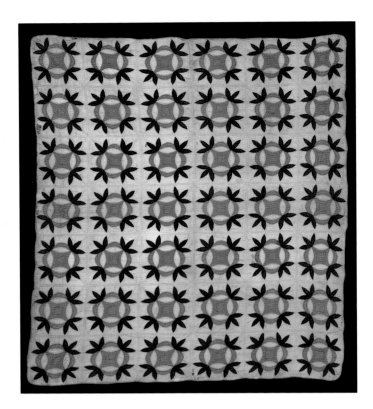

Q–26. Oak Leaf and Reel. Pieced quilt. Made by Mary Harrison (1835–1927). Harrison, Arkansas, c. 1850–60. 77" × 67". *From the collection of the Arkansas Territorial Restoration.*

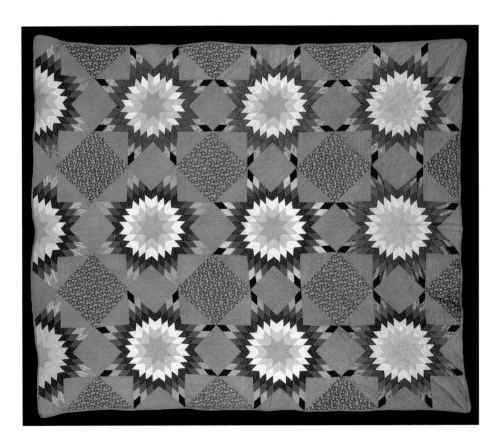

Q–27. Prairie Star, also known as Harvest Sun in the Midwest and the Ship's Wheel in New England. Pieced quilt. Made by Liza Slater Wallace. Junction City, Union County, Arkansas, c. 1870. 84" × 79". *From the collection of the Arkansas Territorial Restoration.*

Q–28. Star of Bethlehem and unknown stylized foliate pattern. Pieced and appliquéd (flowers). Made by Mary Jane Vincent. White County, Arkansas, 1860. 74½" × 71". *From the collection of the Arkansas Territorial Restoration.*

Q–29.   Chips and Whetstone. Appliquéd and pieced quilt. Made by Elizabeth Anne Washington Rogers. Arkadelphia, Clark County, Arkansas, third quarter of the nineteenth century. 76″ × 60″. *Courtesy of Elizabeth Wright.*

Q–30.   Feathered Star. Pieced Quilt. Made by Elizabeth and Sarah Jane Askew. College Hill, Columbia County, c. 1870–80. 88″ × 69″. *From the collection of the Arkansas Territorial Restoration.*

Compare this "Feathered Star" pattern variant with the form shown in Figure Q–15a, which is routinely shown as "Princess Feather."

ARKANSAS
SILVER

Silversmithing, Goldsmithing, Clockmaking, Jewelrymaking, and Watchmaking in Arkansas

Baptist minister Silas T. Toncray brought with him a trade as alien to the wilds of Arkansas Territory as the Gospel—he was a silversmith. It seems that, in the great scheme of things, an apparent superfluity such as silversmithing would wait for accumulated wealth and high society. As a matter of fact, as recently as 1968 the curator of a major museum show on Southern silver had yet to see any silver at all from Arkansas.[1]

A closer look finds Silas Toncray working both souls and silver, only one of the earliest of many silversmiths who practiced in Arkansas, even as mass production began making them obsolete. Toncray, with a versatility typical of his profession, delved into several enterprises; and while his stay west of the Mississippi was brief, some of Toncray's Arkansas work survived: the legacy of a fine artisan.[2]

Silversmith, Etc.

In 1829 Toncray advertised himself as "Clock and Watchmaker, Silversmith, Jeweller and Engraver."[3] Thus he listed for us the professions we must cover before doing justice to silversmithing. Skill at working precious metals is the common denominator, and while silver may seem superfluous, watches and clocks certainly are not,

except maybe on the farm. In 1798 one writer claimed that almanacs were used "by nine tenths of mankind and in fair weather are far more sure and regular than the best time piece."[4] The rising and setting of the sun and the station of the moon and the other heavenly bodies commanded the attention of the farmer, while clock time needed to be nothing more than an entertaining diversion.

But place folks in obligation to other folks for simultaneous mutual activity, and the timepiece says when. If Eli Terry and Seth Thomas had limited their sales territory to America's urban centers, where minutes ticked heavy with importance, Arkansas might have welcomed fewer silversmiths. Of course they did not. Yankee peddlers took their Connecticut clocks to the isolated outposts of civilization and created a market for clockmakers and watchmakers.

In 1802 Eli Terry built a factory which used waterpower to speed clock production. Over the years his innovations in design, manufacture, and marketing sent wooden clocks on their way at an average price nationally of less than seven dollars and fifty cents. By the time the brass-works clock industry geared up, the price had fallen to two dollars per clock.[5]

Watchmaking and clockmaking go hand in hand—the works differ in scale, but the desired result is the same. Chances are, few of either timepiece were made in Arkansas. Assembled, yes. When George Allen's watch was stolen in 1856, he described it in an advertised request for its return: "one heavy Gold Hunting Watch, No. 65303, Joseph Johnson maker."[6] This was, probably, a "hunter watch" with not only a front cover—over the glass-faced dial—but also a hinged back cover, to protect the decorated inner cover, assembled with case work by Joseph Johnson of Sevier County, and with movement by a northeastern manufacturer.

Some artisans who advertised as watchmakers admitted that repair was their real business. "Watchmaker" William H. Howe of Hempstead County promised only to "give prompt personal attention to all articles left in his charge. Watches, Clock, Jewelry, etc., neatly and promptly repaired."[7] James M. Kirk moved to Ft. Smith "for the purpose of repairing watches and clocks."[8]

The retail aspect of the business shined through as early as 1825, when Cresswell and Edwards offered "Gentlemen's and Ladies Patent Lever, Horizontal, Repeating, Duplex, and all kinds of fancy Watches, Clocks and Chronometers, repaired and warranted" to the town of Washington.[9] In 1859 William Anthony especially recommended to Fayetteville the American watch, "the safest and most reliable Time Piece now made," as well as "English and Swiss Levers, Lepine and Duplex Watches." You could get a Seth Thomas clock as low as $8, and he finally added, "Watches, Clocks and Jewelry, cleaned and repaired. . . ."[10]

A related category is that of jeweler. William Anthony, while hawking the American watch, advertised jewelry "made to order."[11] G. H. Stinson, "watch-maker and j e w e l l e r" of Camden, dealt in "Watches, Clocks, Jewelry, Silver-ware, Fine Cutlery, Musical Instruments and Fancy Goods generally." He then promised watch work.[12] Today Stinson's company still serves Camden. H. J. Bishop, in clarifying his payment policy, said "Old Gold and Silver taken in exchange for jewelry or work." Precious metals were to be reworked by another "Watch & Clock maker and Jeweler."[13]

To round out those artisans who should be considered with silversmiths, we must add goldsmiths and engravers. In terms of their professions, more claimed to be either watch- and clockmakers or jewelers than silversmiths. Only a few claimed engraving or gold work, although

Toncray's first advertisement in Arkansas—while he still lived in Kentucky—touted his services as an engraver.

Some men displayed other skills not necessarily closely associated with silversmithing, but worthy of mention, nevertheless. Watch- and clockmaker David Austin of Little Rock was one of several who advertised work on spectacles. Austin also promised "all kinds of gold and silver work."[14] I. Souter and his brother set up a "Picture Gallery" in the town of Washington to execute likenesses and to repair watches and jewelry.[15] William Anthony, whose primary line was watches and jewelry, ended his ad with the postscript that he was also "well prepared to take Pictures in all their various styles."[16] Another man with a variety of skills was Joe McNeill, a former slave in Clark County who made and repaired equipment on Rosedale plantation. McNeill was a cabinetmaker, but he also, and thus his inclusion here, made spoons out of silver dollars.[17]

Technology and Silversmithing

Silversmithing was radically transformed by the nineteenth century. At the beginning of the century, the craft shop still dominated production. Coined or old silver was melted and formed into ingots, to be hammered until they reached the proper thinness. The metal hardened during the process, so the smith had to return the piece to the fire several times to anneal it to keep it workable. Using hammers and stakes appropriate to the form to be fashioned, the smith beat the metal into shape, finally filing and burnishing it to achieve a finished product. Some pieces required the soldering of cast pieces and ornamentation by embossing or engraving. The work did not go quickly: a skilled workman took three to four days to make a dozen tablespoons.[18]

With the innovation of sheet silver, the potential of mass production moved closer for the ambitious silversmith. The uniform thickness and the smooth surface of the sheets cut hours of tedious hammering from production time. The same kinds of machines that rolled sheets could produce beading and other relief ornament. Presses could shape ornamentation, and, more radically, promised the ultimate forming of a whole piece of flatware.

Before such a machine was perfected, another technological advance transformed silver production. In 1840 the process for electroplating was discovered in England. Electroplating deposits a thin layer of a precious metal onto a base metal by the use of an electric current. Within twenty years the value of plated ware produced in the United States surpassed that of solid silver, and, given the lower cost of silver plate, considerably more of it was being made.[19] The story of nineteenth-century silver is the story of increased production by major manufacturers through ever more sophisticated means.

Arkansas Silversmiths

The technological advances brought about the end of the artisan tradition, but not until after that tradition made an impact upon Arkansas.

As might be expected, the fifteen silversmiths born in Tennessee outnumbered those from any other state. C. A. Harris, one watchmaker born in the Volunteer State, found his way to Atlanta, in Prairie County, where in 1861 he manufactured a sword to be presented to Capt. T. J. Payne of the McKeever Guards. He is the only swordmaker yet documented in Arkansas.[20] Tennessee, and also Kentucky, had an influence on Arkansas beyond that of the native-born silversmiths. James J. Mulkey, though born in Georgia, came to Phillips County from Chattanooga. He set up shop in Helena with a gunsmith, advertising "watches, clocks and jewelry, and all kinds of guns made or repaired." He soon started out on his own by buying out J. W. Demby's jewelry shop. He was listed in the 1860 census as a silversmith.[21] Demby, himself, was a North Carolinian who moved from Phillips to Jefferson County. After Federal forces took Little Rock in September of 1863, a J. W. Demby briefly published a loyalist newspaper,

the *National Union*, in the recently inactive offices of the *Arkansas Gazette*.[22]

Silas T. Toncray, while born in Maryland, practiced, and probably learned, his trade in Kentucky. During the period from 1789 until 1824 when Toncray left Kentucky, at least forty shops are known to have produced silver within a forty-mile radius of Shelbyville. Shelbyville rests between Frankfort, the state capital, and Louisville, and Toncray's shop sat on Shelbyville's Main Street.[23] Toncray's introduction to Little Rock appeared in an *Arkansas Gazette* advertisement of April 14, 1821, in which he offered engraving to banking institutions on the frontier—from Shelbyville. Three years later, he followed his sister Maria and her husband Isaac Watkins to Little Rock.

Preaching and silversmithing apparently couldn't pay all the bills. Toncray purchased both a merchant's and a ferry license and offered a variety of retail goods, including "old monongahela whiskey" at forty-five cents per gallon. He promised that the "highest price will be given for furs and peltries."[24] After gaining an appointive position as postmaster of Conway (County) Court House, he ran for the territorial legislature. His reform campaign failed, as he won only twenty-four votes, placing third to the winner's eighty-three.[25] Later that year, on November 14, 1827, Toncray's niece, Jane Eliza Mills, married William E. Woodruff, founder of the *Arkansas Gazette*. Toncray's silver made up part of the bride's trousseau.

The legacy of silver left by Silas Toncray shines in importance for the study of the state's artisans, but the life he led in Memphis, after leaving Arkansas Territory, more profoundly touched many souls. He served on the town council, followed his trades—adding druggist, dentist, sign painter, inventor, and doctor—and he preached. He served a predominantly black congregation, building the African Church (first known as Toncray's church) which survived until progress razed it in the 1960s. (Toncray's alley, which today still runs from Main to Front Street, sports a historical marker, honoring not the Reverend Mr. Toncray, but rather Old Bell Tavern.)[26]

The memories of contemporaries offer a picture of a complex person. James D. Davis praised his church as being the "best specimen of architecture on the bluff," but found much to criticize in the man. "Toncray was a very inconsistent man, ignorant in everything except mechanism. . . ." Davis praised the patience that allowed Toncray to devote weeks to the construction of a miniature ship inside of a bottle, but noted that his patience did not always extend past the inanimate. "He was petulant with those he considered beneath him, and addicted to too frequent use of the cowhide in his own family." Davis didn't even care for Toncray's ministerial style, saying, "He performed the service of baptism as though it were an ordinary business transaction."[27]

Dr. J. B. Mallory found more to praise in this man "of universal genius and various callings."[28] Indeed, his obituary labelled Toncray as one of the "most . . . useful members of the community . . . he was at the head, of that primitive sect of the Baptist persuasion, commonly known as the 'hard-side,' or old-fashioned Baptist. . . . We mourn his loss as that of a man who, while living, we were proud to call friend."[29]

D. C. Fulton also used Kentucky as a jumping-off point to the frontier. Fulton was born in Pennsylvania but operated a "jewelry and fancy store" in Louisville. In fact, while Fulton's Kentucky stay was brief compared with his time in Arkansas, he is known in silver-collecting circles today as a Kentucky silversmith.[30] Such is the comparative record of scholarship in the two states. The 1850 Pulaski County census called him a fancy merchant, as, indeed, this 1842 advertisement in the *Arkansas Gazette* established:

> The undersigned respectfully announces to the citizens of Little Rock and vicinity, his return from the East, with a new and fashionable stock of JEWELRY and FANCY GOODS, consisting in part of Gold and Silver Lever Watches and Mantel Clocks; gold Guard and Fob Chains and Keys; Pink Topaz, Amethyst, and enameled Pins and Rings (new style); Gold and Silver Spectacles and Pencils; Pink Topaz and Enameled Bracelets; Silver and German Silver Table and Tea Spoons; Britannia Coffee and Tea Pots; Castors, Pint Mugs and Cups for children; Roger's Fine Congress and other Pen-knives and Scissors; a variety of Musical Instruments; Riding Whips and Canes; Ladies' and Gentlemen's fine Kid Gloves; and a handsome assortment of Ladies' black and white satin and fancy Kid Slippers; with a variety of other fancy articles in the above line, all of the very latest fashion.

> Clocks and Watches Repaired.
> Having a superior workman, I pledge myself that all Watches and jewelry repaired in my store shall be done in the best possible manner.
> Old Gold and Silver taken in exchange also a superior article of Segars and James River Chewing Tobacco, expressly for retail.
>   D. C. Fulton

Little Rock, November 29, 1842

Fulton did very well in his adoptive state. By 1857 he owned $3,700 worth of city lots in Little Rock, a pleasure carriage, and a horse.[31] During the Civil War, he served with two other silversmiths—Albert Cohen and Jesse V. Zimmerman—in Little Rock's Capitol Guards, which became Company A, 6th Arkansas Voluntary Infantry. His rank was second lieutenant, until after the Battle of Shiloh. Fulton was one of several persons sued for false arrest by Elisha Baxter in 1865. He soon moved to Memphis. Fulton died at the home of his sister in Philadelphia on September 17, 1869.[32]

It may be surprising that foreign-born silversmiths accounted for over twenty-three percent of those whose birth places are known. English and German immigrants, especially, brought their skills to Arkansas. An example is German Marcus Dotter who was a "silversmith" in the 1850 Arkansas census; he was active in the community—an officer in both the Odd Fellows and the fire department—and in 1870 he was enumerated as jewelry/watchmaker.[33]

In all, current research counts 183 silversmiths, etc., in Arkansas 1819–70. This can compare to over three hundred in Tennessee and 911 found in Kentucky.[34] The richest heritage rests in the older and more established states. But, in all three states, the tradition folds at the same time. "The out break of hostilities [in the Civil War] was the death knell of the individual silversmith" in Kentucky,[35] as it was in Tennessee and Arkansas. Even in New Orleans, the home of Hyde and Goodrich, whose silver spread throughout the Mississippi Valley, silversmithing had become a "moribund craft" by the 1870s.[36] The South could not compete with Gorham, Tiffany, and other northeastern manufacturers.

Arkansas Silver

In one of the vivid passages from George Featherstonhaugh's journal of travels in rural Arkansas, the author ate at a table set with five frontier forks and described them, using names related by the hostess's servant and "aide de cuisine," Nisby.

> And Nisby was right. *Stump Handle* was there, and was by far the most forkable-looking concern, for it consisted of one prong of an old fork stuck into a stumpy piece of wood. *Crooky Prongs* was curled over on each side, adapting itself in an admirable manner to catch cod-fish, but rather foreign to the purpose of sticking into anything. *Horny* had apparently never been at Sheffield or Birmingham, as it was a sort of imitation of a fork made out of a cow's horn. *Big Pewter* was made of the handle of a spoon with the bowl broken off; and *Little Pickey* was a dear interesting looking little thing, something like a cobbler's awl fastened in a thick piece of wood.[37]

One had to "make do" on the frontier, and this small tavern did with a homely set of utensils. We might be reminded of the rather limited market for silver. For most early citizens, the owning of silver was a status to which to aspire. For the over 440 cabinetmakers who worked here, we find fewer than 190 silversmiths. A look at what they made, or at least promised to make, might suggest more Arkansas-produced forks of the "Stump Handle" variety than of the silver.

Arkansas was not unique in the comparative rarity of fork production. Silver forks made their debut from Kentucky shops around 1830 and were not produced in great numbers, and dinner or luncheon knives apparently were never made in Kentucky.[38] Forks and knives were used, but they were not of silver.

To give a couple of examples, an unknown thief struck Nicholas Peay's Little Rock sideboard in 1834. Table, dessert, tea, and cream spoons, and ladles and sugar tongs made up the missing silverware.[39] No silver forks or knives were there to be taken. Senator William Savin Fulton died ten years later after sleeping in a freshly painted room. His probate inventory acknowledges much silver, in the form of desert spoons, tea spoons, table spoons, salt spoons, a

butter knife, and sugar tongs, a cream pot, sugar dish, ladle, and cup. But, again, no silver forks, or knives. His forks were German silver and silver plated, and he had ivory-handled knives and forks.[40]

In all the advertisements surveyed in the current research project, only one silversmith specifically offered to make forks. John H. Baldwin, of Washington, called himself a "clock and watchmaker" and asserted that he was "prepared to manufacture silver spoons, forks and all other articles in his line of business." As if to emphasize his work with precious metal, he offered "The highest cash price for old gold and silver."[41] H. M. Carter of Arkadelphia, another watchmaker and jeweler, offered much in the precious metal line but no forks. He advertised to "make to order, silver spoons and cups, silver and gold cane heads, and medals, gold spectacles, gold jewelry, etc., of every description," as well as engagement and wedding rings.[42]

The investigator would hope to find Arkansas-made examples of each of these products, and tea services as well. Seven counties had over ten silversmiths working in them at some point in the artisan period—Pulaski alone had thirty-two—and these men must have produced a variety of work.

But only a small amount of Arkansas silver has come to light. The documented silver shows no departure from the traditions immediately to the east. The spatulate or "fiddle" pattern predominates in the flatware. The evidence found thus far suggests that Arkansas smiths produced a modest output of utilitarian silver without major embellishment.

One especially valuable source of information on artisans should be the probate inventory. The tools, the supplies and materials, the wares ready for sale, even the unfulfilled obligations of the deceased can offer evidence of the kind and extent of manufacture, and a great deal more.

The only inventory yet to surface of one of these artisans in precious metals is that of William W. Parsons. Parsons was a watchmaker and jeweler in Little Rock, and his was not an active silversmith's shop; rather it is indicative of the retail trade, which welcomed so many artisans whose handiwork lost its market.

The only tools and materials listed related to watch repair, and the inventory is clearly jewelry store merchandise: chains, pins, rings, watches, and some flatware. Perhaps most interesting are the bills from three wholesalers: H. Ducommun and Farr and Thompson of Philadelphia, and Richardson and Hicks and Co. of Providence and New York.[43] Arkansas was clearly tied to the national economy, and the local artisan could no longer compete.

Silversmiths, Locations in Arkansas

County	Date Founded	Number of Makers
Arkansas	1813	
Ashley	1848	1
Benton	1836	1
Boone	1869	1
Bradley	1840	
Calhoun	1850	
Carroll	1833	1
Chicot	1823	1
Clark	1818	7
Columbia	1852	1
Conway	1825	1
Craighead	1859	1
Crawford	1820	14
Crittenden	1825	
Cross	1862	
Dallas	1845	
Desha	1838	2
Drew	1846	3
Franklin	1837	3
Fulton	1842	
Grant	1869	
Greene	1833	1
Hempstead	1818	13
Hot Spring	1829	2
Independence	1820	13
Izard	1825	1
Jackson	1829	5
Jefferson	1829	11
Johnson	1833	2
Lafayette	1827	
Lawrence	1815	

County	Date Founded	Number of Makers
Little River	1867	
Madison	1836	2
Marion	1836	
Miller	1820	
Mississippi	1833	
Monroe	1829	1
Montgomery	1842	
Newton	1842	
Ouachita	1842	5
Perry	1840	
Phillips	1820	17
Pike	1833	
Poinsett	1838	1
Polk	1844	
Pope	1829	1
Prairie	1846	6
Pulaski	1818	33
Randolph	1835	2
Saline	1835	
Scott	1833	
Searcy	1835	
Sebastian	1851	10
Sevier	1828	3
Sharp	1868	
St. Francis	1827	1
Union	1829	4
Van Buren	1833	1
Washington	1828	8
White	1835	2
Woodruff	1862	3
Yell	1840	1

Total number of locations listed: 186
Total number of listings in biographical appendix: 183

Two facts of Arkansas silver remain. The first, and this is true of other Southern states especially, is that history has not contributed to the preservation of locally-made—or any—silver. The invasion that Arkansas suffered at the end of the artisan period placed many valuables at risk: food, firearms, silver, etc. Stories about buried silver, looted, stolen, or simply never recovered, are real. Desperate times elicit desperate measures, and silver as heirloom can easily become silver as commodity in time of hardship. Add to that the usual threats to the longtime survival of anything, and much has been lost.

The second fact offers some solace. More Arkansas silver is out there waiting to be identified, and Arkansas is waiting to reclaim a bit more of its heritage.

Count of Arkansas Silversmiths by Place of Birth

UNITED STATES BORN

Alabama	2
Arkansas	3
Connecticut	2
Delaware	2
Florida	1
Georgia	5
Illinois	3
Indiana	6
Kentucky	11
Louisiana	3
Maine	3
Massachusetts	2
Maryland	1
Michigan	3
Mississippi	4
Missouri	1
New York	4
North Carolina	5
Ohio	7
Pennsylvania	7
South Carolina	2
Texas	1
Tennessee	14
Virginia	7
Vermont	1

FOREIGN BORN

Austria	1
England	8
France	3
Germany	14
Ireland	1
Poland	1
Sweden	1
Switzerland	3

Total number of birth places documented: 132

Of the sixty-two counties created by 1870, thirty-nine welcomed silversmiths. Very little evidence exists of the movement of smiths within Arkansas. Current research shows only two smiths who were documented in their trade in two different Arkansas counties. All locations thus far documented to silversmithing activities are listed.

Many of the silversmiths, whose places of birth are known, were foreign born. While Tennessee and Kentucky contributed more silversmiths than any other state, the northern states of Ohio, Pennsylvania, and Indiana made a larger impact on silversmithing in Arkansas than Georgia, the Carolinas, and several other Southern states. Knowledge of where these men learned their trade would be particularly valuable in understanding the tradition of silversmithing in the United States, but such information is available only in a few cases. Census data provided most of these birth places, and a smith was listed here only when a source claimed to provide birth place, as opposed to "he was from" or other similar statements.

NOTES

1. David Warren, *Southern Silver* (Houston: The Museum of Fine Arts, 1968).

2. *See* Biographical Appendix

3. *Arkansas Gazette*, 8 April 1829.

4. Quoted in Milton Drake, comp., *Almanacs of the United States* (New York, 1962), in Brooke Hindle and Steven Lubar, *Engines of Change* (Washington, D.C.: Smithsonian Institution Press, 1985) 220.

5. Hindle and Lubar, 223–26.

6. *Arkansas Gazette*, 20 September 1856.

7. *Washington Telegraph*, 25 November 1857.

8. *Fort Smith Herald*, 13 December 1848.

9. *Arkansas Gazette*, 13 September 1825.

10. *Arkansian*, 18 June 1859.

11. Ibid.

12. *Ouachita Herald*, 29 July 1858.

13. *Helena Democrat Star*, 15 March 1854.

14. *Arkansas Gazette*, 4 June 1828.

15. *Washington Telegraph*, 28 June 1857.

16. *Arkansian*, 18 June 1859.

17. Wanda Martin and H. B. Arnold, "Col. Joseph Allen Whitaker and the 'Rosedale' Plantation," *Clark County Historical Journal* (Arkadelphia: Clark County Historical Association, Winter 1979–80) 260.

18. Deborah Dependahl Waters, "From Pure Coin, The Manufacture of American Silver Flatware 1800–1860," *Winterthur Portfolio 12* (Charlottesville: University Press of Virginia, 1977) 27.

19. Stephen K. Victor, "'From the Shop to the Manufactory': Silver and Industry, 1800–1970," *Silver in American Life* (New York: The American Federation of Arts, 1979) 20.

20. *True Democrat*, 31 October 1861. *See also* Biographical Appendix

21. *See* Biographical Appendix

22. *Southern Shield*, 23 February 1856; Margaret Ross, *Arkansas Gazette: The Early Years* (Little Rock: Arkansas Gazette Foundation, 1969) 386. *See also* Biographical Appendix

23. "Silas T. Toncray and his wife . . ." January 22, 1817; Record of Deeds (T1–132), Office of County Clerk, Shelby County, Kentucky.

24. *Arkansas Gazette*, 16 November 1824, and 11 April 1826.

25. *Arkansas Gazette*, 7 August 1827.

26. Memphis *Weekly Appeal*, 19 February 1847; James D. Davis, *History of Memphis* (Memphis, 1873) 230–32; Linton Weeks, *Memphis: A Folk History* (Little Rock: Parkhurst, 1982) 132.

27. Davis, 230–32.

28. Davis, 120.

29. Memphis *Weekly Appeal*, 19 February 1847.

30. Marquis Boultinghouse, *Silversmiths, Jewelers, Clock and Watch Makers of Kentucky 1785–1900* (Lexington, Kentucky: Marquis Boultinghouse, 1980) 128–301.

31. *See* Biographical Appendix

32. JoAnn Alves, "A Muster Roll of 1862," *Arkansas Historical Quarterly*, Vol. XIII (Fayetteville: Arkansas Historical Association, 1954) 131. Ted R. Worley, ed., "Documents Relating to Elisha Baxter's Imprisonment," *Arkansas Historical Quarterly*, Vol. XVI (Fayetteville: Arkansas Historical Association, 1957) 101. *Arkansas Gazette*, 26 September 1869.

33. *Arkansas Gazette*, 24 October 1857. *See also* Biographical Appendix

34. Derita Coleman Williams, *A View of Tennessee Silversmiths* (Memphis: Dixon Gallery and Gardens, 1983) 6. Boultinghouse, 26–296, 345 (total listings–911).

35. Boultinghouse, 26.

36. Carey T. Mackie, H. Parrott Bacot, and Charles L. Mackie, *Crescent City Silver* (New Orleans: The Historic New Orleans Collection, 1980) iv.

37. George W. Featherstonhaugh, *Excursion through the Slave States* (New York: Negro University Press, 1968) 105.

38. Boultinghouse, 13–15.

39. *Arkansas Gazette*, 4 February 1834.

40. "Inventory of Property of Estate, W. S. Fulton," November 15, 1844, Small Manuscript Records, William S. Fulton Papers, Arkansas History Commission.

41. *Washington Telegraph*, 25 March 1842.

42. *See* Biographical Appendix

43. *See* Biographical Appendix

A Biographical Appendix of Arkansas Silversmiths, Goldsmiths, Clockmakers, Jewelers, and Watchmakers

Abrahamson, Isaac J.

Watch repairman, A.60, B.Poland: MCR 1870 Pulaski Co., Roll 62, AHC. "Abrahamson, J. J. jeweller, 615 Main." LRCD, 1871, 3.

Adams, Martin H.

Silversmith, A.34, B.TN: MCR 1870 Woodruff Co. (Augusta), Roll 67, AHC. Also listed in WCTR 1866, Roll 52, 1867–68, 1873, and 1876–77, Roll 53, AHC.

Adams, Morgan

Jewler, A.25, B.TN: MCR 1860 Jackson Co. (Augusta), Roll 44, AHC. "Clock, Watchmaker & Jeweler." *DAC* 2–29–60.

Alexander, William W.

Watchmaker, A.39, B.SC: MCR 1860 Independence Co. (Batesville), Roll 43, AHC. Listed 1855–70 ICTR, Rolls 58–64, AHC. Also listed in ICTR 1855, Roll 58, 1858, 1861, and 1866, Roll 60, 1869–71, Roll 64, and 1875, Roll 65, AHC.

Angel, James P.

Jeweller, A.32, B.AL: MCR 1870 Jefferson Co. (Pine Bluff), Roll 56, AHC. Also listed in JCTR 1870–76, Roll 143, AHC.

Anthony, William

"Watches and Jewelry, At Greatly Reduced Prices at Anthony's: East of Court Square—Fayetteville, Arkansas. I am on hand this season, and intend to remain: having a large and well assorted stock of Watches, Clocks, and Jewelry, which are offered to the public, at lower prices, than ever before offered in this market. I would call your particular attention to the American Watch which is the safest and most reliable Time Piece now made: If you want a Good Clock! Give Anthony a call, and get one of Seth Thomas' make. They never get out of order, and are warranted for eighteen months! at From Eight to Ten Dollars!! Jewelry of all descriptions, always on hand, and made to order. Watches, Clocks and Jewelry, cleaned and repaired on short notice and reasonable terms. . . . Old Gold and Silver always received in exchange for new articles. . . ." *FA* 6–18–59.

Arnold, F. R.

Watchmaker and Jeweler, A.25, B.OH: MCR 1860 Jefferson Co. (Pine Bluff), Roll 44, AHC.

Assmins, Constant

Watchmaker, A.20, B.Prussia: MCR 1870 Phillips Co. (Helena), Roll 60, AHC.

Austin, David

"Clock and Watch Repairing. . . . Particular attention will be paid to repairing Spectacles, and fitting them with new glasses to suitable eyes . . . Little Rock." *AG* 6–4–28.

Austin, James M.

Silversmith, A.25, B.AR: MCR 1860 Madison Co., Roll 45, AHC.

Badgley, Anthony S.

"Anthony S. Badgley, Clock and Watch Maker, And Gold And Silver Smith. Respectfully informs the citizens of Little Rock . . . and the Territory generally, that he has commenced his business in this town." *AG* 1–4–22. "Died—In this place . . . Mr. Anthony S. Badgley, watch-maker, age about 40. . . ." *AG* 5–2–32.

Baldwin, John H.

"Clock and Watchmaker John H. Baldwin, Respectfully informs his old friends and the public that his health is so restored as to enable him to attend strictly to the duties of his profession. He is prepared to manufacture silver spoons, forks, and all other articles in his line of business. Watches and jewelry sent from a distance will be punctually attended to. The highest cash price given for old gold and silver." *WT* 5–25–42. Also advertised *AG* 7–4–38 and 6–6–38 and in *HSC* 7–15–69.

Barnes, Charles E.

Watchmaker and Repairer, Hot Springs, Ark. The Hot Springs Business Directory as printed in the first edition of the *HSC* 7–15–69.

Battersby, James

"Watchmaker. . . . Jeweler and dealer in fine Duplex lever and other watches. Every style of jewelry, silverware, cutlery, and c. cheap for cash only. N.B. watches, clocks, and jewelry repaired and guaranteed." *FSH* 1–3–57. Listed in SCTR 1858, Roll 46, AHC. Silversmith, A.40, B.England: MCR 1860 Sebastian Co., Roll 50, AHC.

Bernay, Louis C.

Watchmaker, Jeweler, A.22, B.France: MCR 1870 Pulaski Co., Roll 62, AHC. "Bernay, L C watchmaker, 7 e Markham, bds 109 e Fourth." LRCD, 1871, 39.

Bishop, H. J.

"Watch and Clock Maker and Jeweler. . . . Helena . . . Finger and Ear-rings, Breast-pins, Port-monaies, & C. . . . Jewelry, Music Boxes, Accordions, etc. repaired. . . ." *DS* 3–15–54.

Blake, George

Jeweler with the Knickerbocker Exploring Co. from New York in 1849. *FSH* 3–21–49.

Bollun, Henry

Watchmaker, A.43, B.Schleswig-Holstein: MCR 1870 Jefferson Co., Roll 56, AHC.

Boolinger, J.

Clock mender, A.30, B.Germany: MCR 1860 Jackson Co., Roll 44, AHC.

Borge, Peter

Watchmaker, A.31, B.NY: MCR 1870 Pulaski Co., Roll 62, AHC.

Bowden, T. W.

Silversmith, A.35, B.GA: MCR 1870 Monroe Co., Roll 59, AHC.

Boyle, J. H.

Watchmaker, A.29, B.Ireland: MCR 1870 Chicot Co., Roll 49, AHC.

Brown, G. S.

Jeweler, A.25, B.MI: MCR 1860 Sebastian Co., Roll 50, AHC.

Can—eld, William

Jeweler, part of the Knickerbocker Exploring Co. from New York in 1849. *FSH* 3–21–49.

Carter, Henry H.

"Watchmaker & Jeweler, Arkadelphia, Arkansas. Every description of fine Watches, Clocks and Jewelry repaired, and warranted to give satisfaction. Pure Gold Engagement and Wedding Rings made to order at short notice. Henry M. Carter . . . will make to order, Silver Spoons and cups, Silver and Gold Cane Heads, and Medals; Gold Spectacles, Gold Jewelry & C. of every description. Clocks and Watches promptly repaired. Masonic, I.O.F. and Corporative seals, and every description of Engraving executed with neatness and despatch." *OCJ* 7–4–61.

Chaffin, Q.

Jeweler, A.50, B.NC: MCR 1860 Prairie Co., Roll 48, AHC.

Charles, G. H.

Silversmith, A.25, B.Unknown: MCR 1850 Ashley Co., Roll 25, AHC.

Chester, F. L.

Watchmaker, A.22, B. England: MCR 1860 Drew Co., Roll 41, AHC.

Church, Charles H.

Watchmaker, A.25, B.England: MCR 1860 Independence Co. (Batesville), Roll 43, AHC.

Cline, T.

Jewell A.25, B.Germany: MCR 1860 Prairie Co., Roll 48, AHC.

Clower, Daniel

Silversmith, A.25, B.AL: MCR 1860 Ouachita Co., Roll 47, AHC.

Coe, Abner

Silversmith, A.26, B.NY: MCR 1870 Franklin Co., Roll 53, AHC.

Cohen, Albert

"Jewelry, Clocks & Watches." *AG* 6–13–57. "Fashionable Jewelry Establishment." *AG* 9–5–57. "Cohen's Jewelry Store." *AG* 10–17–57. "Jeweler." *AG* 10–30–66. "Meteorological Observations, by Albert Cohen, Watchmaker and Jeweler." *AG* 10–2–70. "Albert Cohen, Practical Watchmaker and Jeweler . . . Dealer in Clocks, Watches, Jewelry, Silver Ware, Plated Ware, Pistols and Ammunition, Fancy Goods, etc. . . ." LRCD 1871, 96. Cohen, A., Watchmaker 1850. Carey Turner Mackie and Charles Le June Mackie, *New Orleans Silversmiths, Goldsmiths, Jewelers, Clock and Watchmakers. 1720–1870,* 1979, 31.

Constantine, William

Watchmaker, A.21, B.MI: MCR 1870 Pulaski Co., Roll 62, AHC.

Crawford, Jonathan

Jeweler, A.46, B.VT: MCR 1850 Union Co. (El Dorado), Roll 30, AHC.

Cresswell, James S.

"Cresswell and Edwards, Clock and Watch Makers, and Gold and Silver Smiths . . . permanently located themselves in the Town of Washington. . . . Gentlemen's and Ladies Patent Lever, Horizontal, Repeating, Duplex, and all kinds of fancy Watches, Clocks, and Chronometers, repaired and waranted . . . Gold and Silver work of all kinds, executed with neatness, and at reduced prices. Having a correspondent in New Orleans, they will be able to keep on hand a general assortment of all the best materials. . . ." *AG* 9–13–25. A James Cresswell is listed as a watchmaker in New Orleans in 1824, Mackie, 34.

Crouch, Augustus M.

Watchmaker, A.28, B.DE: MCR 1850 Hempstead Co., Roll 26, AHC. "Co-Partnership, Watch Makers and Jewelers, C. White and A. M. Crouch." *WT* 7–31–50. "Dissolution of Partnership, C. White-Crouch." *WT* 3–24–52. A mid-November issue of the *WT* said of Crouch: "though still living . . . a citizen of the state nearly 50 years. Came to Arkansas from Georgia . . . first locating in Little Rock and removing to Washington in 1842. He was a soldier in the Mexican War, a bugler in Capt. Albert Pike's Co. and fought at Buena Vista. Perhaps never had a superior as a watchmaker."

Crouch, William A.

[Jeweler] Artist, A.28, B.TN: MCR 1860 Independence Co., Roll 43, AHC. "W. A. Crouch, Silversmith." *NAT* 4–21–66. "Crouch and Durbin, Watchmakers and Jewelers, Batesville, Arkansas." *NAT* 12–8–66. Crouch died in Batesville in 1877. *BG* 2–2–77.

Dearing, R. S.

Silversmith, A.24, B.GA: MCR 1870 Washington Co., Roll 66, AHC.

Delaroderie, R. G.

"Time Watches and Jewelry . . . R. G. Delaroderie & C. J. Garner having associated themselves for the purpose of conducting the watch making and jewelry business in the well known stand on Main Street . . . they are prepared to repair all kinds of clocks, watches, jewelry, & c. . . ." *AG* 2–16–46. "R. G. Delaroderie." *AG* 3–30–48.

Demby, Josiah H.

Watchmaker, A.21, B.GA: MCR 1860 Jefferson Co. (Pine Bluff), Roll 44, AHC. Served in the Civil War, Co. G, 4th Rdg. AR Cavalry, U.S. Army, discharged 6–30–1865 at Little Rock. He remained in Arkansas for the remainder of his life. He also represented Scott, Polk, Montgomery, and Hot Spring counties in the General Assembly in 1868 and Montgomery County in 1879. He died in Hot Springs 2–13–1918. SMC Box VII, #8. Collection of Louise Demby Shull, SMC, Box VII, #8, AHC.

Demby, J. W.

Watchmaker, A.43, B.NC: MCR 1860 Jefferson Co., Roll 44, AHC. Also listed in JCTR 1857–60, Roll 116, 1861, and Roll 117, 1865, Roll 118, AHC.

De St. Martin, Emiele P.

Watchmaker, A.25, B.TX: MCR 1870 Desha Co., Roll 52, AHC.

Dimonds, John

Silversmith, A.26, B.LA: MCR 1860 Poinsett Co., Roll 48, AHC. There are several Dimonds listed under Silversmiths of New York City 1815–1841, NYCD.

Dodge, John

Jeweler, A.36, B.ME: MCR 1860 Ouachita Co. (Camden), Roll 47, AHC. "Watchmaker and Jewler, John Dodge." *OH* 6–23–60.

Dotter, Marcus

Silversmith, A.34, B.Germany: MCR 1850 Pulaski Co., Roll 49, AHC. "Clock, Watchmaking & Silversmithing." *AG* 11–21–51. "Notice—Marcus Dotter, elected Secretary & Treasurer of the Fire Department of the city of Little Rock. . . ." *AG* 1–16–58. Silversmith, A.44, B.Germany: MCR 1860 Pulaski Co., Roll 49, AHC. "Marcus Dotter, Watchmaker & Jeweler." *AG* 10–2–70. Jeweler/Watchmaker, A.54, B.Germany: MCR 1870 Pulaski Co., Roll 62, AHC.

Durbin, H. H.

[Silversmith] Durbin was listed in Independence Co. tax records 1867, Roll 64, AHC. *See* W. A. Crouch

Dyke, Henry

Watchmaker, A.18, B.PA: MCR 1850 Washington Co., Roll 31, AHC. Watchmaker, A.28, B.PA: MCR 1860 Washington Co., Roll 52, AHC.

Edwards, ?

See Cresswell

Ellis, D. J.

Jeweler, A.45, B.KY: MCR 1870 Washington Co., Roll 66, AHC.

English, William K.

"Watches & Clocks . . . in Little Rock. . . ." *AG* 9–28–31. "Notice." *AG* 2–1–32.

Erwin, John

Silversmith, A.38, B.TN: MCR 1870 Woodruff Co., Roll 67, AHC.

Estes, John

Jeweler and Tinker, A.28, B.AR: MCR 1870 Madison Co., Roll 58, AHC.

Estis, John Wesley

Watch repairer, A.25, B.AR: MCR 1870 Carroll Co., Roll 49, AHC.

Fadley, J. M.

Silversmith. Fadley was listed in Pulaski Co. tax records 1849, Roll 2, ATR. Hotel Keeper, A.30, B.VA: MCR 1850 Phillips Co. (Helena), Roll 29, AHC. "Clock and Watch Making." *SS* 4–6–50. Fadley, John M. 1857. 217 Main Street, Memphis, Shelby Co. Jeweler. Benjamin H. Caldwell, Jr., "Tennessee Silversmiths Prior to 1860: A Check List." *Antiques*, December, 1971, 909.

Fellmer (Phelman), Joseph

"Watchmaker & Jeweler, Fellmer & Graf." *AI* 5–15–57. "Watches and Jewelry." *VBP* 7–13–59. "L. Graf & J. Fellmer Jewelers in Fort Smith and Van Buren." *VBP* 1–5–60. Jeweler, A.33, B.Wartenberg [Wurttemberg], Germany: MCR 1860 Crawford Co. (Van Buren), Roll 40, AHC. "Jewelry Store," *VBP* 5–8–61. "Jeweler—Joseph Fellmer." *VBP* 9–25–61. Also listed in CCTR 1860 and 1866–68, Roll 23, AHC.

Ford, Henry

"Silversmith & Jeweler, Henry Ford." *A* 3–26–59. Watchmaker, A.25, B.KY: MCR 1860 Washington Co. (Fayetteville), Roll 52, AHC.

Foster, Charles

Engraver, A.24, B.England: MCR 1850 Franklin Co., Roll 26, AHC. Also listed in FCTR 1852, Roll 14, AHC.

Freers, Samuel

Watchmaker, A.25, B.Bavaria: MCR 1860 Independence Co., Roll 43, AHC.

Fulton, D. C.

[Silversmith] Fancy Merchant, A.39, B.PA: MCR 1850 Pulaski Co., Roll 29, AHC. "Beautiful and Fancy Goods." *AG* 12–7–42. Ad in *AG* 10–12–55. Also listed in PCTR 1843–48, Roll 1, ATR and 1850–52, 1854, and 1856, Roll 2, ATR. "Emporium." *AG* 5–22–58.

Furst, Samuel

Watchmaker, A.25, B.Bavaria: MCR Independence Co., Roll 43, AHC. Also listed in ICTR 1852–57, Roll 58, 1850–58, Roll 59, and 1858, 1861, and 1866, Roll 60, AHC. "Dissolution of Partnership Furst & Lewis, Samuel Furst, W. J. Lewis." *DS* 7–26—59. Furst, Samuel. 1855. Memphis, Shelby Co. Watchmaker. Caldwell, 913.

Garner, C. J.

[Silversmith] listed in Pulaski Co. tax records 1839 and 1845–46, Roll 1, ATR. "Watchmaking & Jewelry Business." *AG* 6–9–45. "Watchmaking & Jewelry Establishment." *AG* 1–9–47. *See* Delaroderie

Garrett, J. W.

Silversmith, A.23, B.GA: MCR 1860 Clark Co., Roll 39, AHC.

Gaskill, David

"Clocks & Watches Repaired." *BE* 12–19–48. Farmer, A.21, B.IN: MCR 1850 Independence Co., Roll 26, AHC. Also listed in ICTR 1849 and 1852–57, Roll 56, AHC.

Gentin, Louis

"Watch and Clockmaker." *ATA* 11–27–37. "Louis Gentin Watch & Clockmaker from Geneva . . . [Little Rock] . . . ." *AG* 11–28–27.

Girard, Othenin

"Watch & Clock Maker . . . opened a shop in Ashley's brick row on Markham. . . . Jewelry, Music boxes, etc. repaired at the shortest notice and in the best manner." *AG* 8–10–42.

Gooch, Albert

Engraver, A.21, B.England: MCR 1860 Pulaski Co., Roll 49, AHC.

Gordon, W. L.

Jeweler, A.39, B.TN: MCR 1870 Randolph Co., Roll 63, AHC.

Goss, J. B.

Jeweler, A.65, B.OH: MCR 1870 Prairie Co., Roll 61, AHC.

Graf (Graff), Louis (Lewis)

Watchmaker, A.32, B.Saxony, Germany: MCR 1860 Crawford Co., Roll 40, AHC. "Jeweler and Watchmaker." *VBP* 4–17–61. Also listed in CCTR 1858–60 and 1865–68, Roll 23, AHC. Mr. L. Graff, Funeral, Van Buren c. 1907. Eno Collection of Funeral Notices, Biography Files, Drawer 20, AHC. *See* Fellmer

Greenleaf, D.

"Greenleaf & Bro., Wathmakers and Jewelers Washington, Arkansas." *WT* 1–15–62.

Greenleaf, S.

See D. Greenleaf

Hamblin, P. G.

Clockmaker, A.49, B.VA: MCR 1860 Van Buren Co., Roll 51, AHC.

Harrington, Samuel

Jeweler, A.40, B.MA: MCR 1860 Crawford Co., Roll 40, AHC. "Watchmaker and Jeweler." *VBP* 2–10–60.

Harris, A. L.

"Watchmaker and Jeweler . . . office on Buena Vista Street, opposite the nucleus house, Des Arc, Ark. Clocks, Watches and jewelry repaired with neatness and dispatch. . . ." *DAC* 11–20–58. "Watchmaker and Jeweler." *DAC* 1–4–60.

Harris, C. A.

Watchmaker, A.43, B.TN: MCR 1860 Prairie Co., Roll 48, AHC.

Hartin, John

Watchmaker, A.30, B.MI: MCR 1870 Drew Co., Roll 52, AHC.

Henry, James A.

"New Jewelry and Watch-Repairing Establishment." *AG* 10–4–56.

Henry, William

Silversmith, A.56, B.CT: MCR 1860 Desha Co., Roll 41, AHC.

Hobbs, Jesse

Watchmaker, A.29, B.KY: MCR 1870 Benton Co., Roll 47, AHC.

Holland, M. H.

Jeweler, A.23, B.Germany: MCR 1860 Drew Co., Roll 41, AHC.

Holland, Martain

Silversmith, A.25, B.England: MCR 1860 Columbia Co., Roll 39, AHC.

Howe, William H.

"Watchmaker and Jeweler . . . has permanently located himself in Washington and will give prompt personal attention to all articles left in his charge. Watches, Clocks, Jewelry, & c. neatly and promptly repaired." *WT* 11–25–57.

Hughes, Frederick

Silversmith, A.27, B.VA: MCR 1870 Pulaski Co., Roll 62, AHC.

Irelan, J. L.

Jeweler, A.43, B.PA: MCR 1870 Sebastian Co., Roll 64, AHC.

Johnson, A. B.

Goldsmith, A.21, B.IL: MCR 1860 Johnson Co., Roll 44, AHC.

Johnson, James B.

"Watches & Clocks . . . silversmith and jeweler . . . permanently located in Helena, is prepared to do any work in his line. . . ." *SS* 5–1–52.

Johnson, Joseph

Whitesmith and watchmaker, A.26, B.NC: MCR 1850 Sevier Co., Roll 30, AHC. His name also appeared in this advertisement: "Stolen—$50 Reward— Taken from Hot Springs, Aug. 8th—one heavy Gold Hunting Watch, No. 65303, Joseph Johnson, maker. The above reward & no question asked, will be paid by leaving it at this office. George Allen." *AG* 9–20–56.

Jordan, C. T.

"Jewelry Repaired. . . . If you want jewelry repaired, Go to '93,' C. T. Jordan." *UU* 7–27–65.

Kirk, J. M. (James)

"Watch and Clock Maker. . . , respectfully informs the citizens of Ft. Smith and vicinity that he has located himself in this place for the purpose of repairing watches and clocks. . . ." *FSH* 12–13–48. Also listed in Crawford Co. tax records 1844–47 and 1849–50, Roll 22, AHC.

Kirk, John

Watchmaker, A.42, B.England: MCR 1860 Independence Co. (Batesville), Roll 43, AHC. Also listed in ICTR 1858, 1861, and 1866, Roll 60, AHC.

Klein, Franklin (Frederick) J.

[Silversmith] Klein became a U.S. citizen in 1855. Pulaski Co. Circuit Court Naturalization Records, Roll 322, AHC. Silversmith, A.30, B.Bavaria: MCR 1870 Woodruff Co., Roll 53, AHC. Also listed in WCTR 1873 and 1877, Roll 53, AHC. Capt. Klein was a member of the 'well-known' jewelry firm of Klein & Fink, founded in 1878. He died in Fort Smith in 1913. *SA* 4–1–1913.

Kock, Joseph

Silversmith, A.34, B.KY: MCR 1850 Independence Co., Roll 26, AHC.

Lampret, C.

Silversmith, A.22, B.TN: MCR 1860 White Co., Roll 52, AHC.

Lathrop, S.

Jeweler, A.30, B.KY: MCR 1860 Jackson Co., Roll 44, AHC. A Jacksonport fire destroyed many businesses, including the jewelry store of S. Lathrop. *AG* 4–7–60.

Leper, Joseph

Jeweler, A.22, B.LA: MCR 1860 Crawford Co., Roll 40, AHC.

Leptienan, (Leptrin) (Leptien) (Leptin), F. or T.

"F. Leptien Clock and Watch Maker and Jeweller." *DAC* 11–13–58. Jeweler, A.32, B.Germany: MCR 1860 Prairie Co. [Des Arc], Roll 48, AHC. Also listed PCTR 1861, Roll 53, 1862–63, Roll 55, 1865–66, Roll 53, 1868, Roll 54, and 1869–70, Roll 57, AHC. Watchmaker, A.42, B.Germany: MCR 1870 Prairie Co., Roll 61, AHC.

Levy, Jonas

[Silversmith] Listed in Pulaski Co. tax records 1841–48, Roll 1, and 1849–51, Roll 2, ATR. "Fire and Marine Insurance. Camden Insurance Co., New Jersey. . . . Jonas Levy. . . . Watchmaker, Markham St." *AG* 2–8–50. Secondary Sources: A Jonas Levy was listed as a jeweler in New York, N.Y., between 1836 and 1838. Ernest M. Currier, *Marks of Early American Silversmiths* (distributed by Century House) (Watkins Glen, New York: The American Life Foundation, 1938) 88. A Jonas Levy was listed as a watchmaker/jeweler in Memphis, Tennessee, between 1855 and 1860. Caldwell, 462. A Jonas Levy, from England, was listed as a watchmaker and silversmith in Cincinnati between 1825 and 1829. Elizabeth D. Beckman. *Cincinnati Silversmiths, Jewelers, Watch and Clockmakers.* (Cincinnati: B&B Company, 1975) 89. A J. Levy (Levi) was listed as a jeweler and watchmaker in New Orleans in 1858–1868. Mackie, 107.

Lewis, W. J.

"Watchmaker & Jeweler." *DS* 7–26–59. "New Jewelry Store." *DS* 8–2–59. Watchmaker, A.25, B.VA: MCR 1860 Independence Co. (Batesville), Roll 43, AHC. Also listed in ICTR 1856, Roll 58, and 1861, Roll 60, AHC. *See* Furst

Linebaugh, Benjamin

"Watches & Jewelry. B & H. W. Linebaugh." *AG* 4–10–33. "Watches & Jewelry." *AG* 2–11–34. "New Jewelry." *AG* 2–17–35. "Dissolution of Co-Partnership. . . . Benj. Linebaugh, H. W. Linebaugh. . . . Benj. Linebaugh would respectfully inform his friends and customers, that he will continue the business. . . ." *AG* 11–3–35. "New Jewelry, Watches & C." *AG* 3–22–36. "New Jewelry." *AG* 1–2–38. Also listed in Pulaski Co. tax records 1836–45, Roll 1, ATR.

Linebaugh, Henry W.

See B. Linebaugh

Linebaugh (Linebough), Robert A.

"Jeweler, Silversmith, Clock & Watchmaker. . . . Helena. . . ." *ASD* 12–24–40. Also listed in the 1840 Phillips Co. census, Roll 19, AHC.

Maloney, Edward B. (P.)

Watchrepairer, A.33, B.KY: MCR 1870 Pulaski Co., Roll 62, AHC. Maloney, E. P., watchmaker, 110 Main. LRCD, 1871, 90.

Marchland, Louis E.

Silversmith, A.62, B.LA: MCR 1850 Crawford Co., Roll 25 AHC. A Louis Marchland is listed as a goldsmith in New Orleans in 1824. Mackie, 113.

Marold, Theodore

Jeweler, Watchmaker and Silversmith . . . Ft. Smith . . . at the store of A. G. Meyers of Garrison Avenue. *SWI* 2–17–55.

Mayer, L. D.

Watchmaker, A.23, B.France: MCR 1860 Jefferson Co. (Pine Bluff), Roll 44, AHC.

McCaughn, Daniel C.

Silversmith, A.33, B.KY: MCR 1850 Independence Co., Roll 26, AHC.

McGuire, Jonathan

Clocktinker, A.37, B.VA: MCR 1860 Randolph Co., Roll 49, AHC.

McMahon, William

Watchmaker, MCR 1870 Arkansas Industrial Census, Phillips Co., Helena, Roll 60, AHC.

McNeill (Niell), Joe

[Silversmith] "Uncle Joe McNeill was in charge of the horses and harness on Sam Strong Sr.'s farm. McNeill made the horse collars and equipment and plows for working the fields and built a cotton gin for the plantation. He also made silver spoons from silver dollars that are in the Sam Strong family today." Amy Jean Green. *The Clark County Historical Journal* (The Clark County Historical Association, Winter 1979–80) 260.

Michot, Eugene

Watchmaker, A.45, B.Switzerland: MCR 1870 Phillips Co. (Helena), Roll 60, AHC.

Miller, Lemuel

Silversmith, A.22, B.KY: MCR 1860 Greene Co., Roll 42, AHC.

Mitchell, Francis

Jeweller, A.30, B.KY: MCR 1850 Union Co. (El Dorado), Roll 30, AHC.

Mitchell, J. W.

"Watchmaker and Jeweler." *WT* 12–22–58. Jeweler, A.24, B.England: MCR 1860 Hempstead Co. (Washington), Roll 42, AHC. Also listed in HCTR 1860, Roll 75, AHC.

Morehead (Moorhead), W. T.

Wachmaker, A.25, B.TN: MCR 1860 Clark Co. (Arkadelphia), Roll 39, AHC. Also listed in CCTR 1857 and 1861, Roll 56, and 1866–68, Roll 57, AHC.

Mulkey, James J.

"Watches, Clocks, Jewelry. Guns—Repaired. . . . Mulkey & Neil." *SS* 10–20–55. "New Jewelry Store J. I. Mulkey & Co." *SS* 2–23–56. Silversmith, A.41, B.GA: MCR 1860 Phillips Co. [Helena], Roll 47, AHC. Also listed PCTR 1859 and 1866–67, Roll 89, AHC. A James J. Mulkey was listed as a watchmaker/jeweler in Chattanooga, Tennessee, Hamilton Co., between 1849 and 1850. Caldwell, 462.

Neil, James H.

[Silversmith] Listed in Phillips Co. tax records 1850–58, Roll 88, AHC. *See* Mulkey

Nickerson, Thomas

Silversmith, A.23, B.IN: MCR 1870 Phillips Co. (Helena), Roll 60, AHC.

Nickerson, Thomas J.

Watchmaker, A.50, B.IN: MCR 1870 Phillips Co. (Helena), Roll 60, AHC.

Nixon, Thomas J. or T. P.

Silversmith, A.40, B.IN: MCR 1860 Phillips Co. (Helena), Roll 47, AHC. Also listed in PCTR 1859–60 and 1866–67, Roll 89, AHC.

Noel (Noll), Washington

"New Jewlery. . . . N. B.—Mr. L[Benj. Linebaugh] has engaged Mr. Noel . . . , whose well-known character as a superior watch-maker, enables him to say . . . that any business in this line entrusted to him shall be executed in a style which cannot be surpassed in any part of the Union." *AG* 1–2–38. "Watchmaker." *AB* 9–23–43. Also listed in Pulaski Co. tax records 1840–41 and 1845, Roll 1, ATR. A Washington Noel was listed as working as a silversmith in Louisville, Ky., in 1836. Marquis Boultinghouse, *Silversmiths, Jewelers, Clock and Watch Makers of Kentucky 1785–1900*, copyright 1980 by Marquis Boultinghouse, 211. A W. Noel was listed as a watchmaker/jeweler in Davidson Co., Nashville, Tennessee, 1857–60. Caldwell, 463.

Nordman, Eugene

Watchmaker, A.22, B.Switzerland: MCR 1860 Jefferson Co. [Pine Bluff], Roll 44, AHC.

Norton, William H.

Jeweler, A.45, B.TN: MCR 1860 Jefferson Co. (Pine Bluff), Roll 44, AHC. Also listed in JCTR 1855–60 (pt.), Roll 116, and 1860 (pt.)–65 (pt.), Roll 117, AHC. In addition to his family, Norton had 21 people living with him, including Henry Von Seckendorff, Artist; F. R. Arnold, watchmaker/jeweler, and J. H. Demby, watchmaker.

Oakley, Oliver B.

[Silver plater] Oakley was with the Knickerbocker Exploring Co., NYC. *FSH* 3–21–49.

Parks, Albert A.

Silversmith, A.37, B.TN: MCR 1860 Conway Co., Roll 39, AHC.

Parsons, William W.

[Silversmith] Listed in Pulaski Co. tax records 1852 and 1856, Roll 2, ATR. "New Jewelry and Watch-repairing Establishment." *AG* 10–4–56. Parsons died in Little Rock on January 28, 1857, Pulaski Co. Probate Court Records, Book "D," 1857–59, Rolls 59 and 60, AHC.

Paxton, William

[Silversmith] "Died-Recently in Pyatt township, in this county (Pulaski). Mr. William Paxton, Watchmaker." *AG* 9–19–26.

Powee (Porree), Melvin

Jeweler, A.33, B.OH: MCR 1870 Jefferson Co., Roll 56, AHC.

Prat (Pratt), Edward

"Watchmaker, Jeweler Edward Pratt Located in the Quarels Bldg. Fayetteville." *FA* 12–9–59. Watchmaker, A.26, B.MA: MCR 1860 Washington Co. (Fayetteville), Roll 52, AHC.

Purrell, G. C.

Engraver, A.30, B.IN: MCR 1860 Hot Spring Co., Roll 42, AHC.

Raleigh, Phillip

Silversmith, A.32, B.KY: MCR 1860 Union Co., Roll 51, AHC.

Reeves, David S.

See J. Baldwin

Rhorerbacker, C. A.

Engraver, A.22, B.NY: MCR 1860 Craighead Co., Roll 40, AHC.

Richmond, Washington

Jeweller, A.37, B.MS: MCR 1870 Crawford Co., Roll 51, AHC.

Roberts, Franklin

Wachmaker, A.39, B.PA: MCR 1860 Clark Co., Roll 39, AHC. Watchmaker and jeweler, *OCJ* 7–4–61.

Roberts, Jeremiah H.

"Watchmaker and Jeweler." *AI* 1–16–47. Watchmaker, A.27, B.IL: MCR 1850 Crawford Co. (Van Buren), Roll 25, AHC.

Robertson, L.

Silversmith, A.33, B.TN: MCR 1860 White Co., Roll 52, AHC.

Robinson, William P.

Jeweler, A.32, B.IL: MCR 1870 Jackson Co. (Jacksonport), Roll 56, AHC.

Roch, F.

"Roch, F., Watchmaker, bds 11 Rock." LRCD 1871, 104.

Rock, Joseph

Silversmith, A.34, B.KY: MCR 1850 Independence Co., Roll 26, AHC.

Roeck, Francis

Watchmaker, A.32, B.Bavaria: MCR 1870 Pulaski Co., Roll 62, AHC. "Roeck, Francis, Watchmaker, 7 e Markham." LRCD 1871, 104.

Rogers, S.

Watch repairer, A.23, B.ME: MCR 1870 Ouachita Co., Roll 59, AHC.

Rollins, Thomas

Watchmaker, A.46, B.SC: MCR 1960 Washington Co., Roll 52, AHC.

Rosenberg, Ferdinand

Silversmith, A.69, B.France: MCR 1870 Johnson Co., Roll 57, AHC.

Rudisell, John

Silversmith, A.18, B.MS: MCR 1850 Phillips Co. (Helena), Roll 29, AHC. A John Rudissile was listed as a silversmith in Memphis in 1850. Caldwell, 148.

Rudisil, L. A.

Wachmaker, A.25, B.MS: MCR 1860 Clark Co., Roll 39, AHC.

Rudasill (Rudisell) (Rudisill), Samuel A.

Watch & Clock repairer, A.34, B.TN: MCR 1870 Clark Co. (Arkadelphia), Roll 49, AHC. Also listed in CCTR 1861, Roll 56, and 1866–67, Roll 57, AHC. "S. A. Rudisill Watchmaker & Jeweler." SS 1–5–84.

Sewald (Seewald), W. H.

Jeweller/Watchmaker, A.24, B.OH: MCR 1860 Sebastian Co. (Ft. Smith), Roll 50, AHC. Jeweler, A.33, B.OH: MCR 1870 Sebastian Co. (Ft. Smith), Roll 64, AHC.

Sewell, A. F.

Watchmaker, A.63, B.TN: MCR 1870 Boone Co., Roll 48, AHC.

Shaw, W. W.

Silversmith, A.25, B.MO: MCR 1860 Franklin Co., Roll 41, AHC. Also listed in FCTR 1861, Roll 14, AHC.

Shuster, Anton

Watchmaker, A.40, B.Austria: MCR 1870 Sebastian Co. (Ft. Smith), Roll 64, AHC.

Simmons, Charles

Silversmith, A.52, B.NY: MCR 1860 Pope Co., Roll 48, AHC.

Smith, J. G.

Silversmith, A.24, B.OH: MCR 1860 Union Co., Roll 51, AHC. Listed in UCTR 1859 and 1867, Roll 62, AHC. Also listed in Union Co. Probate Court Records, Book "M," 1883–93, Roll 20, AHC.

Smith, Lea T.

"Watches and Jewelry . . . at the old stand of Dr. White's Drug store next door to the Court House. New store, new goods, new prices." *VBP* 12–23–59. "Jeweler." *VBP* 1–5–60.

Smith, Seander F.

Silversmith, A.Unknown. B.MS: MCR 1860 Yell Co., Roll 52, AHC.

Souter, I. and Brother

Repaired watches & jewelry along with their photography trade.

Stallcup, John

Jeweler, A.24, B.NC: MCR 1870 Jackson Co., Roll 56, AHC.

Steiner, Alexander

Jeweler, A.23, B.Wurtenberg[Wurttemberg]: MCR 1860 Sebastian Co. (Ft. Smith), Roll 50, AHC. Listed in SCTR, 1866, Roll 46, AHC. "Watchmaker & Jeweler." *FSNE* 9–18–67. Watchmaker, A.33, B.Wurtenberg: MCR 1870 Sebastian Co. (Ft. Smith), Roll 64, AHC. Also listed SCTR 1875, Roll 23, AHC.

Stinson, George

Jeweler, A.23, B.MC: MCR 1850 Ouachita Co. (Camden), Roll 28, AHC. "Watchmaker & Jeweller." *OH* 7–29–58. Watchmaker, A.33, B.ME: MCR 1870 Ouachita Co. (Camden), Roll 47, AHC. Listed in OCTR 1849–51, 1853, 1855, and 1857(pt.), Roll 35, also 1857(pt.)–59, 1861, and 1867, Roll 36, AHC.

Strappy, G. W.

Silversmith, A.26, B.IN: MCR 1860 Phillips Co. (Helena), Roll 44, AHC.

Strong, Cushing

Silversmith, A.29, B.OH: MCR 1860 Izard Co., Roll 43, AHC.

Toncray, Silas T.

[Silversmith] "Baptist Church. . . . Silas T. Toncray, a Minister of the regular Baptist Church. Little Rock, (A.T.) July 5, 1824." *AG* 7–6–24. "S. T. Toncray, Clock and Watchmaker, Silversmith, Jeweller and Engraver . . . Little Rock. . . ." *AG* 4–15–29. "Moving Away. I expect to leave this Territory, for Memphis, Tennessee. . . ." *AG* 7–7–30. Also listed in Pulaski Co. tax records [Though living in Memphis] 1836 and 1840, Roll 1, ATR.

Torrey, J. M.

"J. M. Torrey, Watchmaker and Jeweler . . . may be found at the north-east corner of the public square (Fayetteville)." *SWI* 2–17–55.

Turner, Chapman

"Watchmaker and Jeweler." *SS* 10–2–56.
Silversmith, A.30, B.MD: MCR 1860 Phillips Co. (Helena), Roll 44, AHC. "Watchmaker and Jeweler." *SS* 1–28–60.

Tyree, Thomas F.

Watchmaker, A.47 B.VA: MCR 1870 Pulaski Co., Roll 62, AHC.

Vanhorn, George D.

Jeweler, A.30, B.PA: MCR 1870 Independence Co. (Batesville), Roll 55, AHC.

Varce, Melvin

Watchmaker, A.22, B.OH: MCR 1860 Jefferson Co. (Pine Bluff), Roll 42, AHC. Listed in JCTR 1860, Roll 117, and 1866 and 1868, Roll 118, AHC. Jewler, A.33, B.OH: MCR 1870 Jefferson Co., Roll 56, AHC.

Viler, Thomas

Clockmaker, A.31, B.NC: MCR 1860 St. Francis Co., Roll 49, AHC.

Walker, David T.

"County Seals David T. Walker . . . engaged in Casting and Engraving official seals . . . being now absent . . . has left the business with the subscriber—who is now prepared to execute orders for Seals or Presses. . . . Samuel B. Wilson." *AG* 7–15–20.

Welden, D.

Clock Workman, A.52, B.CT: MCR 1860 Sebastian Co. (Ft. Smith), Roll 50, AHC.

Welte, A. F.

"Watchmaker . . . Permanently located in Helena . . . , patent levers, common watches, brass and wooden clocks and jewelry repaired, fine gold jewelry for sale. . . ." *SS* 1–25–51.

Wendell, Thomas L.

"Watchmaker. . . . Washington House Washington Arkansas." *WT* 12–17–62.

White, Charles

"New Watchmaker, Washington." *WT* 3–25–46. Watchmaker, A.35, B.TN: MCR 1850 Hempstead Co.

(Washington), Roll 26, AHC. Watchmaker, A.55, B.TN: MCR 1870 Ouachita Co., Roll 59, AHC. *See* A. M. Crouch

Whiteford, John

"Watchmaker's card. Notice is Hereby given to the public of Fort Smith, that I will work at my trade again. . . ." *FSNE* 7–2–64.

Wiggins, S. A.

"Wiggins, S. A., engraver, bds 9 e Fourth." LRCD 1871, 116. Invoice to Samuel A. Williams Estate for burial of deceased from James Cook & Co. 1/14/1903, SMC Pulaski Co. Probate Records, General File, AHC.

Wilkins, Marcus

Silversmith, A.35, B.VA: MCR 1850 Sevier Co., Roll 30, AHC.

Wilson, Samuel B.

See D. Walker

Wolfe (Wolf), F. H.

(Silversmith) Listed in Crawford Co. tax records 1849–50, Roll 22, AHC. Gold/Silversmith, A.60, B.DE: MCR 1860 Sebastian Co. (Ft. Smith), Roll 50, AHC. Also listed in SCTR 1855, 1857–60, and 1866, Roll 46, AHC. "Gold & Silversmith *SNE* 9–18–67.

Woolf, Francis F.

Silversmith, A.45, B.PA: MCR 1850 Crawford Co., Roll 25, AHC.

Wood, George

Watchmaker, A.26, B.FL: MCR 1860 Sevier Co., Roll 51, AHC.

Yankus, G. A.

"Silversmith and Jeweler, G. A. Yankus Main St.—opposite Colombus Hotel, prepared to make or repair anything in his line . . . Van Buren." *AI* 12–30–43.

Zimmerman, Jesse V.

"Jewelry Store, J. V. Zimmerman." *AG* 10–23–66. "Zimmerman, J. V., Jeweler, 102 e Markham, res. corner Sixteenth and Commerce." LRCD 1871, 118. Secondary Source: Zimmerman was born in Montgomery County, PA.. He learned the jeweler's trade from the firm of Leibert & Brown. After moving to Little Rock in 1857, he worked for D. C. Fulton, a jeweler and watchmaker. Zimmerman also served as an officer in the Confederate Army and, following the Civil War, opened a jewelry store on Markham Street. *Goodspeed Central Arkansas,* 523 and 524.

Zootland, Gustave

Watchmaker, A.55, B.Sweden: MCR 1860 Jefferson Co., Roll 44, AHC.

An Illustrated Catalog
of Arkansas Silver

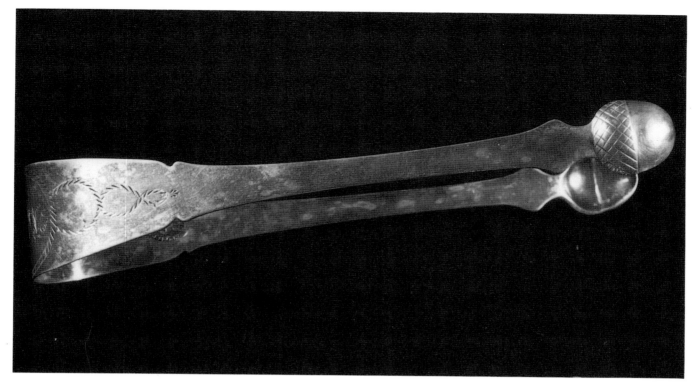

S—1a. Sugar Tongs, monogrammed in bright-cut, oval script "W.J.E.W." (for William and Jane Eliza Woodruff). L: 7¼".

Die-stamped within a rounded cartouche "S. T. Toncray" above an eagle with spread wings clutching an olive branch (symbol of peace) in one talon and a cluster of arrows in the other. Probably Little Rock, c. 1827. *Private collection.*

Formed from a single sheet of coin quality silver, these round spring-strap handled tongs with their fanciful acorn-shaped grips or bowls remain as the only documented Arkansas-made examples. These tongs and several teaspoons, all bearing Toncray's unique mark along with the initials of William and Jane Eliza Woodruff (née Mills), were, according to Woodruff descendants, made for the couple by Toncray as a wedding gift, following their marriage in Little Rock on November 14, 1827. Jane Eliza was in fact Silas Toncray's niece and had arrived here from Kentucky with the Isaac Watkins family in 1821, three years prior to Toncray's arrival in 1824.

S—1b. Detail of the sugar tongs' rounded, stamped mark of "S. T. TONCRAY" above an eagle.

A large, elliptical, bright-cut cartouche or reserve centered on the backstrap of the handles is initialed in script "W.J.E.W." Graduated, bright-cut ornament flanks either side of the central bright-cut bordered reserve.

S–2a. Serving Spoon, top of handle monogrammed "I.W." (Isaac Watkins) in script. L: 8⅞".

Die-stamped "S. T. T." (Silas T. Toncray) in rectangle (second variation). Probably Little Rock, c. 1824–30. *From the collection of the Arkansas Territorial Restoration. Gift of the descendants of the Watkins family.*

One of a set of fiddle-pattern tea, table, and serving spoons, which have descended directly in the Isaac Watkins (1777–1827) family for whom they were made.

Notice that the pointed oval bowl does not have shoulders, or fins as they are sometimes called.

Flatware, especially spoons, in a wide variety of sizes and unique shapes from the eighteenth and nineteenth centuries has survived in much larger quantities than any other form of silverware.

S–2b. View of the back (verso) of the preceding serving spoon showing the rounded imprint of the die punch with the arched mark "S. T. TONCRAY" above an eagle stamped in relief.

This, like the Toncray sugar tongs, is one of two known Toncray marks, which are found both in Arkansas and on his earlier (pre-1824) Kentucky-made silver. Both a James and a Daniel Toncray were working in Kentucky at about the same time. Daniel later moved to Memphis during the late 1820s and was followed by Silas in c. 1830 (Marquis Boultinghouse, *Silversmiths, Jewelers, Watch and Clock Makers of Kentucky, 1875–1900* [Lexington: M. Boultinghouse, 1980], 272–73, 307–08).

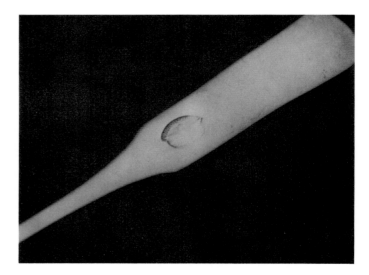

S–3a. Tablespoon, "W" monogrammed in script on front of handle. L: 7⅝".

Die-stamped. Probably Little Rock, c. 1824–30. *Private collection.*

The engraved, monogrammed initial "W" on the fiddle-pattern handle identifies the spoon as having been made for the Isaac Watkins family of Little Rock.

This is one of two matching tablespoons to have the rounded die punch or stamp mark of "S. T. TONCRAY" above an eagle. In addition, both pointed oval spoon bowls have pointed shoulders or fins. None of the identified Toncray pieces have reinforcing drops on the back of the bowls, and all are made in one piece.

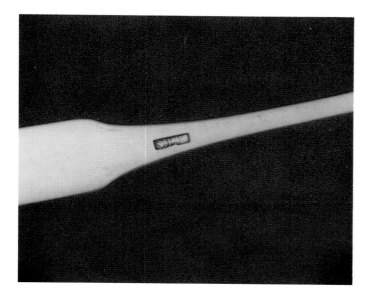

S–3b. Verso of the preceding spoon illustrating the die-stamped "S. T. T." mark in rectangle.

S–4a. Teaspoon, with the engraved monogram "MW" on the front of the spoon handle. L: 5⅜".

Stamped "S. T. T." (Silas T. Toncray) in the rectangle on the back of handle shaft. Probably Little Rock, c. 1824–30. *Private collection.*

Like this diminutive teaspoon, all of the known Isaac Watkins spoons have remained the property of direct family descendants.

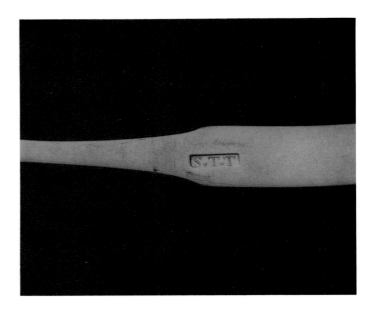

S–4b. Detail view of the previous teaspoon with the die-stamped "S. T. T." mark of Silas T. Toncray raised in rectangle.

S–5a. Teaspoon, monogrammed on handle front "J H W." L: 5 ¹³⁄₁₆".

Die-stamped on verso of handle within rectangle "D. C. FULTON." Possibly Little Rock, c. 1845–61. *From the collection of the Arkansas Territorial Restoration.*

One of a pair of spoons with fiddle-pattern, up-turned handles. The raised-tipped handle ends are a common decorative motif found on spoons in this pattern. If the bowl serves as the head of the spoon then the angularly flared projections between the bowl and the handle are referred to as the shoulders. The spoon has been formed in one piece rather than the soldering together of separate handle and bowl elements. The lack of a reinforcing drop on the back of the bowl where the handle would be joined and soldered to the bowl is often indicative of one-piece construction.

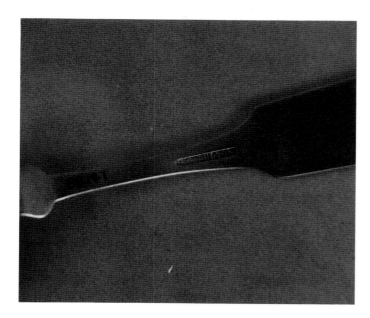

S–5b. Verso of the previous spoon showing D. C. Fulton's rectangular stamped mark.

S–6a. Butter Knife. L: 6¾".

Incuse stamped on blade "D. C. FULTON," "COIN," with pseudohallmark (griffin's head over shield). Possibly Little Rock, c. 1860. *Private collection.*

Molded fiddle-thread pattern handle, with an attenuated scimitar-shaped blade.

The standard mark "coin" is commonly found stamped on American silver from the early decades on through the third quarter of the century. It was used to signify the quality of the silver from which the object was formed. American silversmiths from the late eighteenth century until after the Civil War generally based silver quality upon the government's standards for American silver dollars. From 1792 through 1837 American silver coins were required to be $^{892}/_{1000}$ parts of silver. After 1837 the coin standard was raised to $^{900}/_{1000}$ parts of silver. In other words, a coin or a silversmith's spoon marked "coin" was to be made up of at least 90% silver, the remaining 10% was usually copper for strength. "Pure coin," "dollar," "standard," "premium," or "C" or "D" marks were used interchangeably with the "coin" mark.

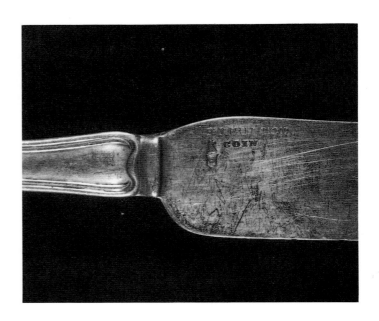

S–6b. Detail of the incuse "D. C. FULTON" mark on the preceding butter knife.

One survey of more than 1,700 silver spoons from the Winterthur museum collection indicates that the great majority of those with incuse type marks seem to date from c. 1845 through the end of the third quarter of the century (Louise Conway Belden, *Marks of American Silversmiths in the Ineson-Bissell Collection* [Charlottesville: University of Virginia Press, 1980] 467).

S—7a. Sugar Shell. L: 7".

Incuse stamped on verso of handle in block capital letters "D. C. FULTON" and "W & H" in calligraphic capitals. W & H stands for the New York City firm of Wood and Hughes, active between 1840 and 1899. Possibly Little Rock or New York City, c. 1860. *Private collection.*

To add more ornament to the surface of this double-swell, fiddle-pattern spoon would be almost impossible. Only the boldly stamped shell-pattern bowl has been spared the smith's whimsy with graver and roulette. The shaft of the spoon is decorated with a continuous figure-eight line of lozenge-shaped gouges. These concave cuts were made with a tool called a roulette. The same roulette-work frames the exuberant, if somewhat disjointed, compositions of foliate engraving surrounding a shield-like cartouche or reserve for a monogram that was never added.

The back of the downturned handle has a brief tipped midrib. At its juncture with the shaft, the incuse mark "W & H" (in engraver's Old English style) has been impressed. This is followed by the incuse stamp of "D. C. FULTON."

The presence of dual marks often denotes that one mark, such as the W & H, is for the maker while the other identifies the retailer of the piece. Fulton did import "Silver Table and Tea Spoons" from the East, as his advertisement stated, and this spoon may be an example. The double swell of the fiddle handle was not a common shape until the mid-century mark, yet it continued in popularity well into the third quarter of the century. Whimsically profuse, the use of bright-cut hand engraving and roulette work is connotative of the less extravagant ornament found on silver of the late eighteenth and early nineteenth centuries.

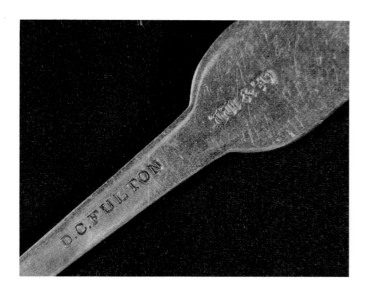

S—7b. Detail of the backmarks on the sugar shell.

S–8. Overall view of five of the seven D. C. Fulton beakers. Note that the second cup from the left has a slightly different and simpler lip and base molding.

S–9a.   Beaker or Cup (one of seven), "Ashley" monogrammed in script on side. H: 3⅞"; D (rim): 3⁵⁄₁₆"; D (base): 2⅞".

Three die-stamped incuse marks on base: "D. C. FULTON/PURE COIN" and three pseudohallmarks: eagle in rectangle, "U" within an ellipse, and a shield. *See* figures S–9b, S–9c, and S–9d for illustrations of the three variations in the marking arrangement. Probably Little Rock, c. 1842–61. *From the collection of the Arkansas Territorial Restoration, purchase of the 1988 Gala fund with the assistance of Elsie and Howard Stebbins.*

One of seven beakers made for either Arkansas's United States Senator (served 1844–48) Chester Ashley (1791–1848) or his son William E. Ashley (1823–1868), both of Little Rock, Arkansas. The cups have descended directly in the Ashley family until acquired recently by the Restoration.

This cup, like the other, has a round body which tapers slightly inward from top to bottom. The body is joined by a vertical silver-soldered seam at one side. Drawn-wire molding at the lip and base is also soldered to the hollowware body.

S—9b. Detail of the first of three variations in the marks found on the D. C. Fulton beakers.

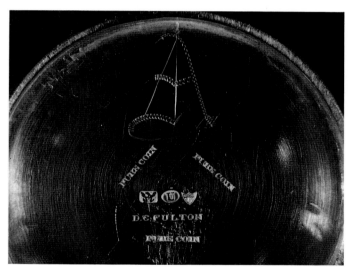

S—9c. View of the second of three variations in the marks found on the D. C. Fulton beakers, with the addition of a large, bright, roulette-cut script "A," above the stamped marks. Note that the words "PURE COIN" are used three times.

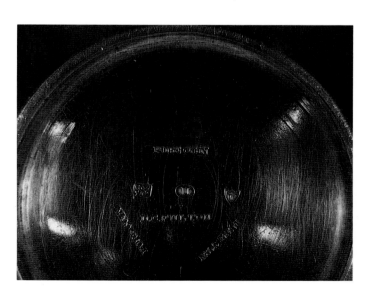

S—9d. Detail view of the third and final variation in marks on the Fulton beakers. "PURE COIN" is again stamped three times, twice on the diagonal on either side of the other marks, as is the case for the second variation.

S−10a. Ladle. L: 10⁹⁄₁₆″.

Incuse stamped on handle "D. C. FULTON," with a relief-stamped pseudohallmark griffin's head above a shield. Little Rock, c. 1860. *Private collection.*

The upturned handle of the ladle is made in the fiddle pattern and has a stamped, shell-design bowl. As in the case of the coin beakers shown in figure S−8, this ladle has descended in the family of Chester Ashley of Little Rock.

S−10b. Detail of the marks on the previous ladle.

ARKANSAS
POTTERY

Potterymaking in Arkansas

The Birds

"Manufactured by Joseph and Nathaniel Bird in the State of Arkansas, Clark County, May 22, 1843." Thus begins the documented story of potterymaking in Arkansas. These Bird brothers will allow no mistake in interpretation of a salt-glazed stoneware churn which they so carefully marked. Through it they set the earliest time-post for Arkansas potting in the European tradition, the native American tradition being beyond the scope of this study.

By 1843 gunsmiths, silversmiths, portrait artists, even daguerrean artists had plied Arkansas for up to two decades. Where were the potters? Wasn't their product an essential part of the agrarian way of life? Food had to be contained, preserved, cooked, and served. Milk needed to be processed into cream and butter, meat, vegetables, and jams stored, libations poured, faces washed. Crocks and churns, bowls and pitchers, jars and jugs had their place in the nineteenth-century household.

The absence of potters until seven years after statehood can be explained with a mixture of fact and speculation. As soon as riverboats traveled up some of Arkansas's larger rivers, no one was far from objects of trade. Imported pottery arrived with other goods from the outside world. This fact, and the need for the potter to find the right clay, acquire the land, and build the kiln, etc., could delay his commitment to the frontier. Further, there probably were potters in Arkansas earlier, but without the listing of occupation in censuses before 1850, and since many potters were loath to advertise, even on their own creations, these potters have not come to light. Pots were, it should be added, utilitarian ware. Their beauty remained secondary to their function, and many folks aspired to silver and glass, and imported ceramics. Pottery was seldom saved on its own merits.

To document the earliest presence of potters in Arkansas, and provide a comprehensive view of their trade, more research must be performed. Because of the mark potting makes on the land—the kiln and spoil piles especially—archeology will ultimately tell us the story that remains to be told. This study will rely on more conventional historical evidence for a more modest survey.

Dallas County

The Annual Report of the Geological Survey of Arkansas for 1891 emphasized Dallas County and offered a brief history of the pottery industry there. *The Annual Report* claimed that William Lafayette Bird set up his first pottery operation in 1843, contemporary to that of his brothers Joseph and Nathaniel, and that James, another brother, did the same one year later in Grant County.[1]

We do know from the 1850 Dallas County census that father William Cornelius Bird, sixty-two years of age, was a tanner, and James, twenty-two, was living in his father's household. Next door lived Joseph, twenty-eight, who was now "milling" and William Lafayette Bird, twenty-four, a potter; one household away, potter Nat Bird, twenty-six, resided.[2]

The first Bird kiln sat on a gravel bridge overlooking a tributary of the west fork of Tulip Creek. Sometime in the 1850s the Birds moved closer to the growing town of Princeton. The pottery site there had long use. In 1860 William L. Bird served a three-month term as sheriff, and John C. Welch took over the pottery. The property transaction was recorded in 1861. Welch was listed as a farmer in 1860 but had learned the pottery trade from Bird. William L. Bird went back into the business after the war. In a letter to William Paisley, Henry Butler in Tulip, Arkansas, confirmed that he had "seen Mr. Bird in regard to the ware. . . . He will burn a kiln this week and I think I can send it over (together with the Bedsteads) next week."[3]

The Welch era lasted long enough to produce both pottery and statistics. Such statistics in pottery are given in gallons, the total capacity of the wares in question. In 1870 the kiln operated for seven months and produced six thousand gallons.[4] In 1891, though fallen into disuse, the kiln had a capacity of fifteen hundred gallons. The factory had two wheels and could produce ten thousand to fifteen thousand gallons a year.[5]

Nathaniel J. Culberson (Culverson), who came to Arkansas by way of Georgia, was a farmer who learned the potting trade in his adoptive Dallas County home, only to backtrack to Tennessee, apparently, in his later years and produce pottery in McNairy County.[6]

A brief but noteworthy Dallas County pottery venture involved Lafayette Glass. Glass, originally from Tennessee, had moved on to Texas before the Civil War to farm. He apparently learned the pottery business from slave Oliver C. Harris (Hanson) who had learned the trade in servitude. After the war, Glass and Harris supposedly fired some kilns in Dallas and Pike counties before setting out for Saline County where, by 1870, they established the industry. Another site, the "Oliver C. Hanson" pottery between Hope and Spring Hill in Hempstead County, was taken over by the Foley family in 1879.[7]

Add to this list of potters a "foreigner named Etl," and Dallas County demonstrated a very active pottery industry, the earliest documented in Arkansas.[8]

Other Potters

Dallas County attracted a plurality of Arkansas's potters, but potters' clay could be found in other areas, and so could potters. A young potter, while visiting relatives in Washington County, found clay very similar to the pipe clay he and his father worked in White County, Tennessee. The Crawley family, spelled Crowley in Tennessee, were potters in a part of White County that became Putnam County in 1854. James C. of the 1840 census is likely James T. of 1850, from the similarity in census data and is probably the father of William S. It was William S. Crawley, who, when just a teenager, started manufacturing crockery in Washington County in 1846. Crawley worked until 1875, distributing his wares all around northwest Arkansas. He had twenty-one children by two wives and participated in the Civil War. While well known as a potter, he was recorded in the census as a farmer.[9]

Although he didn't stay nearly as long, Robert A. Caldwell plied the same trade in Washington County. The son of a farmer-potter, Caldwell was listed as a farmer in the Missouri census of 1850 and as a potter there in 1860. Apparently, in the next year he and his family moved to the Cane Hill area of Washington County where they stayed for several years, moving permanently to Sebastian County around 1870 where he made pottery at Greenwood.

At least one of the next generation of Caldwells kept clay in the family. Henry T. learned the trade from his father, and, according to *Goodspeed*, had charge of the state pottery factory in Louisiana at the close of the Civil War. He returned to work with his father in Sebastian County before setting out on his own in Saline County. He manufactured pottery in Benton before going retail and becoming one of the leading merchants of the county.[10]

J. D. Wilbur, also of Washington County, was born into a large family of potters in Muskingum County, Ohio. J. D. is probably James (son of Thomas) who was sixteen in 1850.[11] He appears in the 1870 census for Cane Hill township as a potter. Wilbur was one of the few in Arkansas to mark his pieces, with a star and "Boonsboro, Ark" under his name. He must have been in partnership with a Mr. Roark at one time, because pottery survives marked "Roark and Wilbur Boonsboro, Ark."

A. E. Wilbur, who was somehow related to J. D., worked in Saline County potteries in the years after 1870, and the Wilbur family continued such work in Arkansas and Texas well into this century. Eighty-three-year-old A. E. Wilbur (probably Jr.) of Dallas, Texas, remembered in 1972 that his uncles Art and Charles ended their careers at the Dickey Sewer Pipe Company in San Antonio. An Art and a Charles can be found listed as babies in the 1850 Ohio census in the same household as Ichabod Wilbur, potter, and Ezra Wilbur, ventriloquist.[12] They were likely issue of the ventriloquist.

Three more potters who worked for a time in Arkansas also made it to Texas: Missourians George W. Cranston and J. W. and W. H. Donaldson who stopped off in Franklin County for a while before heading to the Lone Star State.[13]

As one might guess, Tennessee made its impact on pottery in Arkansas. Alexander Sehone, L. M. Simmons and J. R. H. P. Craven were born in Tennessee, and John M. Craven and John Pearson worked there before setting out to the west. The Craven clan was well known for their pottery work in North Carolina where Peter, especially, worked in Randolph County. His grandson Thomas brought the trade to Henderson County, Tennessee. Thomas's son, John M. Craven, a thirty-two-year-old potter in the 1850 Henderson County census was found in Independence County, Arkansas, in 1860.[14] J. R. H. P. Craven, probably John's nephew, joined him in Arkansas. John W. Pearson, born in Kentucky, was enumerated as a potter in Polk County, Tennessee, in 1850.[15] Ten years later he was a potter in Van Buren County, Arkansas.

The possibility of a connection exists between Arkansas and Alabama potters. The Cribbs family actively pursued the trade there in the middle of the last century. A Joseph Cribbs was reported to be in Hempstead County in the 1840s; and Major Cribbs, a slave potter before the Civil War, apparently set out for Arkansas after he gained his freedom.[16] The Cribbs connection awaits more research.

Production

The 1870 Industrial Census listed all the materials J. D. Wilbur used in his enterprise: wood, clay, and salt, basic, simple materials. But they belie a complex process. The transformation of earth to ware requires the right raw material, properly prepared and appropriately shaped. A set temperature level must be reached for the drying out and hardening of the clay, and a glaze is usually applied to coat the surface of the pot, in many instances salt.

A good clay is free of soluble impurities—lime, excess sand, and other mineral fragments—and contains little organic material. Any of these become an inherent vice in the clay, waiting to cause problems during potterymaking or excessive brittleness after the pot is fired. The clay must exhibit a certain plasticity and must maintain its shape when put into its final form. The clay should allow a certain firing range without warping or cracking and should not shrink excessively.

The Annual Report of the Geological Survey in 1891 provided a detailed analysis of a variety of clays in Dallas County, an analysis which would be important for major commercial operations. An example is the Welch clay:

		PERCENT
Silica (SiO_2)		71.27
Alumina (Al_2O_3)		16.86
Ferrous oxide (FeO)		2.14
Titanic oxide (TiO_2)		1.75
Lime (CaO)		.73
Magnesia (MgO)		.77
Soda (Na_2O)		.46
Potash (K_2O)		.44
Loss on ignition		6.54
Total		100.96
Hygroscopic moisture at 115 C		1.78
Sand in air-dried clay		30.50
Refractoriness by Bischof's revised formula		.31[17]

The experienced potter needed no such analysis—the test was in the look, the feel, the firing, and even the taste.

The clays emphasized in *The Annual Report* were potters' clays, clays which slowly melt together without losing their shape when fired at a temperature between twelve hundred degrees and thirteen hundred degrees c. The ware produced is dense and hard, thus the name stoneware. Earthenware, a product more brittle, more porous, and of broader world-wide use, is fired at a lower temperature, somewhere between one thousand and twelve hundred degrees c. Earthenware's permeability makes it less desirable for many kinds of food storage and other uses requiring clean smooth surfaces, but earthenware retained some related uses in nineteenth-century Arkansas and remained better adapted to cooking than stoneware, because of the expansion and contraction that can occur in its more porous structure. Both stoneware and earthenware were produced in Arkansas. William S. Crawley is said to have used common earthenware clay, while most of the other potters at least aspired to stoneware, though archeology will be the ultimate judge of who made what.

Once a clay was chosen, it required cleaning and manipulation into an appropriate, even texture, free of air pockets. One of William Crawley's sons described the process used at Crawley's operation: "We would go to the clay bank for clay in the early spring, but if there happened to be late freeze it would all have to be dumped and a new supply brought in. No pottery could be made from frozen clay. We would put the clay in the pen, dry it out with a big wheel roller, grind it to a dust then sieve it, put it through a dirt mill, then place it in a box."[18] Not all cleaning and preparation dried out the clay. Sometimes water was added to create a creamy solution or "slip" to be screened before being mixed for throwing. In the case of Crawley's clay, water would be added when the potter was ready to prepare the clay for throwing. Throwing a pot required, and still requires, a developed skill and a great sensitivity to the clay. The clay was manipulated on the wheel as it turned, with a consistency of structure as the goal.

No certain documentation exists regarding the kinds of kilns used in mid–nineteenth-century Arkansas, but the "ground hog" kiln was probably most common.[19] The most modest looking of kiln structures, the low, elongated ground hog was generally built into, and insulated by, the side of a hill. "Green" pottery sat on a platform within the kiln, and the heat from the fire, built in the firebox at the open loading end was pulled past the pottery by a crossdraft and out the chimney at the other end. The cramped chamber had portholes to aid combustion, and, in a sense, the kiln was one long flue.

The beehive kiln was also used in Tennessee, and probably in Arkansas, during the period of this study. The beehive was an updraft kiln, as heat from the firebox(es) rose through the chamber and the stacked pottery, and out the roof. In the later downdraft kiln, the heat from fireboxes on the perimeter of the kiln rose to the roof, to be drawn down to floor level and the opening of the flue into the chimney. The chimney could be in the kiln itself or outside the kiln, connected by a flue in the form of a tunnel.

A certain art was required even in the stacking of the raw pottery before firing. Heat, evenly distributed, needed to reach an appropriate level at the right time, and the vast spoil piles at several known sites speak eloquently of the challenge of firing the kiln.

Stoneware, by vitrifying or melting on the surface, theoretically didn't need glazing to satisfy many of the functions that the ware served. But potters commonly glazed their work. Common table salt, entering the kiln through the ports and fire box during the firing, vaporized and glazed onto whatever surfaces were approaching vitrification: kiln bricks, kiln furniture, and the pottery itself. The resulting combination of sodium and silica from the clay produced sodium silicate. Practically all of the Dallas County pottery—and most Arkansas pottery—was salt glazed, though the glazing often did not reach into the hollow of the pieces. The potter had the option of leaving the interior unglazed or applying a slip glaze before firing. The slip glaze, a creamy solution, relied on the different melting temperature of clays. The trick was to find a clay which would melt to form a glaze at the same temperature that the clay of the pot began to vitrify. Albany slip became the most popular of the slip glazes of the nineteenth century. Shiny brown is the most common color for these glazes.

A third glaze, and, for its use in the United States, a uniquely Southern phenomenon, is the ash, or alkaline, glaze. Appearing first in the Edgefield District of South Carolina, the use of ash glazes spread across the South. The beauty of the glaze was in the simplicity of the materials required: wood ash, sand, and clay. The only drawback was the extra trouble required in preparation. Ash, like slip glaze, was applied to greenware before firing. Nathaniel J. Culverson may have used ash glaze at his site in Dallas County. Some ash-glazed shards have also been found at his later home in McNairy County, Tennessee.[20]

Perhaps the most tempting place to look for ash glazes in Arkansas would be in Union County. The Leopard family hailed from the Edgefield area in South Carolina.[21] Did H. H. Leopard bring the technique with him?

Modern Technology and Rural Tradition

No trade failed to be touched by mass production in the nineteenth century. The change in potterymaking was less dramatic than in some fields where major technological breakthroughs revolutionized the product or production. The decline of locally made pottery came as a result of incre-

mental challenges to the market. It certainly is true that mass production and mass distribution took a major toll over the years as ceramics manufacturers emerged at such places as Bennington, Vermont, East Liverpool, Ohio, and Trenton, New Jersey. Tinware took certain household functions, such as that of the pottery milk pan. The cost of glass fell significantly in the last century, and glass pitchers, flasks, and jars stole a bit more of the potters' market. Advances in lighting, food processing, and storage—the list could continue—left the potter with a smaller variety of saleable items.

Nevertheless, the Southern pottery tradition continued. In 1891, C. E. Siebenthal commented that the "future of the pottery industry in Dallas County depends therefore upon the facility of transportation of the product to markets."[22] The quality of the clay or of the product was not in question. Market competition was the major factor in his mind. Several potters held out well into this century, never able to compete as Siebenthal hoped, but at least able to make a living at their trade.

The Product

Pottery had to function, and the Birds and Welch produced churns, jugs, flower pots, crocks, jars, and pitchers. Evidence at the Culverson site suggests that plates and pipes might have been made there.[23] According to the *Annual Report* in 1891, Mr. Etl made ordinary crockery and flower pots with vines and flowers in relief on the sides.[24] Washington County potters produced much of the same utilitarian ware, to which can be added grease lamps, by William S. Crawley, and "Quaint and artistic vases, milk pitchers and lamps" by J. D. Wilbur.[25]

An irony of potterymaking in the rural state of Arkansas is that its best-known product is not a traditional form, but rather an art pottery made in this century: Niloak pottery from Saline County. The pottery industry in the Benton area, which blossomed after 1870, is not in the scope of this study, but the Caldwell, Glass, Hanson, and Wilbur names come together there.

Pottery's Future

The future of pottery manufacturing in Arkansas, exclusive of the recent arts and crafts revival, rests in discovering more of its past. For example, potters shared a "groundedness" with farmers, and many alternated those occupations as the season or the market suggested. This dual economy bears more investigation.

A strong kinship pattern is evident also, with only the cursory research that has been completed. Families were tied to potterymaking, and the pottery traditions flowed across the South and across Arkansas. It was a craft late to become established on the frontier and late to disappear as a few families held on to their trade when so many others fell to national and international competition based upon higher technology and mass production.

Potters, Locations in Arkansas

County	Date Founded	Number of Makers
Arkansas	1813	
Ashley	1848	
Benton	1836	
Boone	1869	
Bradley	1840	
Calhoun	1850	
Carroll	1833	1
Chicot	1823	
Clark	1818	
Columbia	1852	
Conway	1825	1
Craighead	1859	
Crawford	1820	
Crittenden	1825	
Cross	1862	
Dallas	1845	9
Desha	1838	
Drew	1846	
Franklin	1837	3
Fulton	1842	
Grant	1869	

County	Date Founded	Number of Makers
Greene	1833	
Hempstead	1818	1
Hot Spring	1829	
Independence	1820	2
Izard	1825	
Jackson	1829	
Jefferson	1829	
Johnson	1833	
Lafayette	1827	
Lawrence	1815	
Little River	1867	
Madison	1836	
Marion	1836	
Miller	1820	
Mississippi	1844	
Monroe	1829	
Montgomery	1842	
Newton	1842	
Ouachita	1842	
Perry	1840	
Phillips	1820	
Pike	1833	2
Poinsett	1838	
Polk	1844	
Pope	1829	
Prairie	1846	
Pulaski	1818	3
Randolph	1835	
Saline	1835	4
Scott	1833	2
Searcy	1835	
Sebastian	1851	2
Sevier	1828	
Sharp	1868	
St. Francis	1827	
Union	1829	1
Van Buren	1833	1
Washington	1828	3
White	1835	1
Woodruff	1862	
Yell	1840	

Total number of locations listed: 36
Total number of listings in biographical appendix: 29

The final story of pottery will not be told until more research can seek out the original ownership of pottery sites and evaluate the shards in waste piles hidden by brambles and measure and study kilns in various stages of disintegration. Also, homes in Union, Washington, Dallas, and Hempstead counties will yield more pieces of our heritage, preserved where the makers originally sold their wares.

Several of these potters moved around, as the text discusses, and each location is listed here to show the extent that potterymaking touched the state. In the period after 1870, Saline County actually dominated pottery production in the state, just as Dallas County did earlier.

Count of Arkansas Potters by Place of Birth

UNITED STATES BORN

Arkansas	1
Georgia	2
Indiana	1
Kentucky	2
Missouri	4
North Carolina	6
Ohio	1
South Carolina	1
Tennessee	5
Virginia	1

FOREIGN BORN

Belgium	2
Prussia	1

Total number of birth places documented: 27

Most of this information came from census data. For example, two potters enumerated in 1870 hailed from Belgium, with names quite similar, but with ages just different enough to be included. The information in one of the census citations might only be a landlord's best guess. Possibly because of their necessary commitment to the land in the form of property, kiln, etc., we know more about a higher percentage of potters than any other artisan class.

NOTES

1. C. E. Siebenthal, "The Geology of Dallas County," John C. Banner, ed., *Annual Report of the Geological Survey of Arkansas for 1891*, Vol. II (Little Rock: Brown Printing Company, 1894) 317–18.
2. Manuscript Census, Smith Township, Dallas County, 1850. *See also* Biographical Appendix.
3. Dallas County Deed Records, Book E, p. 125 (12 March 1861); Siebenthal, 317; Dallas County Court Records, Book B, pp. 22, 26, 27; Manuscript Census, Smith Township, Dallas County, 1860; Beverly Watkins, "The Bird and Welch Potteries: Small Industry in Nineteenth Century Arkansas," presented at the Society for Historical Archeology's annual meeting, January, 1980; Albuquerque, New Mexico, 2; Elizabeth Paisley Huckaby and Ethel C. Simpson, eds., *Tulip Evermore* (Fayetteville: The University of Arkansas Press, 1985) 87.
4. Watkins, 3, citing 1870 Industrial Census.
5. Siebenthal, 317–18.
6. Samuel D. Smith and Stephen T. Rogers, *A Survey of Historic Pottery Making in Tennessee* (Nashville: Division of Archeology, 1979) 117. *See also* Biographical Appendix
7. *Arkansas Democrat*, 7 April 1940; Hardy L. Winburn, Jr., *Seven Years of Saline County Pottery* (Benton: Niloak Pottery Company, 1938) 6–7.
8. Siebenthal, 318.
9. *Arkansas Gazette*, 16 January 1938; Smith and Rogers, 74, 128.
10. Jeffery A. Blakely, "The 19th Century Pottery Industry in Sebastian County, Arkansas," prepared for presentation at the Arkansas Historical Association's annual meeting in 1989, Hope, Arkansas, 7–9. *See also* Biographical Appendix
11. Manuscript Census: Muskingum County, Ohio, Putnam-Springfield Township, 1850.
12. Ibid.; Georgeanna H. Greer, letter of February 17, 1972, to Patrick E. Martin, Fayetteville, Arkansas.
13. Georgeanna H. Greer, letter to Jeffery Blakely dated November 16, 1988, quoted in Blakely, 20.
14. Smith and Rogers, 110–11, 128. *See also* Biographical Appendix
15. Smith and Rogers, 52, 132.
16. E. Henry Willett and Joey Brackner, *The Traditional Pottery of Alabama* (Montgomery: Montgomery Museum of Fine Arts, 1983) 38. *See also* Biographical Appendix
17. Siebenthal, 296.
18. *Arkansas Gazette*, 16 January 1938.
19. Winburn 9; Nancy Sweezy, *Raised in Clay: The Southern Pottery Tradition* (Washington D. C.: Smithsonian Institution Press, 1984) 60–76.
20. Watkins, 7–8; Smith and Rogers, 117.
21. Willett and Brackner, 31.
22. Siebenthal, 292.
23. Watkins, 8.
24. Siebenthal, 318.
25. *Arkansas Gazette*, 16 January 1938.

Biographical Appendix of Arkansas Potters

Barthel, Mathew

Potter, A.27, B.Prussia: MCR 1870 Pulaski Co., Roll 62, AHC. Barthel & Derx, potters, Pulaski Co., *Products of Industry* 1870, Roll 18, AHC.

Bird, James

"In 1844 James Bird . . . erected a pottery just over the line in Grant County. . . . He had burned but a few kilns when he sold out, and the business was discontinued. He used clay from a bed close by the shop." John C. Branner, *Annual Report of the Geological Survey of Arkansas for 1891,* Volume II (Little Rock: Brown Printing Company, 1894), 317.

Bird, Joseph

[Potter] Listed in Dallas Co. tax records 1845–48, 1850–51, and 1853, Roll 45, AHC. "The first pottery plant to be set up in Dallas County was operated by Joseph and Nathaniel Bird in 1843 in the northern part of the county. . . . William Bird, another member of the same family, established a pottery in 1843 about 15 miles north of Princeton. . . . In 1861 he sold his plant to John Welch. . . ." *FWN* 3–10–1938–1–6.

Bird, Nathaniel

Potter, A.26, B.NC: MCR 1850 Dallas Co., Roll 26, AHC. Listed in Dallas Co. tax records 1845–46, 1848, 1850–51, 1853, and 1857–58, Roll 45, AHC. *See* Joseph Bird

Bird, William Lafayette

Potter, A.24, B.NC: MCR 1850 Dallas Co., Roll 26, AHC. Listed in Dallas Co. tax records 1845, 1847–48, 1850–51, 1853, 1857–58, 1861–62, and 1867, Roll 45, 1865, Roll 46, and 1870, Roll 47, AHC. Potter, A.54, B.NC: MCR 1880 Dallas Co., Roll 42, AHC. *See* Joseph Bird

Caldwell, Henry T.

Secondary Source: After the War (Civil) he carried on the pottery business in Sebastian County, Ark., until 1870, when he moved to Benton, Saline County, Ark., there continuing the same business until 1872. *Goodspeed Central Arkansas,* 249.

Caldwell, Robert A.

Potter, A.56, B.KY: MCR 1870 Sebastian Co., Roll 64, AHC. Listed in SCTR 1875, 1888, and 1890, Roll 23, AHC. Secondary Sources: "Caldwell Pottery. A small deposit of bluish-white sandy clay . . . was at one time clay to supply a pottery at Greenwood owned by Mr. Caldwell, but clay from this place has not been used for a number of years." John C. Branner, *The Clays of Arkansas* (Washington Government Printing Office, 1908), 218. Major Robert A. and Mary R. Caldwell (wife) came to Washington Co., Arkansas, in 1861, and in 1869 they moved to Sebastian Co., where Caldwell died in 1888. *Goodspeed Central Arkansas,* 249.

Cranston, George Washington

Potter, A.22. B.MO: MCR 1860 Franklin Co., Roll 41, AHC.

Craven, J. R. H. P.

Potter, A.24, B.TN: MCR 1860 Independence Co., Roll 43, AHC.

Craven (Cravin), John M.

Potter, A.42, B.NC: MCR 1860 Independence Co., Roll 43, AHC. Also listed in ICTR 1857–60, Roll 61, and 1861–66, Roll 62, AHC.

Crawley (Crowley), William S.

[Potter] Farmer, A.32, B.TN: MCR 1860 Washington Co., Roll 52, AHC. Farmer, A.41, B.TN: MCR 1870 Washington Co., Roll 66, AHC. Also listed in WCTR 1852–55, Roll 62, and 1856 and 1859–60, Roll 63, AHC. "Old Pottery Makers of Hills Recalled. . . . In 1845 William S. Crawley came on horseback to Washington County. There he found a clay deposit on the Virgil Guthrie farm similar to the pipe clay he and his father had used for making pottery in Tennessee. He soon was making pottery, jars, jugs, crocks, churns and clay pipes. . . . The clay Mr. Crawley used was called common earthenware. It was free from grit and had enough plasticity to being turned by the potter. The clay turned a red or cream color, and took a good glaze.

Mr. Crawley built his large kiln in the back of his log cabin. The kiln was 10 ft. across with outside walls over 4 ft. with a high round beehive shaped dome with air vents. The furnace was under the floor. For 26 years he made an average of 750 pieces of pottery annually. . . ." *AG* 1–16–1938.

Culverson (Culberson), Nathaniel J.

Manufacturer of Crockery, A.36, B.NC: MCR 1860 Dallas Co., Roll 40, AHC. Also listed in DCTR 1859 and 1861, Roll 45, and 1870, Roll 47, AHC. ". . . Culverson worked a while with Welch, and then entered the business for himself, operating a pottery three miles northeast of Princeton from 1858 until 1865. His ware was thick and porus. . . ." *FWN* 3–10–1938–1–6.

Cribbs, Joseph

Secondary Source: "Joseph Cribbs or 'Cribbs the potter' as he was known came to Hempstead County at an early day. He lived in the region of Spring Hill, where he built a pottery, and manufactured and sold jugs and other kinds of stoneware. He went to California in 1849." Mary Medearis, ed., *Sam Williams: Printer's Devil* (Hope, Arkansas: Etter Printing Company, 1979), 266.

Davis, E. L.

Potter, A.45, B.VA: MCR 1850 Scott Co., Roll 30, AHC.

Derricks, Leonard

Potter, A.33, B.Belgium: MCR 1870 Pulaski Co., Roll 62, AHC. *See* Derx

Derx, Leonard

Potter, A.42, B.Belgium: MCR 1870 Pulaski Co., Roll 62, AHC. *See* M. Barthel

Donaldson, J. W.

Potter, A.30, B.MO: MCR 1860 Franklin Co., Roll 41, AHC. Also listed in FCTR 1861, Roll 14, AHC.

Donaldson, W. H.

Potter, A.25, B.MO: MCR 1860 Franklin Co., Roll 41, AHC.

Etl, ?

"In 1859 or 1860 a foreigner named Etl, established a pottery . . . and operated it for about three years. Besides ordinary crockery he made flower pots with vines and flowers in relief on the sides." Branner, 318.

Garrison, James

[Potter] Farmer, A.35, B.GA: MCR 1860 Conway Co., Roll 39, AHC. Also listed CCTR 1857, Roll 44, 1858, 1860–62, and 1865–67, Roll 45, AHC. Secondary Source: Garrison lived in Georgia and Alabama until 1856 when he came to Conway County, Arkansas, where he manufactured pottery, which was perhaps the first enterprise of that kind in the county. He died in Conway Co. in 1862. *Goodspeed Western Arkansas*, 68.

Glass, Lafayette

Manufacturer Stoneware, Saline Co., *Products of Industry* 1870, Roll 18, AHC. Merchant-Ret.(Retail?), A.39, B.TN: MCR 1870 Saline Co. (Benton), Roll 63, AHC. Also listed in SCTR 1869–72, Roll 33 and 1873–74 and 1876, Roll 34, AHC. Secondary Source: "Lafayette Glass was a farmer near Mansfield, Arkansas. On his return from the war, he found nothing of his former possessions but his land. He had owned a slave [Oliver Harris] which he had purchased at New Orleans, Louisiana. The slave had worked in a pottery shop . . . he taught Glass how to make pottery. When he returned from the war he invested in a small pottery shop. The slave returned to him and went with him to obtain employment in pottery at Princeton . . . in 1868 they went to Benton, Arkansas and invested in pottery plants there. The Niloak Company at Benton was the result of clay technology which began with Oliver Harris and Lafayette Glass." Norman Goodner, *A Scott County Scrapbook* (Mansfield, Arkansas: Frank Boyd, 1982), 55.

Harris (Hanson), Oliver C.

Potter, A.31, B.AR: MCR 1870 Saline Co., Roll 63, AHC. *See* Lafayette Glass

Leopard, H. H.

Potter, A.50, B.SC: MCR 1860 Union Co., Roll 51, AHC. Farmer, A.61, B.SC: MCR 1870 Union Co., Roll 65, AHC. Listed in UCTR 1859, Roll 62, AHC. Also listed in Union Co. Deed Records, Books "M–N," 1869–71, Roll 40, and Books "Q–R," 1873–74, Roll 42, AHC.

Pearson, John

Potter, A.46, B.KY: MCR 1860 Van Buren Co., Roll 51, AHC. Also listed in VBCTR 1866, Roll 17, AHC.

Sehone, Alexander

Potter, A.55, B.TN: MCR 1850 Scott Co., Roll 30, AHC.

Simmons, L. M.

Potter, A.27, B.TN: MCR 1870 White Co., Roll 67, AHC. Also listed in WCTR 1870–76, Roll 58, AHC.

Todd, Abbott L.

Potter, A.29, B.IN: MCR 1850 Carroll Co., Roll 25, AHC. Also listed in CCTR 1851, Roll 25, AHC.

Welch, John C.

[Potter] A.19, B.GA: MCR 1850 Dallas Co., Roll 26, AHC. Also listed in DCTR 1857–61, Roll 45, 1865, Roll 46, 1867 and 1870, Roll 47, and 1883, Roll 48, AHC. Secondary Sources: "John C. Welch . . . learned the trade under William Bird, and in 1861 bought him out and continued the business . . . The kiln had a capacity of 1,500 gallons. Two wheels were run and the average annual output was 10,000 or 15,000 gallons. The product was in the form of jugs, jars, churns, and crocks, which found a market in neighboring towns. . . . Mr. Welch at first used clay from the Cheatham beds, but later found and worked the Welch bed. His ware was hard, close-bodied, and thin." Branner, 88.

In 1855 Welch started in the pottery business. He had a variety of vessels made from clay—churns, crocks, jugs, flower-pots, etc. This was the only pottery in the county. Welch also owned fifteen hundred acres of land and kept most of his acreage under cultivation. During the Civil War he was on detached duty at the pottery. *Goodspeed Southern Arkansas* 1890, 737.

Wilbur, J. D.

Potter, A.36, B.OH: MCR 1870 Washington Co., Roll 66, AHC. Also listed in WCTR 1878–79, Roll 65, AHC. Potter, A.46, B.OH: MCR 1880 Washington Co., Roll 58, AHC. "Old Pottery Makers of Hills Recalled. . . . Older citizens at Cane Hill recall the 'little old man' Wilbur, who would sit at his wheel at Wilbur Falls on the bank of the creek, watching with intent childish interest the potter 'with pin-point ease,' sitting there with one foot on the pedal and a small paddle in his hand moulding his pieces while the water trickled down over the jar, jug, or pitcher being shaped. Mr. Wilbur marked all of his pottery not only with the 'Wilbur,' but also a star and the name 'Boonsboro.' . . . Most of the Wilbur pieces are dark, dull brown. He made not only crocks, jugs, jars, and churns, but also quaint and artistic vases, milk pitchers and lamps. . . ." *AG* 1–16–1938.

J. D. Wilbur of Washington County was the only Arkansas potter to be enumerated in the 1870 *United States Census for the Products of Industry for Arkansas.* (1870, United States Census, Schedule for the Products of Industry, Washington County. AHC Roll 18). The enumerator reported that Wilbur worked alone, at a yearly wage of two hundred and fifty dollars, and with an investment of five hundred dollars he produced wares valued at one thousand dollars. That Wilbur was strictly a salt-glaze potter at the time seems apparent, for the materials he used to produce his wares were listed as being "wood, clay and salt."

An Illustrated Catalog of Arkansas Pottery

The Potter, a woodblock engraving from Edward
Hazen, *The Panorama or Professions and Trades*
(Philadelphia: Uriah Hunt, 1837) 234.

P–1a.   Pitcher. Incuse stamp on the shoulder and beneath the spout: "J. D. WILBUR/Boonsboro, Ark." Wheel-turned, gray-green, salt-glazed stoneware body. H: 8⅛", D (rim): 6", D (base): 4¹³⁄₁₆". C. 1870–89. *Courtesy of Charles W. McNair.*

Several unmarked pitchers similar to this one and with dark Albany-like slip have remained in private collections (*see* figure P–8) in the Cane Hill/Boonsboro vicinity. All of these baluster-shaped, "pinch-necked" pitchers are attributed to the pottery wheel of J. D. Wilbur.

P–1b.   Detail of mark.

P–2a.   Jar. Stamped on shoulder in incuse fashion: "J. D. WILBUR/Boonsboro, Ark." Wheel-turned, gray-green, salt-glazed body. H: 9⅜", D (rim): 7⅛", D (base): 6½". C. 1870–89. *Courtesy of Charles W. McNair.*

Wilbur's rectangular incuse mark is the second of two known variations, the other being his more commonly arched J. D.WILBUR over BOONSBORO, ARK. (in capitals). In addition, he would occasionally include a five-pointed star or the numbers "2" or "3" to indicate capacity of a piece in gallons.

P–2b.   Detail of mark.

P–3a.   Jar. Stamp on shoulder of J. D. WILBUR over BOONSBORO (centered above) ARK. Notice that Wilbur has over-struck his recurring five-pointed star (centered between the lettering) and BOONSBORO with a "2" gallon capacity stamp.

Wheel-turned, salt-glazed stoneware body. H: 11¼", D (rim): 7⁵⁄₁₆", D (base): 7⅛". C. 1870–89. *Courtesy of Charles W. McNair.*

P–3b.   Detail of mark.

P–4.   Jar. Incuse stamp on shoulder: "J. D. WILBUR/ 2/Boonsboro, Ark." Wheel-turned, reddish stoneware body, partially salt-glazed and bisque exterior surface, interior unglazed. H: 9⅛", D (rim): 6¼", D (base): 6⅜". C. 1870–89. *Courtesy of the Arkansas Territorial Restoration.*

Few all bisque (unglazed) forms by Wilbur have surfaced. In the main, his pieces are always salt glazed. This standard form of Wilbur jar is darkened and lightly (possibly salt) glazed on its left side from the shoulder to the base. Several problems in firing, such as an uneven application of glazing salt or a too low reducing fire within the kiln may have resulted in the bisque state of this food storage jar. In addition, if the clay body of the jar contained too little silica for the formation of a glaze in combination with the salt vapors, no visible glossy glaze area will be apparent. However, the absence of glaze on slip-glazed pieces is to be expected, for they were wiped clean before firing since any glaze contact between pieces during firing may cause them to fuse together. Georgeanna H. Greer, *American Stonewares, The Art and Craft of Utilitarian Potters* (Exton, Penn.: Schiffer Publishing, 1981), 232–35.

P–5. Jar. Stamped with an incuse die on the shoulder: "J. D.WILBUR/Boonsboro, Ark." Wheel-turned, gray-green, salt-glazed exterior body, interior unglazed. H: 7⅞", D (rim): 2⅝", D (base): 5⅜". C. 1870–89. *Courtesy of the Arkansas Territorial Restoration.*

The cracks or "dunts" near the base of the cylindrical body of the jar may very well be due to too rapid cooling of the kiln after it was fired or to steam expansion during the firing process.

The projecting flange-like molding of the base is seen on numerous Wilbur small-hollowware forms of jars.

The mark of "ROARK & WILBUR" (*see* figure P–10) has been found on a similar jar from the Cane Hill/Boonsboro area.

P–6. Jar. Incuse stamp on shoulder: "J. D. WILBUR/BOONSBORO, ARK./3." Wheel-turned, brown, salt-glazed stoneware body, interior unglazed. H: 14", D (rim): 7½", D (base): 7¾". C. 1870–89. *Private collection.*

Large capacity jars such as this could be used as small churns, in addition to their routine relegation as food storage ware. The flared rim has a dropped ledge (galleried rim) for a now missing lid. The "lug" style applied handles are common accoutrements for carrying such large containers.

The stamped "3" again denotes gallon capacity. Many of these die-stamps used to impress the makers name, locale, and gallon size were themselves made of ceramic by the potter.

P–7. Jar. Incuse arched stamp on shoulder: "J. D. WILBUR/BOONSBORO, Ark./2." Brown stoneware body, wheel-turned, salt-glazed exterior, interior unglazed. H: 11¾", D (rim): 7½", D (base): 7¼". C. 1870–89. *Private collection.*

Much of this pottery with Wilbur's mark and its particular brownish salt-glazed exterior finish has survived in private collections throughout Washington County and the Cane Hill/Boonsboro Community.

This particular jar has a flared molded galleried rim. The galleried rim refers to the interior recessed ledge, situated at the base of the flared rim, which supported a fitted ceramic lid, now missing.

The large die-stamped "2" on the shoulder of the jar denotes the number of gallons the container will hold.

P–8. Pitcher. Stoneware body, wheel-turned, with reddish-brown Albany exterior slip glaze (possibly with a salt overglaze). Interior unglazed. H: 8½", D (rim): 5¼", D (base): 5½". C. 1870–1900. Attributed to the pottery of J. D. Wilbur, Boonsboro, Washington County. *Private collection.*

It is difficult, if not impossible, to date this slightly squat, baluster-shaped pitcher form or say that it is unique to Arkansas or the South. In fact, such pitchers, with their applied-strap handles and pinched-neck pouring spouts, were a ubiquitous, utilitarian form of holloware produced by potters throughout the land during the last half of the century. It reflects the American need for functional wares, with their typical thick form of construction.

Numerous other pitchers of an identical form having either this reddish slip glaze or a salt glaze over a gray-green body have been located in close proximity to Wilbur's pottery near the western Washington County community of Cane Hill.

P–9.   Jar. Incuse arched stamp on shoulder: "J. D. WILBUR/BOONSBORO, Ark." Wheel-turned, brown, salt-glazed stoneware body, interior unglazed. H: 11¼", D (rim): 7½", D (base): 7¾". C. 1870–89. *Courtesy of the Arkansas Territorial Restoration.*

P–10.   Jar. Detailed view of the incuse-stamped shoulder mark of "ROARK & WILBUR/Boonsboro, Ark." Wheel-turned, brown, salt-glazed stoneware body. H: 6¼", D (rim): 2¾", D (base): 4". C. 1870–89. *Courtesy of Charles W. McNair.*

This small-mouth food container has been wired for use as a lamp. The cylindrical body is rounded at the shoulders, below which the vessel tapers slightly inward to a projecting ⅜" wide base molding.

Only this one marked jar and a single deed reference have surfaced to connect Wilbur and Roark in what may have been a short-lived partnership. In January, 1871, a J. M. Roark sold J. D. Wilbur a parcel of one hundred and twenty acres of land northwest of the town of Cane Hill in Washington County and contiguous to the small community of Boonsboro. The illusive J. M. Roark does not appear on Washington County tax rolls, nor in any of the census schedules for population through 1880.

P—11b.   Detail of the churn base and its inscription, "Joseph & Nathaniel Bird, 1843."

P—11a.   Churn. Stamped on rim "8" within a dotted circle, to indicate gallon capacity. Stamped on shoulder: "J. & N. BIRD" within rectangle. Wheel-turned, brown, salt-glazed body. H: 22¾", D (rim): 8¾", D (base): 9½", 1843. *Courtesy of the Henderson State University Museum.*

Joseph and Nathaniel Bird, two of Dallas County's most well-known potters, left future researchers an exquisite documented reference to their presence on the base of this tall churn. Prior to firing, one of the Birds scratched the following legend into the base of the piece: "Manufactured by Joseph & Nathaniel Bird in the State of Arkansas, Clark County, May 1843." Unfortunately, it is at the present time the only whole signed piece of Bird pottery to have come to light.

Between 1843 and c. 1887 brothers Joseph, Nathaniel, William, and James Bird operated several small potteries in Dallas County. Two other potters working there during the second half of the century were John C. Welch (active c. 1860–1910) who was trained by William Bird, and Nathaniel Culberson, an apprentice of Bird's or Welch's (active c. 1860–65). Culberson eventually moved to Tennessee and established a pottery in McNairy County.

P—11c.   Detail view of the "J. & N. BIRD" stamp on the shoulder of the churn.

P—12a.   Jar. Incuse stamped on shoulder "2" and "W". (mark for John C. Welch). Wheel-turned, brown, salt-glazed body, interior partially unglazed. H: 11½", D (rim): 6¾", D (base): 6⅜". C. 1860–1870. *From the collection of the Arkansas Territorial Restoration.*

The tapered ovoid shape of Mr. Welch's jar was a popular form for storage jars and jugs during the first half of the century. And it would remain a much used holloware jar form among isolated rural potters of the South into the present century.

As in the case of the Bird churn, this jar remains as the only piece of stamped Welch pottery to have come to light. Family descendants have kept a number of unmarked pieces which are attributed to his shop.

John Welch (1832–1910) was active in Dallas County, Arkansas, from c. 1860 up until the time of his death. Welch may have been trained by Dallas County potter William Bird whose brothers Joseph, Nathaniel, and James were also active potters in the vicinity (active c. 1843–87). In 1860, Welch did purchase William Bird's pottery site. His great-grandson in a 1972 interview stated that sometime after 1891 he moved his kiln site to the Waverly Community, west of Princeton, onto his son's property, and there finished out his days making pottery for the local trade.

P—12b.   Detail illustration of the incuse stamped "2" and "W" on the John C. Welch jar.

P–13a. Jug. Incuse stamp on handle of "WB." Green alkaline glaze over stoneware body. H: 7⅞", D (base): 5½". C. 1860. *Collection of Edward Tardy.*

This is the only whole documented example to date of alkaline-glazed ware made by the well known Bird family of potters of Dallas County, Arkansas. The tradition of employing this uniquely simple, attractive glazing compound was widely used, especially by Southern potters in the Carolinas, Georgia, and Alabama during the nineteenth century. Few Arkansas-made pieces have been located despite the fact that several of our potters were from these states.

P–13b. Detail of the "WB" stamp on the handle of the jug.

ARKANSAS FIREARMS

Gunsmithing in Arkansas

The Reverend Eli Lindsey, bringing the Gospel to pre-territorial Arkansas, was in mid-sermon when the hunting dogs outside the church took up the bay. "The service is adjourned in order that the men may kill that bear," he announced. After the successful hunt, Lindsey renewed the sermon, thanking God "for men who know how to shoot and for women who know how to pray."[1] Prayers were important on the frontier, but guns, perhaps, retained the greater utility.

Arkansas became the "bear state," and the hunting there became legendary. In "the most celebrated anecdote ever published" about the state,[2] Thomas Bangs Thorpe's hero finally bags "The Big Bear of Arkansas." Col. C. F. M. Noland's Pete Whetstone regularly commented on hunting, defining himself to the electorate in his first stump speech as "a professional bear hunter and scientific bee-hunter.—Pete is no orator, but when it comes to killing a bear or finding a bee tree, he is *there*."[3]

The legends rested on the facts of frontier life. All of the chroniclers of early Arkansas, such as Thomas Nuttall,[4] Henry Rowe Schoolcraft,[5] George W. Featherstonhaugh,[6] and Friedrich Gerstäcker,[7] note the importance and the prevalence of firearms for hunting and personal protection. Further, the ownership of firearms took a significant role in the protection of the community. Given means to avoid it, "every able bodied free white male inhabitant" was legally bound to duty in the militia. Each man was to provide himself "with a musket, cartridge box, and nine charges of powder and ball . . . or rifle, powder horn and shot pouch" plus accessories, unless the acquisition of this equipment exceeded the means of the militiaman.[8] The persistent perceived threat came from the native Americans recently removed beyond Arkansas's western border. In 1825 William E. Woodruff editorialized that "no portion of the Union presents more vulnerable points for sudden attack from a savage foe."[9] But the militiamen were called to arms in earnest only for the major conflicts of the era—the Texas Revolution, the Mexican War, and the Civil War.

Not only did marksmanship have survival value, but it also had competitive value. Shooting matches, often for beef or other awards, enlivened many communities. Albert Pike, trying to begin a subscription school on Little Piney Creek, was advised to attend a beef shoot the next morning, because "nearly all the settlement will be there." Sure enough, Pike had twenty scholars signed up by the day's end.[10] Peter Kuykendall, a settler in the Arkansas River valley, said, "Rude farming and hunting were the occupations of these early settlers, and they were good marksmen; almost every Saturday there would be a shooting match. We'd put up a big beef, and shoot sides for it. One of the largest stakes to be won was $100, at a match between the Lanthams, Couches, myself and others, in which I won in seven shots."[11]

The well-used image of pioneers marching off with ax and rifle to tame the wilderness fits those early settlers who moved west beyond the Mississippi. Schoolcraft makes a good argument for the addition of the hunting dog to that picture, but the "rifle-gun" was clearly a tool of these representatives of civilization who labored to extend its boundaries.

Not all the uses of firearms reflected civilization, of course. Critics charged that the frontier represented a haven from law and order for antisocial types who used guns for selfish or unpleasant reasons. Territorial Governor William Savin Fulton warned that the "practice of carrying deadly weapons . . . has been the cause of much bloodshed in Arkansas, and has greatly injured the character of this Territory abroad."[12] Duels and other criminal activities left a lingering reputation for violence, a reputation which far outlasted the frontier period. For better or worse, it is safe to say that the rifle-gun was part and parcel of every man's baggage on the frontier.

The Armories

The context and inspiration for the Arkansas gunsmith is found in the work of the U.S. armories at Springfield, Massachusetts, and Harper's Ferry, Virginia. These institutions pioneered and incorporated amazing changes in both firearms and their production, and these changes ultimately resulted in the decline of the individual artisan throughout the country.

When George Washington chose the Springfield and Harper's Ferry sites as United States armories and arsenals, he was taking a step towards a stronger union and a self-sufficient nation. By the mid-1790s England and France were no longer possible sources of firearms, and this nation's stance as an equal international power needed reinforcing with the proper military supplies and equipment.

The initial arms production reflected the operation of a large craft shop, and the manual process displayed a minimal division of labor. For example, by 1815 in Springfield the construction of a firearm involved thirty-six different operational specialties; by 1825 there were one hundred, as more and more men worked on each gun.[13]

Complementing this division of labor was the introduction of machinery which both sped the process and increased the accuracy in the preparation of the individual parts. This was a special goal of the military, a goal irrelevant to the average gunsmith and his customer. Great precision in parts production permitted interchangeability. Repairs or replacements in the heat of battle could be made only if a musket could receive new parts standardized to the old ones. John Hall at Harper's Ferry stated the ideal this way: "to make every similar part of every gun so much alike that it will suit every gun, so that if a thousand guns were taken apart and their limbs thrown promiscuously together in one heap, they may be taken promiscuously from the heap and will all come right."[14] Eli Whitney had been the major advocate of this principle, but it was John Hall, using his improvement of a milling machine produced at Simeon North's arms factory in Connecticut, who by 1825 achieved the goal.[15] Large-scale arms production was never the same again.

The Product

The means of production were transformed, and the products underwent substantial changes. For a century and a half the flintlock musket had been the standard firearm, especially for the military. Loaded through the muzzle of the barrel, the musket used a flint ignition system, in which the flint, attached to the spring-driven hammer, struck the steel frizzen, sending sparks into a flash pan full of powder. The powder would burn through the touch hole into the base of the barrel to ignite the main charge, which would then send the patched ball out of the barrel toward the target.

The mainspring rested under the lock plate in front of the hammer (front action lock), and the barrel was smooth bore. This barrel was not terribly accurate, but it was fairly easy to load and offered the versatility of being loaded with shot as well as musket ball. The wooden stock extended the full length of the barrel and is therefore called "full stock."

In a few years John Hall had produced a workable breech-loaded flintlock, which was made for the United States military between 1823 and 1839.[16] The Sharps rifle followed soon after, and perfected breech loading just in time for the Civil War. Meanwhile, Samuel Colt created his revolver, another leap toward shooting efficiency. Then the 1850s witnessed a series of advances in bullets and cartridges, including the contributions of Messrs. Smith and Wesson, as rim-fired metallic cartridges were readied for, again, the Civil War. The first "modern" war was well supplied with "modern" weapons.

But these remarkable innovations barely touched Arkansas. Admittedly, as early as 1834 the 1st Dragoons at Ft. Gibson were supplied with caliber .50 John Hall carbines manufactured by Simeon North,[17] after originally being "armed with Rifles to be provided by themselves, and at their own expense."[18] Colt and the other manufacturers did sell their wares through local gunsmiths, and Arkansas Confederates were on the wrong end of Sharps and Spencer rifles. But the changes to the flintlock musket relevant to Arkansas gunsmiths were not so dramatic.

Rifling, the cutting of spiral grooves in the interior of the barrel, gave the projectile greater stability in flight. Rifles and muskets served in the Revolutionary War stock by stock. The faster loaded muskets, preferred by the professional military, were complemented by the more accurate rifles of the hunter frontiersmen.

The "Pennsylvania" or "Kentucky" rifle drew its inspiration from the German jaeger rifle, elaborated for American needs. The barrel was made longer, the bore smaller, and the stock lighter. The result was the graceful and legendary long rifle, clearly a precursor to the Arkansas rifle.

From 1803 on, Harper's Ferry produced rifles as well as muskets, recognizing the strengths of each. The model 1803 rifle had another significant innovation for mass-produced arms: the half stock. On this rifle the stock extended less than halfway down the barrel. The logic of the change rested in a lighter firearm, easier to make and less liable to forestock damage, all accomplished without sacrificing accuracy. The half stock, combined with a barrel shorter than that of the "long rifle," made the 1803 handy for horseback and scabbard.[19] The Arkansas half-stock rifle was probably influenced by the model 1803.

The flint ignition system, successfully used for years and years, had its drawbacks. The pan had to be loaded with powder just as did the barrel, but a heavy rain or continuous drizzle could easily dampen the effort to ignite the main charge. The discovery by Scottish clergyman Alexander Forsythe that a certain chemical mixture could be readily ignited by a blow led to the development of the percussion cap. This self-contained primer had only to be struck with adequate force to send a flame through a tube into the barrel, to ignite that charge waiting to hurl the projectile at its target. Samuel Colt's revolver, and other innovations, required this more efficient ignition system. The U.S. Government did not adopt the percussion cap in any form until the Hall-North breech-loaded carbine, which came west for the use of the Dragoons. The flintlock could fairly easily be adapted to the caplock system, but by the time Arkansas gunsmiths began production in earnest, the caplock was a standard feature.

The final innovation in gun design which materially affected the rifles produced in Arkansas was the development of the back action percussion lock. Instead of the mainspring extending forward from the hammer as on the front action flintlock, it extended back, resulting in a lighter, simpler mechanism that was cheaper to manufacture.

The Makers

Metallurgy, engraving, machining, blacksmithing, woodworking, a knowledge of ordnance, and sometimes even silversmithing were required to make firearms. Praise might be due the man who mastered the gunsmith's art, and respect due the artisan who can at least "get by."

At the top of the list of master gunsmiths in Arkansas must be John Pearson. His was a typical frontier story. Born in England, Pearson became a successful tradesman in Baltimore before moving west. Ending up on Arkansas's western border, he was an artisan, property owner, and member of a Masonic Lodge. He may have been the John Pearson who joined the great mid-century adventure and trekked temporarily to California.

Pearson's claim to fame rests in his relationship with inventor Samuel Colt. Colt patented the first workable application of the new percussion ignition system to the revolver, and his "number one gunsmith and consultant in developing the first revolvers" was John Pearson.[20] Pearson, though, had the unfortunate desire to be paid for his work, and Colt, the tendency to neglect bills from the gunsmith. Correspondence from Pearson to Colt invariably included progress reports on the development of the prototypes along with requests for money: "I worked night and day almost, so I would not disappoint you and what have I got for it—why vexatation and trouble." His final letter while in Colt's employment included an ultimatum: "I shall expect some money next week or I wil stop work for I can get Half a Dozen places of work and get my pay every week. You are in a Devil of a hurry but not to pay your men. . . ."[21]

That was in May of 1836, and by August 15, 1837, Pearson had located in Little Rock, advertising himself as "Gunsmith and Cutler."[22] Two years later he sold his business to Henry Griffiths and moved to Crawford County where he set up shop in Van Buren. By 1850 he had settled across the Arkansas River in Ft. Smith, living there for the remainder of his life. During the Civil War, Pearson applied his trade for the Confederacy as a master armorer. In the census of 1860, sixteen-year-old John Pearson, Jr., is listed as a gunsmith

in his father's home, as is William in 1870, but the trade had little future in a time of increased industrialization. John Pearson died in Ft. Smith in 1883.[23]

Henry Griffiths followed Pearson in Little Rock after learning his trade at the famous gunworks in Harper's Ferry, Virginia. He served as city constable through most of the 1850s and early 1860s, continuing the gunsmith business. He faired well enough to be taxed for three city lots, a horse, and gold/jewelry worth $2,700 in 1861. After the war, he advertised for customers to "call on the old GunSmith" for everything in the gun line.[24] Griffiths died in 1868 at the age of 51.

Another Arkansas gunsmith with ties to a renowned gun manufacturer was Edward A. Linzel who worked in the shop of H. E. Dimick of St. Louis, whose name, for some, became synonymous with the Plains rifle. A ledger covering 1862 and part of the following year shows that in addition to hiring outside contractors for certain parts and supplies, Dimick had two machinists and one man specializing in rifle barrels, one in rifles and pistols, and one in derringers in his employ. His master gunsmith was E. A. Linzel. One of Linzel's guns won the silver award in the fourth annual Agricultural and Mechanical Fair in St. Louis in 1859.[25]

Linzel arrived in Little Rock in 1869 and was active as a gunsmith and locksmith for the rest of the century. One reason for his longevity in a commercial world increasingly dominated by the large manufacturers was Schutzenverein, the shooting clubs organized by German immigrants. Linzel's greatest legacy from his Arkansas days rests in the fine Schutzen rifles he made after the Civil War, and one Little Rock museum has a small cannon reportedly made by him.[26]

Jacob F. Trumpler was another fine gunsmith whose active years extended beyond Arkansas's artisan period. A half-stock sporting rifle made by Jacob Trumpler in Madison County, Georgia, won the medal for the fifth best rifle in the world at the 1974 National Rifle Association Convention.[27] Trumpler moved to Little Rock by 1860, and he worked with partners John C. Day and, later, William Dabbs for a number of years as one of the state's best gunsmiths. In one of the most discouraging blows that could befall an artisan, Trumpler yielded the contents of his gunsmithing shop to the authorities at a time of governmental crisis and was never justly compensated. This was not in the Civil War, in which he loyally served the Confederate cause through his profession, but in the Brooks-Baxter conflict. Mr. Trumpler "gave to the state the earnings of a lifetime . . . if he is to lose it he will be reduced to poverty, and left to labor in his old age. . . ."[28] He became better known for his never-satisfied claim to the state than for his well-made firearms.

These gunsmiths brought their skills to the frontier from the East. Of 161 Arkansas smiths whose birth places can be determined (primarily from census records), twenty-nine hailed from Tennessee, fourteen from Kentucky, and eleven each from Virginia and North Carolina. Including the eleven native-born gunsmiths, 108 came from below the Mason-Dixon Line, and twenty-one were foreign born.

Where did they settle? Not surprisingly, the larger communities in the state attracted these artisans. The counties embracing Little Rock (thirty), Helena (sixteen), Fayetteville (ten), Pine Bluff (ten), Ft. Smith (nine), Van Buren (eight), and Batesville (seven) attracted almost half of the documented gunsmiths, with Pulaski welcoming a plurality. (This list excludes ordnance work during the Civil War.)

Many of these gunsmiths were highly skilled artisans who managed quite well on the frontier, although gunsmithing was often not the only enterprise which occupied their time. Some advertised as blacksmiths or wagonmakers. Then there was Christian Brumback. Brumback covered those trades, masonry construction, baking and butchering, and, to satisfy social needs, a house of public entertainment. In addition he served as commandant of the Pulaski County regiment of the territorial militia. A Brumback advertisement in 1832 suggests the process of commerce on the frontier: "All kinds of country produce will be received in return for work."[29]

In 1861 Jesse Overton of Arkadelphia claimed eighteen to twenty years of gunsmithing experience. In the meantime, he had served as a carpenter, Clark County judge, and even tavern keeper. For several years he, like several gunsmiths, owned slaves, but the surviving records do not indicate whether they assisted in the gunmaking business.[30]

Some other trades practiced by gunsmiths included knifemaking, horseshoeing, locksmithing, surveying, bell making, steam engine work, and the pervasive pastime of farming.

The Arkansas Shop

In 1834 John Martin sold his blacksmithing and gunsmithing tools, and the inventory of items offered provides a rare glimpse into an Arkansas gunsmith's shop. His first advertisement, over two years earlier, promised little more than repairing firearms and fitting percussion locks on guns and pistols with "common locks." But in 1833 he assured his old customers that he could make as well as repair side arms and surgical instruments. In September, 1834, the sale took place, and apparently Martin was out of business.[31]

The blacksmithing and gunsmithing tools included the following:

2 SETS BLACKSMITH'S TOOLS, CONSISTING OF—

2 pair Bellows	1 screw Plate	2 Shoeing Hammer
2 Anvils	22 Punches	2 Clinchers
2 Vices	1 Swedge and Punch	1 pair Pinchers
5 pair Tongs	1 sledge Hammer	4 Heading Tools
4 hand Hammers	1 set Hammer	1 splitting Chisel
4 Eye Wedges	2 Buttresses	

1 SET GUNSMITH'S TOOLS, TO WIT:

11 Boring Rods	2 pair Composses
8 firmer Chisels	3 pair Nippers
7 Gouges	4 bench Hammers
30 Files	2 hand Vices
3 drawing Knives	1 bench Vice
2 screw Plates	1 breach-pin Wrench
7 Burrs	11 Rifling Rods
18 Taps	8 Planes
1 Brace and 29 Bits	2 Ox Bands
36 Littering Tools	1 Frame and Emery Wheel
20 Cold sets and Chisels	
5 Saws	2 Hatchets
1 pair Shears	1 pair Flasks

Martin was equipped to bore and rifle barrels and do most of the work associated with construction of a gun. Certainly as a blacksmith he could forge the barrel before boring or rifling. Locks and related hardware were likely bought in quantity, to be adapted for use on the rifles constructed in the shop. For example, Overton advertised that he had "received from New York: barrels, locks, triggers, wipers, bullet molds, tubes, cylinders."[32] We may never know the extent of hand manufacture versus assembly work done in Arkansas shops, but obviously a great deal of fine gunsmithing was done in nineteenth-century Arkansas.

The shops that produced this work ultimately could not compete with Colt, Smith and Wesson, Remington, and Winchester. In 1884, only twenty-four smiths advertised in the *Arkansas Gazetteer and Business Directory* statewide.[33] Gunmaking shops became repair and retail shops, and the trade was in sporting goods.

Manufacturing for War

The largest gunsmithing shop in Arkansas was established when outside sources of firearms were cut off during the Civil War. Initially, Confederate forces took possession of the Federal arsenals at Little Rock and Ft. Smith, and, of course, individual soldiers entered military service with their own weapons. A local agent for the cause soon advertised for "all the good Guns in the country . . . not only regulation arms such as Muskets and Rifles, both flint and percussion made for the army, but also Double Barrelled Shot Guns and Country Rifles, Percussion Loads."[34]

The battle of Pea Ridge, in March of 1862, ended Confederate hopes of establishing a western front for the War and insured that Arkansas would be a battleground. Major General Thomas C. Hindman soon took command of the Trans-Mississippi District, intent on bringing order from a chaos of divided command and bleak prospects. Hindman's ruthless administration brought the stark reality of the hardship of war to the citizens of Arkansas. But his resulting unpopularity and his lack of military success do not diminish his organizational skills and vision for maintaining the resistance to Northern invasion.

Hindman knew that his forces needed logistical support, and he chose Arkadelphia as his prime location for factories for the production of those things necessary to wage war. One factory complex of frame and log structures sat near Arkadelphia on the Ouachita River. A furnace and evaporating pans were major components of this salt-making plant put into use by the Confederates.[35]

The Ordnance Works Department was at the heart of what one Federal spy called "the great depot for the Trans-Mississippi Confederate States Army."[36] Confederate Capt. George D. Alexander secured a large, two-story brick building which was originally a merchant's storehouse, to be used by the Confederate Army as an armory. Capt. George S. Polleys, commander of the Ordnance Works, arranged to acquire the adjoining lots with "a large skeleton frame with roof." T. D. Kingsburg built a blacksmith shop "for the rebels" on his own property, and a foundry was constructed by Confederate forces on property on the Maddox estate. Alexander also found a complex for powder manufacturing.[37] In these buildings rested Hindman's hopes for a well-supplied army.

The dream had been stated in bold terms as the war began. A Little Rock editor noted that "we possess, within the borders of the state, materials for the manufacture of firearms sufficient to supply the whole of the Confederate forces."[38] Indeed, "preparations were made for mining and smelting iron,"[39] but workers assembled at Arkadelphia yielded to more modest goals. Twenty-two gunsmiths manufactured small arms and repaired and adapted damaged guns. Barney Paynter, a gunsmith already established in Arkadelphia before this war, was probably the most important smith there, if not for his skill, at least for his material support. He was paid eight dollars a day for himself, "Boy Henry and tools." A. R. Mendenhall, living in Michigan in 1850, found his way to Des Arc, Arkansas, and advertised as a manufacturer of "Rifles, Shot-guns and Pistols."[40] He is best known in gun-collecting circles for his derringers. When the war began he moved to Arkadelphia to work in the Ordnance

Department. Lewis Worschowitz, a Hungarian by birth, and C. G. Rosengreen, a Swede, came to Arkadelphia from Yell and Dallas counties respectively, bringing their talents as gunsmiths with them.[41]

Hindman expressed pride at the quality of their work, but Brig. General W. L. Cabell, whose brigade used Arkadelphia rifles in the battle of Fayetteville, claimed that they were no better than shotguns.[42]

Master mechanics, tinners, carpenters, saddlers, bullet molders, blacksmiths, and men, women, and boy cartridge makers rounded out the crew of the Ordnance Department. The production of percussion caps was of special note, using a machine which formed the cap and inserted the fulminate with a single stroke.[43]

Gunsmiths, Locations in Arkansas

County	Date Founded	Number of Makers
Arkansas	1813	1
Ashley	1848	
Benton	1836	5
Boone	1869	
Bradley	1840	1
Calhoun	1850	
Carroll	1833	1
Chicot	1823	2
Clark	1818	25
Columbia	1852	2
Conway	1825	1
Craighead	1859	4
Crawford	1820	9
Crittenden	1825	1
Cross	1862	
Dallas	1845	1
Desha	1838	4
Drew	1846	2
Franklin	1837	1
Fulton	1842	2
Grant	1869	
Greene	1833	5

County	Date Founded	Number of Makers
Hempstead	1818	3
Hot Spring	1829	2
Independence	1820	7
Izard	1825	2
Jackson	1829	5
Jefferson	1829	10
Johnson	1833	
Lafayette	1827	4
Lawrence	1815	1
Little River	1867	
Madison	1836	1
Marion	1836	1
Miller	1820	1
Mississippi	1844	3
Monroe	1829	2
Montgomery	1842	
Newton	1842	
Ouachita	1842	3
Perry	1840	
Phillips	1820	16
Pike	1833	2
Poinsett	1838	2
Polk	1844	
Pope	1829	1
Prairie	1846	3
Pulaski	1818	52
Randolph	1835	5
Saline	1835	2
Scott	1833	1
Searcy	1835	1
Sebastian	1851	9
Sevier	1828	5
Sharp	1868	
St. Francis	1827	3
Union	1829	
Van Buren	1833	
Washington	1828	10
White	1835	3
Woodruff	1862	
Yell	1840	3
Lincoln		1
Howard		1

Total number of locations documented: 232
Total number of listings in biographical appendix: 224

Not all such enterprises took place in Arkadelphia. For a while there were "works" at several locations, including the arsenal in Little Rock. In August of 1862 four gunsmiths began work in the Little Rock arsenal, and from one to five served until July of 1863, when nineteen "detailed" gunsmiths appeared in the roster.

According to the Little Rock arsenal's thirteen monthly reports, 16,722 small arms—muskets, shotguns, and rifles—were repaired there before Confederate flight from the capital city.[44] The armorers also refurbished several cannons, including eight which had been relegated to service as corner posts. Due to a lack of paper, cartridges were manufactured there using public documents from the state library.[45]

In the last week of August the stores of Little Rock's arsenal were packed and sent toward Arkadelphia. But the Union forces that threatened Little Rock also put Arkadelphia at risk, so those who stopped there did so temporarily. Daniel F. Fones, a tinner in the Little Rock arsenal in July, made Arkadelphia's roster and then found himself in Tyler, Texas, in November. Most of the detailed gunsmiths in Little Rock were in Tyler by October. On October 31, 1863, Union General Frederick Steele reported that "all the machinery, etc., has been removed from Arkadelphia to Marshall, Texas."[46] Whether at Marshall or Tyler, Arkansas gunsmiths became part of the last hope of Confederate forces west of the Mississippi. A. R. Mendenhall, A. Atkinson, and Gains George were three Arkadelphia gunsmiths who ended up in Tyler by the end of 1864.[47]

Arkansas's most intensive gunsmithing effort ended a little more than a year after it had begun: an ill-supported effort for a lost cause. The war forced the state to revert to frontier self-sufficiency at the same time that it drove manufacturers in the North to gear up for mass production. After the war and reunification with the rest of the country, Arkansas's gun market fell under the irresistible influence of the mass producers, and gunsmithing began a slide into obscurity.

Count of Arkansas Gunsmiths by Place of Birth

UNITED STATES BORN

Alabama	11
Arkansas	11
Georgia	4
Illinois	4
Indiana	2
Kentucky	14
Louisiana	1
Maryland	1
Massachusetts	1
Michigan	2
Mississipi	5
Missouri	6
New Hampshire	1
New Jersey	2
New York	1
North Carolina	11
Ohio	4
Pennsylvania	8
South Carolina	10
Tennessee	29
Vermont	1
Virginia	11

FOREIGN BORN

Canada	2
England	4
Germany	11
Hungary	2
Sweden	2

Total number of birth places documented: 161

A cursory glance shows two communities dominating this list: Arkadelphia (Clark County) and Little Rock (Pulaski). Twenty-one gunsmith locations in Clark County were documented solely through Confederate records, leaving four "civilian" gunsmiths found in the county. Without twenty similarly documented Confederate gunsmiths, Pulaski County still attracted thirty-two smiths, more than any other location. Two smiths were not known by their historical residence, accounting for the inclusion of two of the counties which were formed from other counties after 1870 (Lincoln and Howard). Each smith was counted in each location in which he was recorded as gunsmith, to show the extent of the state's contact with gunsmithing. Only a few smiths were recorded in more than one place, suggesting a less transitory nature than one might suspect from this artisan class.

The South contributed a dominant share of the gunsmiths whose birth places are known, and more than twice the gunsmiths came from Tennessee (29) than any other state. Foreign smiths accounted for 21 or 13 percent of the known birth places. A number of gunsmiths are known only by their advertisements, and while some said they came from one place or another, none was listed without a stated place of birth. Occasionally even the major source of birth information, the censuses, can be questioned, as with James P. Johnson whose birth place was either Alabama (1850) or North Carolina (1860). In Johnson's case the earliest citation was used. While place of birth is helpful in revealing migration patterns, for the study of gunsmithing in the United States, it would be more helpful to know where the trade was learned, but we know that in only a few cases.

NOTES

1. Walter N. Vernon, *Methodism in Arkansas 1816–1976* (Little Rock: Joint Committee for the History of Arkansas Methodism, 1976) 18.

2. James R. Masterson, *Arkansas Folklore* (Little Rock: Rose Publishing, 1974) 56.

3. C. F. M. Noland, "The Spirit of the Times," June 3, 1837, reprinted in Leonard Williams, ed., *Cavorting on the Devil's Fork: The Pete Whetstone Letters of C. F. M. Noland* (Memphis: Memphis State University Press, 1979) 68.

4. Thomas Nuttall, *A Journal of Travels into the Arkansa Territory* (Philadelphia: Thomas H. Palmer, 1821) 68.

5. Henry R. Schoolcraft, *A View of the Lead Mines of Missouri* (New York: Charles Wiley & Co., 1819).

6. George W. Featherstonhaugh, *Excursion through the Slave States*, Vol. 2 (London: John Murry, 1844).

7. Friedrich Gerstäcker, Edna L. and Harrison R. Steeves, eds., *Wild Sports in the Far West* (Durham, North Carolina: Duke University Press, 1968).

8. Revised by William McK. Ball and Samuel C. Roane, *Revised Statutes of the State of Arkansas* (Boston: Weeks, Jourdan and Co., 1838) 554, 550, 551, 561.

9. *Arkansas Gazette*, 14 June 1825.

10. Albert Pike, "Letters from Arkansas, No II," *American Monthly Magazine*, I, 25 (Fayetteville, Arkansas: Arkansas Historical Quarterly, Spring, 1951, Vol. X No. 1) 74–75.

11. Boyd Johnson, *The Arkansas Frontier* (Pine Bluff: The Perdue Printing Co., 1957) 100.

12. *Arkansas Gazette*, 6 October 1835.

13. Brooke Hindle and Steven Lubar, *Engines of Change* (Washington, D.C.: Smithsonian Institution Press, 1986) 228.

14. Stuart E. Brown, Jr., *The Guns of Harpers Ferry* (Berryville, Va.: Virginia Book Co., 1968) 69.

15. Brown, 70–71; Hindle and Lubar, 230.

16. Brown, 70, 79.

17. Brown, 81.

18. The secretary of war to Jesse Bean, June 16, 1832, *The Territorial Papers of the United States*, ed. C. E. Carter, Vol. XXI (Washington, D.C.: U.S. Gov't Printing Office, 1954) 512. Capt. Bean was authorized to raise a company of Mounted Rangers in Arkansas. This company became a part of the first U.S. dragoon regiment.

19. Brown, 29–35.

20. R. L. Wilson, *The Colt Heritage* (New York: Simon and Schuster, 1979) 8.

21. William B. Edwards, *The Story of Colt's Revolver* (New York: The Stackpole Company, 1957) 46.

22. *Arkansas Gazette*, 15 August 1837.

23. Clara Eno, *History of Crawford County, Arkansas* (Van Buren, Arkansas: Press-Argus, 1951) 96, 100; David M. Sullivan, "John Albert Pearson, Jr.: Arkansas Soldier and Confederate Marine," *Arkansas Historical Quarterly*, Vol. XLV, 3 (Fayetteville, Arkansas: Arkansas Historical Association, 1968) 250–1; Priscilla McArthur, *Arkansas in the Gold Rush* (Little Rock: August House, 1986) 226; ed. Wilma Jamison, "1883 News," *The Journal*, Vol. VII, 2, (Ft. Smith, Arkansas: Fort Smith Historical Society, September, 1983) 33. *See also* Biographical Appendix

24. *Daily Pantograph*, 3 May 1866; *Arkansas State Gazette*, 21 April 1868. *See also* Biographical Appendix

25. Herschel C. Logan, "H. E. Dimick of St. Louis" in *The American Rifleman*, April, 1958, 31–33.

26. J. J. Wolfe, "Background of German Immigration to Arkansas," *Arkansas Historical Quarterly*, Vol. XXV, 2 (Fayetteville, Arkansas: Arkansas Historical Association, Summer, 1966) 167; The Museum of Science and History in Little Rock has a small cannon possibly made by Linzel.

27. James Webb Smith, *Georgia's Legacy* (The University of Georgia: Georgia Museum of Art, 1985) 216–17.

28. *Arkansas Gazette*, 11 November 1875, 25 November 1899. *See also* Biographical Appendix

29. *Arkansas Gazette*, 24 August 1824, 9 August 1825, 26 January 1830, 11 November 1830, 11 April 1832; *Arkansas Advocate*, 20 June 1833.

30. Barbara Coffee, "Antebellum Arkadelphia," *The Clark County Historical Journal* (Arkadelphia, Arkansas: Clark County Historical Association, Spring 1981) 65; *Ouachita Conference Journal*, Vol. 25, 4 July 1861 (Arkadelphia, Arkansas).

31. *Arkansas Gazette*, 25 January 1832, 1 May 1833, 2 September 1834.

32. *Quachita Conference Journal*, 4 July 1861.

33. *Arkansas Gazetteer and Business Directory* (St. Louis: R. L. Polk, 1884) 767.

34. *Arkansas Gazette*, 14 August 1861.

35. H. B. McKenzie, "Confederate Manufacturers in Southwest Arkansas" (Fayetteville, Arkansas: *Publications of the Arkansas Historical Association*, Vol. 2, 1908) 201–02.

36. Margaret Ross, "Chronicles of Arkansas," *Arkansas Gazette*, 13 February 1963.

37. National Archives, Records, Ass't Commissioner, Arkansas Freedmen's Bureau M. F., Roll 30. Monthly Report of Abandoned or Confiscated Lands, Nov. 30, 1865, Dec. 31, 1865; Monthly report of Lands, Oct. 1865

38. *Arkansas Gazette*, 18 May 1861.

39. Gen. T. C. Hindman report on Trans-Mississippi District, *The War of the Rebellion, A Compilation of the Official Records*, Series 1–Vol. XIII (Washington, D.C.: Government Printing Office, Washington, 1885; Harrisburg, Pa. republished by National Historical Society, 1971) 32. (Hereinafter cited as *Official Records.*)

40. *Des Arc Citizen*, 22 June 1861.

41. "Account book Ordnance Department, Arkadelphia Arkansas," photocopy in Place File, Arkadelphia, Arkansas History Commission.

42. *Official Records*, 32; Margaret Ross, "Chronicles of Arkansas," *Arkansas Gazette*, 14 February 1963.

43. Ross, "Chronicles," 14 February 1963.

44. Little Rock Arsenal Records 1862–63 in Civil War: Misc. Records, National Archives, Gen M/F, Roll 1, Arkansas History Commission.

45. Hindman, 34.

46. *Official Records*, Series I, Vol. 22, part II, 685.

47. Tyler, Texas, Arsenal Records, 1863–1864: Misc. Records, National Archives, Gen M/F, Roll 1, Arkansas History Commission.

A Biographical Appendix of Arkansas Gunsmiths

Atkinson, A.

Gunsmith, Confederate States of America (hereafter cited as CSA), Ordnance Dept., Arkadelphia, AR, 1863, Collection of the Carnegie History Center, Tyler, TX.

Baker, William

Gunsmith, A.45, B.MS: MCR 1850 Chicot Co., Roll 25, AHC.

Bass, J.

Gunsmith, A.30, B.possibly GA: MCR 1860 Clark Co., Roll 39, AHC. Also listed in CCTR 1861–62, Roll 56, AHC.

Baty (Batey), James or Collin James (Isaiah)

Gunsmith, A.42, B.VA: MCR 1870 Sebastian Co., Roll 64, AHC. Also listed in SCTR 1875, Roll 23, AHC.

Bell, Isaac

Gunsmith, A.39, B.GA: MCR 1870 Pike Co., Roll 60, AHC.

Bennett, L. F.

Gunsmith, A.50, B.NJ: MCR 1860 Desha Co., Roll 41, AHC.

Bennett, Robert

Gunsmith, A.30, B.TN: MCR 1860 Independence Co., Roll 43, AHC.

Benthal (Benthall), John C.

[Gunsmith] Blacksmith, A.43, B.TN: MCR 1850 Phillips Co. (Helena), Roll 29, AHC. "Black and Gun Smithing." SS 6–18–53. Also listed in PCTR 1850–58, Roll 88, AHC.

Berrit, Richard

Gunnsmith, A.23, B.KY: MCR 1870 Benton Co., Roll 47, AHC.

Berrit, Thomas

Gunnsmith, A.45, B.KY: MCR 1870 Benton Co., Roll 47, AHC.

Blevins, John M.

Gunsmith, A.33, B.TN: MCR 1850 Washington Co., Roll 31, AHC. Gunsmith, A.43, B.TN: MCR 1860 Washington Co., Roll 52, AHC. Listed in WCTR 1842, Roll 61, AHC. Also listed in Washington Co. Probate Records Books "B–C," 1847–59, Roll 16, AHC.

Bloomgreen, M.

Gunsmith, A.Unknown, B.Sweden: MCR 1860 Jefferson Co., Roll 44, AHC.

Bodine, John

Gunsmith, A.27, B.MO: MCR 1860 Scott Co., Roll 50, AHC.

Brilter, J. G.

Gunsmith, CSA, Ordnance Dept., Arkadelphia, AR, 1863, Collection of the Carnegie History Center, Tyler, TX.

Brown, Leopold

Gunsmith, A.24, B.Germany: MCR 1870 Jefferson Co., Roll 56, AHC.

Brawley, S. S.

Gunsmith, A.36, B.NC: MCR 1850 Ouachita Co. (Camden), Roll 28, AHC. Also listed in OCTR 1846–57, Roll 35, AHC.

Brinsfield, Simpson

Gunsmith, A.40, B.NC: MCR 1860 Fulton Co., Roll 41, AHC.

Brumback, Christian

"Gun-Smith, Little Rock." *AA* 3–21–32. "New Shop . . . Gunsmith, Blacksmith, and Wagon-Making business." *AG* 4–11–32.

Buckham, William

Gunsmith, A.30, B.VA: MCR 1860 Mississippi Co. (Osceola), Roll 46, AHC. Buckham lived with William Webster who was also a gunsmith.

Burke, James

Gun Smith, Little Rock (Confederate) Arsenal Records: 1862–63. Civil War: Misc. Records National Archives, Roll 1.

Burnett, Lemuel Fordham

Gunsmith, A.38, B.NJ: MCR 1850 Desha Co., Roll 26, AHC. Gunsmith, A.50, B.NJ: MCR 1860 Desha Co., Roll 41, AHC. Also listed in DCTR 1840–55, Roll 67, 1856–62, Roll 68, and 1863–65, Roll 69, AHC. "Obituary . . . he apprenticed to gunsmith in Ohio and came to Arkansas in 1832 settled just about where the State House now stands . . . near a creek that crosses on Markham St. and empties into the river . . . there he established the first shop and made the best guns and knives ever made in Little Rock . . . some knives sold for 25 to 30 dollars. . . ." *AM* 6–14–94.

Cameron, David

"David Cameron, from Cincinnati, Ohio, respectfully informs the citizens of Van Buren and the public generally, that he designs carrying on the Gunsmithing Business in all its various branches, in the town of Van Buren. He pledges himself to execute his work in superior style, and at reduced prices." *WFW* 12–9–45.

Carnahan, A.

"A. Carnahan, Gun-Smith, . . . informs the citizens of Little Rock . . . that he has taken the shop, at Mr. Gilbert Barden's, lately occupied by Mr. John Sharlaville [Sherleville], where he purposes carrying on the Gun-Smith business, in all its various branches." *AG* 12–19–26.

Carroll, John

"Blacksmith & Gunsmith, Horseshoeing, Jobwork, Making & Repairing Guns. 95 Main St. Batesville, AR. . . . With careful and experienced workmen, he will dispatch business at sight, and hopes to the satisfaction of his patrons." *AA* 1–16–33.

Charnley, William

Gunsmith, A.31, B.Canada: MCR 1870 Jefferson Co., Roll 56, AHC. Also listed in JCTR 1870–75, Roll 143, AHC.

Cherry, T. B.

Gunsmith, A.23, B.OH: MCR 1870 Sebastian Co. (Fort Smith), Roll 64, AHC.

Clay, S. R.

Gun Smith, Little Rock (Confederate) Arsenal Records: 1862–63. Civil War: Misc. Records National Archives, Roll 1.

Cobb, James

Gunsmith, A.39 B.SC: MCR 1860 Pulaski Co., Roll 49, AHC.

Corey, Chester

Gunsmith, A.55, B.NY: MCR 1870 Crawford Co. (Van Buren), Roll 51, AHC. Also listed in CCTR 1865–68, Roll 23, AHC.

Couch, J. M.

Gunsmith, CSA, Ordnance Dept., Arkadelphia, AR, 1863, Collection of the Carnegie History Center, Tyler, TX.

Cowgill, Addison J. H.

Gunsmith, A.24, B.VA: MCR 1850 Pulaski Co., Roll 29, AHC.

Crawford, Adam

Gunsmith, A.35, B.SC: MCR 1850 Pulaski Co., Roll 29, AHC.

Cross, J. T.

Gunsmith, CSA, Ordnance Dept., Arkadelphia, AR, 1863, Collection of the Carnegie History Center, Tyler, TX.

Dabbs, William

Gunsmith, A.28, B.England: MCR 1870 Pulaski Co., Roll 62, AHC. "Dabbs, William, gunsmith. 108 Main, res. 1510 Lousiana." LRCD 1871, Roll 57. Dabbs was a partner of Jacob F. Trumpler, 1866–71.

Dary, Buy

Gun Smith, Little Rock (Confederate) Arsenal Records: 1862–63. Civil War: Misc. Records National Archives, Roll 1.

Day, Jacob F. F.

Gunsmith, A. 30, B.SC: MCR 1860 Pulaski Co., Roll 49, AHC.

Day, John C.

Gunsmith, A.36, B.GA: MCR 1860 Pulaski Co., Roll 49, AHC. "Rifles, Shotguns, & Pistols! Gun and Locksmith—The Subscribers have opened a shop on Main St. opposite the theatre and are prepared to manufacture Rifles, Shotguns, & Pistols on Short notice. . . ! Trumpler & Day." *AG* 11–24–60. "New Gun Shop." *AG* 4–13–67. Also listed in PCTR 1861–62, Roll 3, ATR. *See* Jacob F. Trumpler

Delph, John

Gunsmith, A.74, B.NC: MCR 1860 Independence Co., Roll 43, AHC. Also listed in ICTR 1840, 1843–44, 1848–49, and 1851, Roll 57, 1852–57, Roll 58, 1857–60, Roll 61, 1861–66, Roll 62, and 1867–72, Roll 64, AHC.

Doil, George

Gunsmith, A.31, B.KY: MCR 1850 Phillips Co., Roll 29, AHC.

Dorris, James

Gunsmith, A.28, B.MO: MCR 1860 Crawford Co., Roll 40, AHC. Also listed in CCTR 1854–68, Roll 23, AHC.

Dougherty (Daugherty), George

Gunsmith, A.30, B.AL: MCR 1850 Sevier Co., Roll 30, AHC. Also listed in SCTR 1846, 1849–54, 1856, and 1861, Roll 47, 1862–63 and 1865–66, Roll 48, AHC; and in Sevier Co. Probate Court Records, Books "8–9," 1862–67, Roll 16, and Books "10–11," 1867–72, Roll 17, AHC.

Dougherty (Daugherty), Parish

Gunsmith, A.34, B.AL: MCR 1850 Sevier Co., Roll 30, AHC. Also listed in SCTR 1846 and 1849–54, Roll 47, and 1865–66, Roll 48, AHC.

Draper, J. J.

Gunsmith, A.45, B.KY: MCR 1850 Arkansas Co., Roll 25, AHC. Also listed in ACTR 1851–58, Roll 66, AHC.

Dunlap, Samuel or Saline

Gunsmith, A.51, B.VT: MCR 1850 Washington Co., Roll 31, AHC. Also listed WCTR 1851, Roll 62, AHC.

English, Andrew

Gunsmith, A.25, B.KY: MCR 1860 St. Francis Co., Roll 49, AHC

Ferdick, Henry

Gunsmith, A.46, B.PA: MCR 1860 Randolph Co., Roll 49, AHC.

Fergun, W. M.

Gun Smith, Little Rock (Confederate) Arsenal Records: 1862–63. Civil War: Misc. Records National Archives, Roll 1.

Fitzpatrick, Thomas

Gunsmith, A.22, B.MS: MCR 1870 Phillips Co., (Helena), Roll 60, AHC.

Follis, W.

Gunsmith, CSA, Ordnance Dept., Arkadelphia, AR, 1863, Collection of the Carnegie History Center, Tyler, TX.

Forgeson, Jacob D.

Gunsmith, A.33, B.TN: MCR 1850 Independence Co., Roll 26, AHC. Also listed in ICTR 1849 and 1851, Roll 57, AHC.

Foster, Martain

Gunsmith, A.40, B.VA: MCR 1850 Desha Co., Roll 26, AHC.

French, W. G.

Gun Smith, Little Rock (Confederate) Arsenal Records: 1862–63. Civil War: Misc. Records National Archives, Roll 1.

Freshhour, Henry

Gunsmith, A.61, B.PA: MCR 1850 Washington Co., Roll 31, AHC. Gunsmith, A.70, B.PA: MCR 1860 Washington Co., Roll 52, AHC. Also listed in WCTR for 1836, Roll 61, 1840, 1842, 1843–45, 1848–49, and 1851–55, Roll 62, and 1856, 1859, 1861, and 1867, Roll 63, AHC.

Gamble, Robert W.

Gunsmith, A.34, B.AL: MCR 1860 Conway Co. (Lewisburg), Roll 39, AHC.

George, Gains

Gunsmith, CSA, Ordnance Dept., Arkadelphia, AR, 1863, Collection of the Carnegie History Center, Tyler, TX.

Gilmose, S. H.

Gunsmith, Little Rock (Confederate), Arsenal Records: 1862–63. Civil War: Misc. Records National Archives, Roll 1.

Givins, J. T.

Gunsmith, A.31, B.AL: MCR 1870 Monroe Co., Roll 59, AHC.

Glidewell, William J.

Gunsmith, A.38, B.TN: MCR 1860 Saline Co., Roll 63, AHC.

Grasse, Fred

Gunsmith, A.35, B.Prussia: MCR 1860 Sebastian Co. (Fort Smith), Roll 50, AHC. Gunsmith, A.45, B.Heolstern, Prussia: MCR 1870 Sebastian Co. (Fort Smith), Roll 64, AHC. Sebastian Co. Probate Records 1872–79, Book "B," Roll 39, AHC, p. 39 mentions Grasse as having his gunsmith tools for sale.

Griffith (Griffiths), Charles.

"Gunsmith Shop." *AG* 3–17–66. The son of Henry Griffiths.

Griffiths, Henry

"Guns, Pistols and Rifles." *AG* 7–3–39. "Gun Smithing and Brass Foundry." *AG* 1–13–41. "Gun-smithing." *AG* 2–10–45. "Ho For California." *AG*

12–14–48. Gunsmith, A.33, B.VA: MCR 1850 Pulaski Co., Roll 29, AHC. "Guns! Guns! Guns!" *AG* 8–24–55. "H. Griffiths, Gunsmith." *AG* 8–29–57. Listed PCTR 1840–48 (pt.), Roll 1, 1848 (pt.)–56, Roll 2, and 1857 and 1861–62, Roll 3, ATR. "Cheap Guns." *DP* 5–3–66. "Gun & Locksmith." *AG* 4–17–67.

Gross, Elbert

Gunsmith, A.25, B.TN: MCR 1860 Washinton Co., Roll 52, AHC.

Gross, Jacob R.

Gunsmith, A.38, B.TN: MCR 1870 Greene Co., Roll 54, AHC.

Gully, John J.

Gunsmith, A.46, B.TN: MCR 1870 Randolph Co., Roll 63, AHC.

Hagen, G. W.

Gun Smith, Little Rock (Confederate) Arsenal Records: 1862–63. Civil War: Misc. Records National Archives, Roll 1.

Hamilton (Hamillton), J. J.

Gunsmith, A.22, B.AR: MCR 1860 Jefferson Co., Roll 44, AHC.

Hamond, Joab

Gunsmith, A.40, B.KY: MCR 1860 Phillips Co., Roll 47, AHC.

Hannah, T. A.

Gunsmith, A.46, B.TN: MCR 1870 Washington Co., Roll 66, AHC.

Harless, Gasper

Gunsmith, A.48, B.VA: MCR 1870 Benton Co., Roll 47, AHC.

Harper, N. J.

Gunsmith, CSA, Ordnance Dept., Arkadelphia, AR, 1863, Collection of the Carnegie History Center, Tyler, TX.

Harrison, Thomas

Gunsmith, A.51, B.VA: MCR 1850 Prairie Co., Roll 29, AHC.

Harrison, Thomas

Gunsmith, A.55, B.OH: MCR 1860 White Co., Roll 52, AHC.

Hart, E.

Gunsmith, A.21, B.Germany: MCR 1860 Hempstead Co. (Fulton), Roll 42, AHC.

Hart, Harkman

Gunsmith, A.23, B.IL: MCR 1860 Hempstead Co., Roll 42, AHC.

Hatchet, E. G.

Gunsmith, A.30, B.TN: MCR 1850 Searcy Co., Roll 30, AHC.

Hazen, William C.

Gunsmith, A.50, B.NC: MCR 1850 Crittenden Co., Roll 25, AHC. Secondary Source: "Hazen, situated on the Little Rock and Memphis Railroad, forty three miles from De Valls Bluff, has a population of about 650, and is the leading commercial point in the county. It was surveyed and laid out in 1873, and named in honor of William C. Hazen, its original proprietor." *Goodspeed Eastern Arkansas*, 674.

Hebberlin, J.

Gunsmith, A.26, B.Germany: MCR 1860 Jackson Co., Roll 44, AHC.

Heberline (Heberlein), August

Gunsmith/Locksmith, A.39, B.Prussia: MCR 1870 Jackson Co., Roll 56, AHC. Also listed in JCTR 1865–66, Roll 46, and 1867, Roll 47, AHC.

Heinemann, Edward

Gunsmith, Little Rock (Confederate) Arsenal Records: 1862–63. Civil War: Misc. Records National Archives, Roll 1.

Herald, Louis

"Herald, Louis, gunsmith, 12 e Markham, bds St. Louis House." LRCD 1871, 75.

Herriott (Herriett), Rutherford

Gunsmith, A.52, B.PA: MCR 1850 Independence Co., Roll 26, AHC. Listed ICTR 1840, 1843–44, 1848–49, and 1851, Roll 57, 1850–58, Roll 59, and 1852–57, Roll 58, AHC. Also listed in Independence Co. Probate Records 1858–69, books "C–D," Roll 15, AHC.

House, Isham

Gunsmith, A.58, B.SC: MCR 1870 Columbia Co., Roll 50, AHC. Secondary Source: I. T. House was elected surveyor of Columbia Co. in 1853 and was listed as surveyor 1853–56. *Goodspeed Southern Arkansas*, 457, 458.

Houston, Robert

Gunsmith, A.65, B.NC: MCR 1850 Carroll Co., Roll 25, AHC.

Howard, William

Secondary Source: William Howard, a gunsmith by trade, was born in Arkansas in 1816. He was the father of nine children, one of which was Joseph H. Howard, who was elected sheriff of Yell Co. in 1890. *Goodspeed Western Arkansas*, 157.

Hudson, John

"Black & Gun Smithing. . . . The undersigned having associated themselves together . . . in the town of Helena . . . are now well prepared to do any and all kinds of work in their line . . . we do our work well and our charges are moderate, and . . . we hope to receive the patronage of the community and the traveling public. . . . William M. Snively, William M. Johnson, John Hudson." SS 5–4–50. Gunsmith, A.34, B.England: MCR 1860 Phillips Co. (Helena), Roll 47, AHC. Secondary Source: The Civil War greatly retarded the settlement of the county (Lee), as it did elsewhere. Among those who once owned a large estate was John Hudson, one of the first blacksmiths to locate in this section. *Goodspeed Eastern Arkansas*, 568.

Humphries, Edward

Gunsmith, A.63, B.NC: MCR 1870 Sevier Co., Roll 64, AHC. Also listed in SCTR 1862–66, Roll 48, and 1867–72, Roll 49, AHC, and Sevier Co. Probate Records 1867–72 Books "10–11," Roll 17, AHC.

Ingram, William W.

Gunsmith, A.39, B.MO: MCR 1870 Independence Co., Roll 55, AHC. Also listed, ICTR 1861–66, Roll 62, and 1867–72, Roll 64, AHC.

Jacob, John

Gunsmith, A.41, B.IL: MCR 1870 Independence Co. (Batesville), Roll 55, AHC.

Jenkins, Andrew

Gunsmith, A.29, B.AR: MCR 1860 Pulaski Co., Roll 49, AHC.

Johnson, A. O.

Gunsmith, CSA, Ordnance Dept., Arkadelphia, AR, 1863, Collection of the Carnegie History Center, Tyler, TX.

Johnson, H. C.

Gunsmith, A.25, B.NH: MCR 1860 Phillips Co. (Helena), Roll 47, AHC.

Johnson, James P.

Gunsmith, A.24, B.AL: MCR 1850 Hempstead Co., Roll 26, AHC. Gunsmith, A.32, B.NC: MCR 1860 Prairie Co., Roll 48, AHC. "James Johnson, Gunsmith, Des Arc, Arkansas. Having permanently located myself, I am prepared to manufacture Guns, Pistols . . . to order. All kinds of Fire-Arms Repaired, on reasonable terms. Locks repaired and Keys made." *DAC* 11–13–58.

Johnson, William M.

Gunsmith & Blacksmith, A.28, B.TN: MCR 1850 Phillips Co., Roll 29, AHC. *See* John Hudson

Jones, B. H.

Gunsmith, Little Rock (Confederate) Arsenal Records: 1862–63. Civil War: Misc. Records National Archives, Roll 1.

Jones, William

Gunsmith, A.27, B.AL: MCR 1850 Lafayette Co., Roll 27, AHC. Also listed in LCTR 1848–49, Roll 44, AHC.

Keller, Joseph W.

Gunsmith, A.49, B.VA: MCR 1870 Pulaski Co., (Little Rock), Roll 62, AHC. "Keller, J W gunsmith 206 w Forth." LRCD 1871, 83.

Kennedy, Nathan

Gunsmith, A.59, B.NC: MCR 1850 Franklin Co., Roll 26, AHC. Gunsmith, A.70, B.NC: MCR 1860 Franklin Co., Roll 41, AHC.

Kerns, Louis

Gunsmith, A.55, B.OH: MCR 1870 Crawford Co., Roll 51, AHC.

Knight, David

Gunsmith, A.71, B.SC: MCR 1850 Izard Co., Roll 27, AHC.

Knotts (Knott), James

Gunsmith/Wagonmaker, A.58, B.SC: MCR 1850 Randolph Co., Roll 30, AHC. Also listed in RCTR 1850–57 and 1859, Roll 18, AHC. Secondary Source: "James Knotts . . . was a farmer and mechanic, though he never served a regular apprenticeship at the trade, but picked it up at odd times, having a natural taste for the work. He was quite an extensive manufacturer of all kinds of implements, such as wagons, axes, guns and the like, in connection with which work he also conducted his farm in an admirable manner, being ably assisted by his wife, who was an excellent business manager." *Goodspeed Northeastern Arkansas*, 407.

Kubler, Godfrey

Gunsmith, A.16, B.IL: MCR 1870 Jefferson Co. (Pine Bluff), Roll 52, AHC.

Kubler, John

"Gun and Locksmith, Markham Street between Main & Louisiana Streets, Little Rock, Ark." *ER* 11–23–67.

Kupler, John

Gunsmith, A.51, B.Wortenburg (Wurttemburg): MCR 1870 Hot Spring Co., Roll 54, AHC.

Lane, William H. H.

Gunsmith, A.35, B.TN: MCR 1850 St. Francis Co., Roll 30, AHC. Also listed in SFCTR 1848–49, Roll 27, AHC.

Lange, Morris

Gunsmith, A.40, B.Bavaria: MCR 1860 Jefferson Co., Roll 44, AHC.

Lawler, J. J.

Gunsmith, Little Rock (Confederate) Arsenal Records: 1862–63. Civil War: Misc. Records National Archives, Roll 1.

Ledbetter, B. M.

"Blacksmithing, Gunsmithing, Bell Making . . . has opened a new shop, opposite to the Advocate office, where he will carry on Blacksmithing, Gunsmithing, and Bell making, in all their various branches. He will also make butcher knives of the best quality at the shortest notice. . . ." *AA* 5–29–33.

Lee, S. M.

Gunsmith, Little Rock (Confederate) Arsenal Records: 1862–63. Civil War: Misc. Records National Archives, Roll 1.

Lewis, Jonathan

Gunsmith, A.55, B.MA: MCR 1860 Pulaski Co., Roll 49, AHC. Also listed in PCTR 1856, Roll 2, and 1857, Roll 3, ATR.

Lindsley (Linsley), Darwin

"Lindsley and Moffett, Blacksmiths, Gun-Smiths, Wagon-Makers and Turners, . . . inform the public, that they have purchased the long row of buildings formerly occupied as the Advocate office, on the corner of Scott and Cherry streets, and have converted them into shops. . . . They are prepared for making, repairing and setting-up . . . Steam Engines, and doing all kinds of Steam-boat work. Every description of Blacksmith's work executed at the shortest notice. Rifles, Muskets, Shot-Guns, and Pistols, made and repaired in neatest style. Carriages, Wagons, Carts, etc. made and repaired . . . all kinds of Turning in Iron, Brass, Ivory, Wood, etc. . . . Constant supply of ploughs, axes, and farming utensils of every description . . . kept on hand for sale . . . Horses shod for $2." *AG* 3–6–33. Also listed in Pulaski County tax records 1837–43, Roll 1, ATR.

Linzel, Edward A.

Gunsmith, A.39, B.Prussia: MCR 1870 Pulaski Co., Roll 62, AHC. "Linzel, E. A., gunsmith, 12 e Markham, res. 6 Rector Avenue." LRCD 1871, 87. "A. E. Linzel, 204 E. Markham street, who came to Little Rock and established his business in 1869, having previously carried on a successful business of the same kind in St. Louis for 15 years." *Little Rock: The City of Roses, and Argenta, Ark. with Rambles in the Path of Industrial and Commercial Circles: Descriptive Review* (Memphis: Historical and Descriptive Publishing Co., 1888) 55.

Lowry, Nimrod C.

Gunsmith, A.23, B.TN: MCR 1850 Jefferson Co. (Pine Bluff), Roll 27, AHC. Blacksmith, A.33, B.TN: MCR 1860 Jefferson Co., Roll 44, AHC. Listed JCTR 1855, Roll 119, 1856–58, Roll 120, and 1860–61, Roll 121. Secondary Source: "Lowry was born in Henry Co. TN. June 1823, the son of Isaac and Rebecca (Crosswell) Lowry, natives of North Carolina and Tennessee respectively. Lowry came to Arkansas in 1840 with his family and spent the rest of his life in the state. Lowry began learning the blacksmith trade soon after he came to AR., and served as an apprentice for three

years. In 1844 he opened his own shop and ran it for approximately eight years. He sold his store and clerked until the War Between the States broke out and then he joined the Confederate forces and served as a mechanic until the war's end. After the war he returned to clerking and in 1848 he married Christina Smart." *Goodspeed Central Arkansas,* 187–88.

Lynsley, A. W.

Gunsmith, CSA, Ordnance Dept., Arkadelphia, AR, 1863, Collection of the Carnegie History Center, Tyler, TX.

Martin, Henry T.

Gunsmith, A.25, B.KY: MCR 1870 Phillips Co. (Helena), Roll 60, AHC.

Martin, John

"Blacksmith & Gunsmith, . . . has settled permanently in Little Rock, where he intends carrying on the trades of Blacksmith and Gunsmith. . . . Fire-arms of every description repaired in the neatest style; and Guns and Pistols with common locks, fitted with percussion locks. . . . shop is situated near the banks of the river, within a few rods [a rod is a unit of length of approximately 66 ft.] of the Ferry landing. . . ." *AG* 1–25–32. "John Martin, Blacksmith, Gun-Smith and Founder." *AG* 5–1–33. "Trust Sale." In 1834, to make good an overdue debt, Martin sold his entire estate at an auction. Among his personal effects was an inventory of gun and blacksmith tools. *AG* 9–2–34.

Martin, Rubin

Gunsmith, A.40, B.VA: MCR 1860 Phillips Co. (Helena), Roll 47, AHC. Also listed in PCTR 1850–58, Roll 88, 1859–60 and 1866–67, Roll 89, AHC.

Martin, W. L.

Gunsmith, CSA, Ordnance Dept., Arkadelphia, AR, 1863, Collection of the Carnegie History Center, Tyler, TX.

McBride, Jacob

Gunsmith, A.28, B.AR: MCR 1850 Monroe Co., Roll 28, AHC.

McGrew, John E.

Gunsmith, A.21, B.NC: MCR 1850 Ouachita Co., Roll 28, AHC.

McDaniel, Solomon

Secondary Source: "Blacksmith, and Gunsmith, b.1820 in TN. McDaniel came to Arkansas in 1839 at the age of 19 with his family. He engaged principally in farming but also worked as a blacksmith and gunsmith. McDaniel's farm was located approximately five miles southwest of Jonesboro and consisted of around 170 acres. He married Juliet White on April 6, 1848 and they had 13 children. Solomon McDaniel died in 1899 and was the first person buried in McDaniel cemetary." Harry Lee Williams, *The History of Craighead County, Arkansas,* 1977 reprint of 1930 ed. (Little Rock: Rose Publishing Co.) 439.

McDonald, Milton

Gunsmith, Little Rock (Confederate) Arsenal Records: 1862–63. Civil War: Misc. Records National Archives, Roll 1.

Mendenhall, A. R.

Gunsmith, A.24, B.MI: 1860 Prairie Co., Roll 48, AHC. "Gunsmith, A. R. Mendenhall." *DAC* 6–22–61. Gunsmith, A.34, B.MI: MCR 1870 Prairie Co., Roll 61, AHC. Gunsmith, CSA, Ordnance Dept., Arkadelphia, AR, 1863. Collection of the Carnegie History Center, Tyler, TX.

Meredith, Frederick

Gunsmith, Little Rock (Confederate) Arsenal Records: 1862–63. Civil War: Misc. Records National Archives, Roll 1.

Mescheke, Edmund

Gunsmith, CSA, Ordnance Dept., Arkadelphia, AR, 1863, Collection of the Carnegie History Center, Tyler, TX.

Miliean, F. M.

Gunsmith, Little Rock (Confederate) Arsenal Records: 1862–63. Civil War: Misc. Records National Archives, Roll 1.

Mitchell, Eli

Gunsmith, A.37, B.AR: MCR 1860 Saline Co., Roll 50, AHC.

Moffett, N. H.

[Gunsmith] Listed in Pulaski Co. tax records 1838 and 1840, Roll 1, ATR. *See* Lindsley

Mooney, Isaac (J.)

Blacksmith/Gunsmith, A.35, B.TN: MCR 1870 Sebastian Co., Roll 64, AHC. Mooney, J. Gunsmith and Blacksmith, Sebastian Co., *Products of Industry* 1870, Roll 18, AHC.

Morgan, Chester Cora

Gunsmith, A.40, B.MO: MCR 1860 Crawford Co., Roll 40, AHC.

Mulkey, J. J.

"Watches, Clocks & Guns repaired, Mulkey and Neil, All kinds of guns made & repaired. . . ." *DS* 9–6–55. "Watches, Clocks, Jewelry, Guns Repaired." *SS* 10–20–55. Also listed in Phillips Co. tax records 1850–58, Roll 88, 1859–60 and 1866–67, Roll 89, AHC. *See* Silversmiths

Musgrove, Alvin

Gunsmith, A.29, B.TN: MCR 1870 Sevier Co., Roll 64, AHC. Lived in the household of his father, Anderson Musgrove, who was a cabinet maker.

Neal, Jesse

Gunsmith, A.40, B.TN: MCR 1860 Washington Co., Roll 52, AHC. Also listed in WCTR 1855, Roll 62, AHC.

Neal, John

Gunsmith, A.23, B.AR: MCR 1860 Washington Co., Roll 52, AHC.

Neely, Richard

Gunsmith, A.62, B.SC: MCR 1850 Bradley Co., Roll 25, AHC.

Neil, ?

Gunsmith, A.35, B.IN: MCR 1870 Phillips Co., Roll 60, AHC. *See* both Mulkey and Silversmiths

Nix, W. S.

Gunsmith, Little Rock (Confederate) Arsenal Records: 1862–63. Civil War: Misc. Records National Archives, Roll 1.

Nobles, George

Gunsmith, A.35, B.IN: MCR 1850 Lafayette Co., Roll 27, AHC.

Norris, Amos M.

Gunsmith, Little Rock (Confederate) Arsenal Records: 1862–63. Civil War: Misc. Records National Archives, Roll 1.

Norris, James A.

Gunsmith, A.37, B.TN: MCR 1870 Pope Co., Roll 61, AHC.

O'Steen, Harvey

[Gunsmith]/Ironsmith, A.50, B.NC: MCR 1860 Craighead Co., Roll 40, AHC. Secondary Source: "Harvey O'Steen is of Scotch origin. He was a blacksmith and also a gunsmith, which occupation he followed up to the time of his death, which was in 1865 in Craighead, Co., Arkansas." *Goodspeed Northeastern Arkansas*, 163, 164.

O'Steen, John

Gunsmith, A.25, B.MO: MCR 1870 Greene Co., Roll 54, AHC. Secondary Source: "John O'Steen was partly reared in Panola County, Miss., but moved with his father [Harvey O'Steen] to Craighead Co., Ark., in 1859. He went to work in the shop learning the gunsmith trade of his father, and now has the reputation of being the finest gunsmith in Northeast Arkansas." *Goodspeed Northeastern Arkansas*, 163.

Overton, Jesse

[Gunsmith]/Carpenter, A.38, B.TN: MCR 1850 Clark Co., Roll 25, AHC. Gunsmith, A.45, B.TN: MCR 1860 Clark Co., Roll 39, AHC. Gunsmith A.56, B.TN: MCR 1870 Clark Co. (Arkadelphia), Roll 49, AHC. Gunsmith, A.68, B.TN: MCR 1880 Clark Co. (Arkadelphia), Roll 40, AHC. Also listed in CCTR 1845–46, 1851, 1853–55, 1857, and 1861, Roll 59, and 1874, Roll 59, AHC.

Paynter (Painter), Barney

Gunsmith, A.32, B.VA: MCR 1860 Clark Co. (Arkadelphia), Roll 39, AHC. Also listed in CCTR 1854–55 and 1857–59, Roll 56, and 1866–68, Roll 57, AHC. Gunsmith, CSA, Ordnance Dept., Arkadelphia, AR, 1863, Collection of the Carnegie History Center, Tyler, TX.

Paynter, Henry

Gunsmith, CSA, Ordnance Dept., Arkadelphia, AR, 1863, Collection of the Carnegie History Center, Tyler, TX.

Payne, Preston

Gunsmith, A.48, B.TN: MCR 1860 Poinsett Co., Roll 48, AHC.

Pearson (Pierson), John

"Gunsmith & Cutler." *AG* 8–15–37. "Guns, Pistols, and Rifles." *AG* 7–7–39. Gunsmith, A.39, B.England: MCR 1850 Crawford Co., Roll 25, AHC. Gunmaker, A.53, B.England: MCR 1860 Sebastian Co., Roll 50, AHC. Gunsmith, A.62, B.England: MCR 1870 Sebastian Co., Roll 64, AHC. Pulaski Co. tax records 1839–40, Roll 1, ATR. Also listed in Crawford Co. tax records 1839–40 and 1845–50, Roll 22, AHC. Sebastian Co. tax records 1851–52, 1855–57, and 1859, Roll 44, and 1866 and 1875, Roll 46, AHC. Secondary Source: Pearson is best known for his association with American weapons pioneer Samuel Colt. Listed several times in *Goodspeed Northwestern Arkansas* (1853–1878).

Pearson, John, Jr.

Gunsmith, A.16, B.AR: MCR 1860 Sebastian Co., Roll 50, AHC. Son of John Pearson, Sr.

Pearson (Pierson), William

Gunsmith, A.17, B.AR: MCR 1870 Sebastian Co., Roll 64, AHC. Son of John Pearson, Sr.

Pepper, Oliver

Gunsmith, A.39, B.Canada: MCR 1850 Jefferson Co., Roll 27, AHC. Also listed in JCTR 1846–48, Roll 115, and 1855, Roll 116, AHC.

Perkins, Milton B.

Gunsmith, A.47, B.KY: MCR 1850 Lafayette Co., Roll 27, AHC. Also listed in LCTR 1845–49, Roll 44, AHC.

Person, William Davis

[Gunsmith] Secondary Source: "William D. Person was born in Shelby Co., Alabama in 1818. The Person family are of Irish descent. He moved with his wife to what is now Lincoln Co. in 1852. Mr. Person devoted much of his time to his plantation, and through many years worked hard as a blacksmith and a gunner." *Goodspeed Southern Arkansas,* 992.

Peyatt, James

Gunsmith, A.27, B.AR: MCR 1860 Washington Co., Roll 52, AHC.

Pike, James

Gunsmith, A.47, B.TN: MCR 1850 Desha Co., Roll 26, AHC. Also listed in the 1860 Desha Co. Census and DCTR 1845–50 and 1854–55, Roll 67, 1856–62, Roll 68, and 1863–65, Roll 69, AHC.

Pollard, John A.

Gunsmith, A.76, B.VA: MCR 1860 Craighead Co., Roll 40, AHC.

Powell, Jacob F.

"Lock and Gun Smith . . . Main St. Van Buren . . . has removed to the shop lately occupied by E. Craig, where he will be . . . repairing guns in superior style . . . He hopes by strictest attention to his business and by working for fair prices to merit a liberal share of patronage. All kinds of produce taken in payment for work." *AI* 3–11–43.

Prather, J.

Gunsmith, CSA, Ordnance Dept., Arkadelphia, AR, 1863, Collection of the Carnegie History Center, Tyler, TX.

Pryor, G. W.

Gunsmith, CSA, Ordnance Dept., Arkadelphia, AR, 1863, Collection of the Carnegie History Center, Tyler, TX.

Qualls, Thomas

Gunsmith, A.44, B.SC: MCR 1850 Benton Co., Roll 25, AHC. Also listed in BCTR 1843–46, 1851–54, 1856, 1859, and 1861, Roll 39, AHC.

Rankin, James D.

Gunsmith apprentice, A.22, B.MS: MCR 1870 Drew Co., Roll 52, AHC. Resided in the household of William Rankin.

Rankin, William

Gunsmith, A.30, B.MS: MCR 1870 Drew Co., Roll 52, AHC.

Reavis, William

Gunsmith, CSA, Ordnance Dept., Arkadelphia, AR, 1863, Collection of the Carnegie History Center, Tyler, TX.

Ribald, Jacob

Gunsmith, Little Rock (Confederate) Arsenal Records: 1862–63. Civil War: Misc. Records National Archives, Roll 1.

Richison, Hiram G.

Gunsmith, A.25, B.PA: MCR 1860 Pulaski Co., Roll 49, AHC.

Richison, T. J.

Gunsmith, A.50, B.PA: MCR 1860 Pulaski Co., Roll 49, AHC. Also listed in PCTR 1855–56, Roll 1, and 1857–58, Roll 2, ATR.

Ridley, H. A.

Gunsmith, Little Rock (Confederate) Arsenal Records: 1862–63. Civil War: Misc. Records National Archives, Roll 1.

Roach, Benjamin

Gunsmith, A.26, B.TN: MCR 1860 Randolph Co., Roll 49, AHC. Also listed in RCTR 1860–67, Roll 19, AHC.

Roberson, James H.

Gunsmith, A.27, B.AR: MCR 1870 Pike Co., Roll 60, AHC.

Robertson, William O.

Gunsmith, A.24, B.AL: MCR 1870 Pulaski Co., Roll 62, AHC.

Rosengreen, C. G.

Gunsmith, A.29, B.Sweden: MCR 1860 Dallas Co., Roll 40, AHC. Gunsmith, CSA, Ordnance Dept., Arkadelphia, AR, 1863, Collection of the Carnegie History Center, Tyler, TX.

Rudolph, A. E.

Gunsmith, A.33, B.TN: MCR 1860 White Co., Roll 52, AHC. Also listed in WCTR 1857–61, Roll 53, 1859–62(pt.), Roll 54, and 1862(pt.)–68, Roll 55, AHC. AN A. E. Rudolph is also listed as a gunsmith working in Canon City, Colorado, 1875–80. A. Merwyn Carey, *American Firearms Makers* (New York: Thomas Y. Crowell Co., 1953) 107.

Rudolph, G. F. L.

Gunsmith, A.45, B.TN: MCR 1870 Washington Co., Roll 66, AHC. ". . . Rudolph remained in Fayetteville until his death in 1916. He was one of Washington County's oldest and most respected citizens." *AS* 3–30–1916.

Rudulph (Rudolph), W. W.

Gunsmith, A.26, B.TN: MCR 1860 Izard Co., Roll 43, AHC. Also listed in ICTR 1861, Roll 16, AHC.

Rupe, Samuel

Gunsmith, A.22, B.OH: MCR 1860 Sebastian Co., Roll 50, AHC. Gunsmith, A.33, B.OH: MCR 1870 Sebastian Co., Roll 64, AHC.

Schuman, Adolph

[Gunsmith] Secondary Source: *Goodspeed Southern Arkansas*, 547. *See* C. A. Schuman

Schuman, C. A.

[Gunsmith] Secondary Source: "C. A. Schuman, a substantial planter of Rocky Comfort, was born in Dresen, Germany on August 19, 1848 . . . he finally selected Jacksonport, Ark., as the scene of his labors, and here he established his residence. He purchased a gun shop, and sent for his brother, Adolph, who was a gun smith by trade, and they conducted this business very successfully until in November, 1873, when their place was visited by fire and entirely destroyed. Then they started for Paris, Tex., but on their way stopped at Rocky Comfort, and being pleased with the location, they opened a gun shop . . . they soon added a line of general merchandise and were conducting these interest, when on May 24, 1876, their store was entered by burglars, and in defending his property the brother, Adolph, was killed . . . Mr. Schuman commenced business on his own responsiblity, dealing in general merchandise, and carried on this business very successfully until 1883, when he gave it up to engage in farming." *Goodspeed Southern Arkansas*, 546, 547.

Scott, Peter S.

Gunsmith, A.56, B.KY: MCR 1870 Benton Co., Roll 49, AHC.

Schooler, B. H.

Gunsmith, CSA, Ordnance Dept., Arkadelphia, AR, 1863, Collection of the Carnegie History Center, Tyler, TX.

Shaw, S. B.

Gunsmith, A.28, B.PA: MCR 1860 Phillips Co., Roll 47, AHC.

Shaw, Samuel M.

Gunsmith, A.23, B.TN: MCR 1850 Fulton Co., Roll 26, AHC. Gunsmith, A.32, B.TN: MCR 1860 Fulton Co., Roll 41, AHC.

Shaw, T. J.

"Blacksmith and Gunsmith Business. The subscribers respectfully inform the citizens of Pulaski County, that they have taken the shop recently occupied by Mr. Benjamin Kellogg, where they intend on carrying on the Blacksmith and Gunsmith business, in all its various branches, and will execute all orders on reasonable terms, for cash only. T. J. Shaw, John Sherleville." *AG* 3–26–28.

Sherleville (Sharlaville), John

See T. J. Shaw and A. Carnahan

Shoars, John

Gunsmith, A.40, B.IL: MCR 1860 Greene Co., Roll 42, AHC.

Siebert, Christian

"Gunmaker." *SS* 12–25–41. A Christian Siebert is also listed as a maker of fine percussion match and target rifles and hunting rifles in Columbus, Ohio, 1851–72. Carey, 113.

Simmons, Thomas

Gunsmith, A.45, B.MD: 1850 Chicot Co., Roll 25, AHC.

Smart, Felecit (Falicit)

Gunsmith, A.23 (22), B.TN: MCR 1850 Jefferson Co. (Pine Buff), Roll 27, AHC.

Smith, C. G.

Gunsmith, A.36, B.SC: MCR 1860 Randolph Co., Roll 49, AHC.

Smith, James C.

Gunsmith, A.43, B.NC: MCR 1860 Poinsett Co., Roll 48, AHC. Secondary Source: J. C. Smith was a gunsmith by trade. He settled in Poinsett Co., Ark., and made Bolivar his home until the county seat was changed to Harrisburg, and he moved there in 1857. In 1863 he moved to Jonesboro and worked there until his death in 1885. *Goodspeed Northeastern Arkansas,* 609.

Smith, Joseph R.

Gunsmith, A.24, B.AR: MCR 1860 St. Francis Co., Roll 49, AHC.

Smith, Uriah

Blacksmith, A.56, B.PA: MCR 1850 Lawrence Co., Roll 27, AHC. Gunsmith, A.68, B.PA: MCR 1860 Lawrence Co., Roll 45, AHC.

Smith, W. N.

"Gunsmith Shop." *AI* 4–16–58. Gunsmith, A.27, B.MO: MCR 1860 Crawford Co., Roll 27, AHC. Also listed in CCTR 1854–68, Roll 23, AHC.

Snively, William M.

"Black & Gun-Smithing. . . . The subscribers still continue the above business. . . , in Helena, where they are prepared to execute every description of work. . . , prices to suit the times. William Snively, John Wilson." *SS* 4–28–49. "Black & Gun Smith." *SS* 4–28–49. Secondary Source: A William Snively is also listed as a gunsmith in Flint Falls, Ohio, 1854–65. Carey, 115. *See* John Hudson

Spangler, Daniel

Gunsmith, A.18, B.Unk: MCR 1850 Crawford Co., Roll 25, AHC. "Gunsmithing." *FSH* 3–21–51. Resided in the household of John Pearson, who was also a gunsmith.

Steel, B. B.

Gunsmith, A.50, B.KY: MCR 1860 Jefferson Co., Roll 44, AHC. Also listed in JCTR 1856–60, Roll 120, 1859–60, Roll 121, and 1861–65, Roll 122, AHC.

Stephens, G. W.

Gunsmith, A.58, B.KY: MCR 1860 Ouachita Co., Roll 47, AHC.

Stout, Jasper N.

Gunsmith, A.33, B.MS: MCR 1870 Sevier Co., Roll 64, AHC. Also listed SCTR, 1867–72, Roll 49, AHC.

Strickland, W. M.

Gunsmith, A.39, B.GA: MCR 1850 Greene Co., Roll 26, AHC. Also listed in GCTR 1851, Roll 22, AHC.

Teaff, Nimrod

Gunsmith & Blacksmith, A.47, B.PA: MCR 1850 Marion Co., Roll 28, AHC. Secondary Source: A Nimrod Teaff is listed as a gunsmith in Stubenville, Ohio, 1861–91. Carey, 222.

Thompson, William

Gunsmith, B.MS: White Co., *Products of Industry*, 1870, Roll 8, AHC.

Thurmin (Thurmine), William

Gunsmith, A.55, B.KY: MCR 1860 Washington Co., Roll 52, AHC.

Titsworth, John

[Gunsmith] Farmer, A.59, B.TN: MCR 1850 Madison Co., Roll 27, AHC.

Tompkins, D. E.

Gunsmith, Little Rock (Confederate) Arsenal Records: 1862–63. Civil War: Misc. Records National Archives, Roll 1.

Towery, Isaac

Secondary Source: Towery was a gunsmith and blacksmith who was born in 1818 in Alabama. He came to Miller County, Arkansas, with the earliest settlers and married Jane Johnson. He also served as a drum major in the Mexican War. Soon after he married, Towery moved his family to Bowie Co., Texas, where remained until his death in 1850. *Goodspeed Southern Arkansas*, 206.

Triffs, David

Gunsmith, A.23, B.MI: MCR 1860 Jackson Co. (Jacksonport), Roll 44, AHC.

Trigg, James M.

"Gunsmithing, James M. Trigg & Co. In all its various branches, neatly and expeditiously executed. . . . Little Rock." *AA* 7–4–34.

Trumpler, George

Gunsmith, A.14, B.GA: MCR 1870 Pulaski Co., Roll 62, AHC. The son of and apprentice to Jacob F. Trumpler.

Trumpler, Jacob F.

"Gun and Lock Smiths." *AG* 11–24–60. Also listed in Pulaski Co. tax records 1861–62, Roll 3, ATR. "J. Trumpler, Gun and Lock Smith." *AP* 5–16–63. "Gunsmith Shop." 3–24–66. "J. F. Trumpler, Gun and Lock Smith." *DC* 4–22–67. Advertisement in *ER* 11–29–67. "Trumpler and Dabbs, Gunsmiths." *AG* 9–17–68. Editorial in *AG* 10–9–70. Gunsmith, A.40, B.SC: MCR 1870 Pulaski Co., Roll 62, AHC. "Trumpler, J. F., gunsmith 108 Main, res 102 w Twelfth." LRCD 1871, 111. "Partnership Notice, . . . J. F. Trumpler & Son, Importers, Manufacturers and Dealers in Fire Arms and Sporting Material. No. 407 1/2 South Main Street." *Commercial and Statistical Review of Little Rock, Arkansas, 1883*, 110. "J. F. Trumpler Fire Arms Co. 405 Main Street." *Descriptive Review*, 135. "Death of Jacob F. Trumpler." *AG* 11–25–99. A Jacob F. Trumpler is also listed as a general gunsmith and dealer in Little Rock, Arkansas, in 1855. Carey, 123.

Walker, W. W.

Gunsmith, Little Rock (Confederate) Arsenal Records: 1862–63. Civil War: Misc. Records National Archives, Roll 1.

Walters, Elbert

Gunsmith, A.42, B.KY: MCR 1860 Hot Spring Co., Roll 42, AHC.

Wave, William W.

Gunsmith, A.38, B.LA: MCR 1870 Columbia Co., Roll 50, AHC.

Webester, William

Gunsmith, A.36, B.AL: MCR 1860 Mississippi Co., Roll 46, AHC.

Wells, A. P.

Gunsmith, A.38, B.AL: MCR 1860 Phillips Co., Roll 47, AHC.

Wheeler, W. Cicero

"Notes from William D. Faulkner (1973)—Cicero Wheeler was a blacksmith who lived with Daniel Faulkner. Wheeler made Daniel a Kentucky rifle over 100 years ago." Students of Umpire High School, *The Unfinished Story of North Howard County* (Umpire, Arkansas: North Howard County Youth Group, 1982) 259.

White, George

Gunsmith, CSA, Ordnance Dept., Arkadelphia, AR, 1863, Collection of the Carnegie History Center, Tyler, TX.

Whitford, D. J.

Gunsmith, CSA, Ordnance Dept., Arkadelphia, AR, 1863, Collection of the Carnegie History Center, Tyler, TX.

Williams, Henry

Gunsmith, A.20, B.KY: MCR 1850 Mississippi Co., Roll 28, AHC.

Wilson, James C.

Gunsmith, A.55, B.NC: MCR 1860 Lafayette Co., Roll 46, AHC. Also listed in LCTR 1854, 1856, and 1858, Roll 44, and 1860–62 and 1865, Roll 45, AHC.

Wilson, John C.

See Snively

Worschowitz, Edmond

Gunsmith, A.26, B.Hungary: MCR 1860 Yell Co., Roll 52, AHC.

Worschowitz, Lewis

Gunsmith, A.20, B.Hungary: MCR 1860 Yell Co., Roll 52, AHC. Gunsmith, CSA, Ordnance Dept., Arkadelphia, AR, 1863, Collection of the Carnegie History Center, Tyler, TX.

Wright, John

Gunsmith, A.66. B.England: MCR 1860 Sebastian Co., Roll 50, AHC. Gunsmith, A.75, B.England: MCR 1870, Sebastian Co., Roll 64, AHC.

Wurderlick, W.

Gunsmith, CSA, Ordnance Dept., Arkadelphia, AR, 1863, Collection of the Carnegie History Center, Tyler, TX.

Yearwood, John

Gunsmith & Blacksmith, A.50, B.TN: MCR 1870 Greene Co., Roll 54, AHC.

Yoest, John B.

Gunsmith, A.23, B.Germany: MCR 1860 Pulaski Co., Roll 49, AHC.

Yoest, John P.

Gunsmith, A.59, B.Germany: MCR 1860 Pulaski Co., Roll 49, AHC. "Black, Lock, and Gun Smithing, The undersigned, late Armorer at the U.S. Arsenal, would respectfully inform the public that he is now prepared to do all kinds of Black and Locksmith work—also repairing of guns etc. His shop is on Rock St. next to the residence of A. George." *AG* 7–30–52. "Card, Informing public that undersigned has taken as partner, Mr. Charles Becker, in blacksmithing business. He will continue his former business of locksmithing & general jobber. Shop corner of Rock & Markham St." *AG* 7–21–60. Yoest died in 1863, at his home in Little Rock. *AP* 1–8–63.

An Illustrated Catalog of Arkansas Firearms

G—1a.   Caplock Pistol, rifled, approximately .45 caliber. Incuse stamped on top flat of barrel "A. R. MENDENHALL/DES ARC. ARK."

LOA (Length overall): 10¾", LOB (length of barrel): 7". C. 1860. *Courtesy of Dixie Gun Works.*

A. R. Mendenhall of Des Arc (Prairie County) was an active gunsmith throughout the period c. 1860–78 (year of death). During the Civil War, Mendenhall served as a gunsmith both at the Confederate arsenal in Arkadelphia (Clark County), and later in Tyler, Texas, when the arsenal was moved there late in 1863.

Mendenhall began advertising his services in the *Des Arc Citizen* (Prairie County) in March, 1861, when he declared himself to be a "Manufacturer of Rifles, Shot guns, & Pistols." *DAC* 6–22–61. This ad ran for several months until Mendenhall became a gunsmith for the Confederate government.

All known pistols by Mendenhall were stamped in identical fashion "A. R. MENDENHALL (centered over) DES ARC. ARK."

The full walnut stock is fitted with an unmarked, cast-iron, back-action lock and hammer, a form which, although known in the late second quarter of the century, did not come into popular use until after c.1850. The pistol is fitted with an iron trigger and guard and an iron breech-plug tang strap which curves down the back of the pistol's grip, terminating in a curve beneath the butt. Ovoid steel escutcheons inlaid into sides of the forestock frame the wedge pin which secures the barrel to the stock. The swelled forestock or "nose" is trimmed by a single silver band and capped by a wide triangular-shaped silver plate.

The cross-hatching or "checking" on the pistol's grip gained widespread popularity during the percussion era (c.1830–70).

The rectangular, wedge-like, "v" slotted front sight is fitted into a slot which was filed out tangential to the barrel length near the muzzle, while the iron rear sight has been welded to the top of the breech plug at its juncture with the tang strap.

G–1b.   Opposite view of the A. R. Mendenhall pistol shown in the previous figure.

Note the inlaid silver ornament just behind the lockplate screw, on which is engraved in script "C to H 1836." A. R. Mendenhall was born in 1836, ruling

out any possibility that he could have made the gun at that early date. The date and initials remain a mystery. This particular inlaid ornament was used on other known Mendenhall handguns dating from c. 1860.

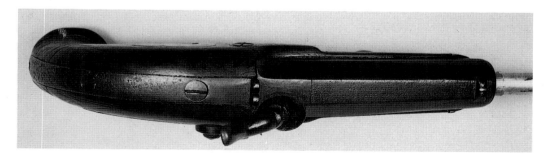

G–1c.   Detail of the top flat of the barrel showing incuse-stamped mark of A. R. Mendenhall situated just forward of the breech plug.

Note that the top half of the barrel has been flattened on three sides, beginning at the breech and

continuing along the top flat to the muzzle. The angular side flats taper out at the wide pin where at this point the barrel appears (from a side view) to be rounded again.

G–2a.   Caplock Pistol, rifled, approximately .50 caliber. Incuse stamped on top barrel flat "A. R. MENDENHALL."

LOA: 7⅝", LOB: 4⅞". C.1860. *Courtesy of Dixie Gun Works.*

The cast-iron back-action lock makes up more than half of the length of the pistol. Iron mounts include the wedge and inlaid escutcheon trigger and trigger guard. Silver mounts include a nosecap and three cloverleaf inlays just behind the tang strap and on the butt of the grip and an inlaid sideplate ornament similar in form to that shown on the Mendenhall pistol in figure 1b. Again, the upper half of the barrel has been flattened along three sides most of the length of the short barrel while the underside remains round. Almost the entire grip of the walnut stock has been decorated in a checkered or crosshatched pattern.

G–2b.   Detail of the opposite side of the A. R. Mendenhall pistol shown in figure G–2a. Silver inlaid mounts may be seen both in front and in back of the single lock-plate screw. The elongated, scrolled shape of the inlay behind the screw is somewhat similar, but with rounded projections, to inlay mount dated "1836" on the pistol in figure G–1b.

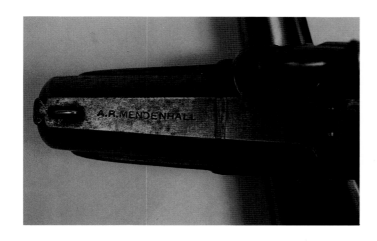

G–2c. Detail of the "A. R. MENDENHALL" stamp along the top flat of the pistol in the previous figure.

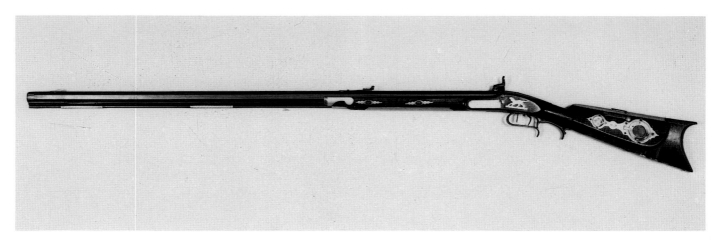

G–3a., b. Caplock Rifle (both sides shown), half-stock, octagonal barrel, approximately .40 caliber. Engraved on a silver-inlaid plate in place of the side plate (opposite the lock plate): "Made by W. O. Robertson/Pulaski County Arkansas. 1870" (figure G–3b).

LOA: 52½", LOB: 38½". *From the collection of the Arkansas Territorial Restoration.*

Robertson's profuse display of inlaid ornament in combination with a novel assortment of hinged and spring-triggered accessories compartments reflects the gunsmith's whimsical ingenuity and skill as a multi-talented artisan.

Almost sparingly, Robertson has used cast brass mounts only for the trigger guard, butt plate, and toe plate, which is more than just a toe plate (figure G–3f). The ramrod, lock and hammer, set, triggers, and back sights are of cast iron. Silver abounds in its use for the ramrod pipes or thimbles, nosecap and wedge pin escutcheons, along with the combination capbox and cloth patch dispenser (figure G–3e).

The length of the top edge of the butt of the stock is referred to as the "comb." A sheath or band of silver covers the length of this rifle's comb to its juncture with the brass butt plate. Beneath, the butt has been partially hollowed to hold the percussion caps with which to ignite the weapon's powder charge. In the center of the silver band, on top of the comb, is an iron, spring-loaded lever which when depressed dispenses a fresh cap into the hand of the shooter (see figure G–3e).

A thin, sheet-silver patch is nailed to the stock directly beneath the hammer and may have been intended to protect and reinforce the wood near the lockplate which was constantly subject to damage from the pounding action of the hammer, ignition sparks, and rifle barrel recoil in firing the weapon. There is an elongated solid bar or piece of silver atop the lock plate immediately in front of the nipple and bolster. This bar was another innovation which was developed for percussion during the mid-nineteenth century. Some locks were made with the bar in place

and were referred to as side-bar locks. Robertson's lock plate, however, is a standard side lock to which he added a silver bar. Side (action) locks and back (action) locks were the two most common ignition systems designed for nineteenth-century percussion weapons.

As already stated, Robertson signed this piece on a silver inlaid plate. In tandem with his signature plate, he added another silver inlay of a hunting dog in profile (figure G–3c).

The set or double triggers found on Robertson's fanciful sporting rifle were commonly used on both flintlock and percussion nonmilitary rifles during part of the eighteenth and most of the nineteenth centuries. To operate, the shooter first pulls upon the rear trigger until it "clicks" meaning the trigger is "set" (thus the term), after which he cocks the rifle hammer. Then, he has only to apply the slightest pressure to the front trigger to cause the gun to fire. An easy pull of the trigger, resulting in less jerking of the weapon, was most necessary when extreme accuracy was required.

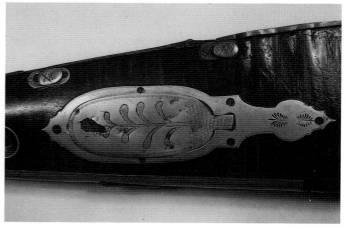

G–3c.   Detail of the inlaid silver plate inscribed "Made by W. O. Robertson/Pulaski County Ark./ 1870," and the ornamental inlay of a hunting dog.

G–3d.   Detail of the Robertson rifle's inlaid compartment for rifle balls. Line and bright-cut engraving have been employed to create the stylized tree and grass, along with abstract foliate designs on the tang or side plate of the patchbox frame. The beveled edges of the patchbox frame have been bright-cut engraved with a silversmith's roulette wheel. The ovoid engraved silver buttons above the patch box serve as release mechanisms to open the various compartments.

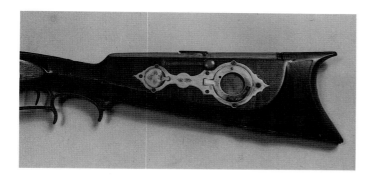

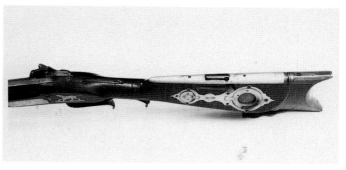

G–3e. Detail of the opposite side of the rifle butt showing combination cap (smaller hinged lid area) and patchbox compartments. The round opening or gate in the patchbox lid was designed so that the sportsman could withdraw, from the wrapped spool of cloth patches inside the box, a continuous tape of patches. Notice the curved-spring steel blade (used to cut short lengths of patches) fixed with a screw to the patchbox lid.

Above the patchbox, a thin three-inch-long strip of brass that is screwed into place at one end and held by a round, dome-shaped button at the other serves as a spring release for the combination screwdriver and nipple wrench recessed into the inlaid silver comb.

G–3g. A close-up view of the long sheath of silver covering most of the comb of the butt. Beneath the silver is located a cavity to hold the combination screwdriver and nipple-wrench tool shown here in its recessed position in the center of the comb.

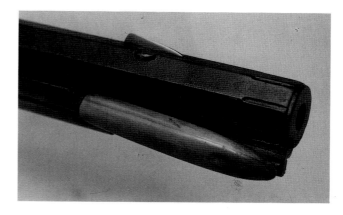

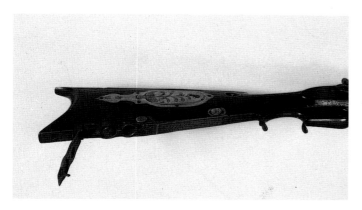

G–3f. A close-up view of the underside of the butt of the stock showing the dual compartments which appear to be an exceptional extension of the toe plate. The open compartment at the back reveals an open metal cup for the highly viscous lubricant used. A second round cavity holds a brass bottle with slotted lid, which still contains oil for the care of the rifle. There is also a hole in which to carry a "gunworm" which attaches to the ramrod for withdrawing misfired balls and cleaning the bore of the barrel. The front compartment (shown closed) with its matching foliate engraved lid was probably used to hold prepared ball and powder charges wrapped in paper. The compartments are opened by pushing the ovoid silver buttons on the side of the stock.

G–3h. Detailed view of the muzzle and its blade-type sight along with a built-in bone-handle patch knife, used to trim off the excess cloth once the patch and ball are seated on the muzzle. Notice too the concave cuts along the angles of the rifle flats and the molded edge around the end of the muzzle. These indicate that Robertson designed his rifle to be fitted with a false muzzle. The false muzzle was an accessory that looked like a small separate section of the barrel of the same caliber, and which was fitted precisely upon the muzzle of the rifle to aid in accurately starting the patched bullet down the barrel without deforming it. It also prevented the muzzle of the gun from being damaged by the countless blows of metal ramrods.

G–4a. Caplock rifle, half stock, octagonal barrel, .36 caliber. Incuse die stamped on top flat of barrel "J. OVERTON/ARKADELPHIA, ARK."

LOA: 56⅜", LOB: 39¾". *From the collection of the Arkansas Territorial Restoration.*

Half-stock rifles, such as this one made by Jesse Overton (active c. 1845–80) of Arkadelphia, with its somewhat shorter barrel and attenuated stock, became the dominant form for sporting shoulder arms made and used along the nineteenth-century frontier of the Trans-Mississippi South. The longer full wooden stocks and barrels of the flint and early percussion Pennsylvania or Kentucky style rifles were not as por-

table as the lighter and more maneuverable half stock. This was an especially important consideration for an American population on the move westward into the frontier of which Arkansas was a much noted part. With the exception of a silver blade-type front sight, the fittings of Overton's rifle are of cast iron and brass, a combination found typically on the many documented examples of his work. The cast-iron mounts consist of a cast lock plate and rear "buckhorn" style sight, along with sheet brass, and include the nosecap, wedge pin, escutcheons, trigger guard, and butt plate. The maple stock has been repaired at the checkering on the wrist.

G–4b. Detail view of the "J. OVERTON/ARKADEL-PHIA, ARK." stamp on the top flat of his rifle shown in the previous figure.

G–5. Caplock pistol, rifled, octagonal barrel, walnut stock, approximately .50 caliber. Unmarked, but at-

tributed to Jesse Overton, Arkadelphia, Clark County. C. 1860.

LOA: 13″, LOB: 9″.

Function rather than form predominates the design criteria for this pistol which is believed to have been made by Arkadelphia gunsmith Jesse Overton.

The pistol's full octagonal barrel and "G. Goulcher" stamped side action lock were originally made for use on half stock sporting rifles. Brass ramrod pipes flank a typically Southern lead nosecap.

G–6a. Caplock rifle, half stock, octagonal barrel, set triggers, .38 caliber. Stamped on top barrel flat "B. PAYNTER/ARKADELPHIA, ARK." On the top flat between the front sight and the muzzle, the incuse stamp of "S. REYNOLDS & CO." appears, while the iron side-action lock plate contains within a cast banner only a partially legible name "JOCEL——," the unidentifiable name of the lockmaker.

LOA: 47″, LOB: 31″. C. 1860. *From the collection of the Arkansas Territorial Restoration.*

Barney Paynter (active 1854–69), like his Arkadelphia counterpart Jesse Overton, did order some of the parts for his half-stock rifles pre-made. In the case of this particular rifle Paynter ordered a lock plate and hammer in a finished, ready-to-use state. Unfortunately, the full name of the lock plate maker (JOCEL——) has been obliterated by rust pitting. The additional barrel mark of S. Reynolds & Co. is the name of an unknown firm who possibly sold the barrel to Paynter completely rifled and in a finished state. Paynter may have had only to add the sights and possibly the breech plug. But, whether or not he actually rifled the barrel in his shop is impossible to ascertain. The use of a wide variety of premade parts became commonplace for many nineteenth-century makers. In fact, an entire weapon, in parts, could be ordered from one of any number of large gun parts manufacturers. At the sign of the "White Gun" in Arkadelphia, Jesse Overton, Paynter's friend and competitor, announced to the public in July, 1861, the various kinds of ready-made parts he had available to make and repair guns "just received from New York . . . Barrels, triggers, locks, wipers [gun worm], bullet moulds, tubes [nipples], [and] cylinders." (*Ouachita Conference Journal*, 4 July 1861)

The rifle mounts or fittings consist in part of a silver-inlaid wedge escutcheon, blade-style front sight, and a replaced pewter nosecap. While the buttplate, trigger guard, rear "buckhorn" type sight, lock and hammer, and the ramrod thimble are of iron.

This is one of the few documented Arkansas rifles to have a unique kind of breech known as the patent breech, one in which the breech plug and nipple seat or bolster are cast in one piece with an upturned hook at the back. This hook is engaged in a slot in a separate tang (attached to the stock). In half-stock rifles, only the wedge pins have to be pulled, so that the barrel lifts easily out, for convenience in repairing or transporting a piece.

G–6b. Detail of the "B. PAYNTER/ARKADELPHIA, ARK." incuse stamp mark.

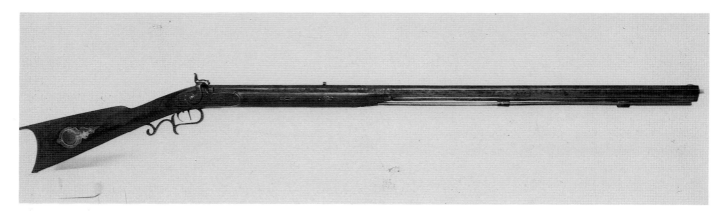

G–7a.   Caplock rifle, half stock, octagonal barrel, set triggers, .40 caliber. Incuse stamped on top barrel flat "G. F. L. RUDOLPH/FAYETTEVILLE, ARK."

LOA: 53⅝", LOB: 37½". C. 1870. *Loan collection of the Arkansas Territorial Restoration, courtesy of David Perdue.*

Except for the silver, front, leaf-type sight (*i.e.,* thimbles, trigger guard, butt plate, patchbox, etc.), all of the mounts for Rudolph's walnut-stock rifle are of iron.

The true origin of the half-stock form has been debated by firearms collectors and historians for many years. Many feel its prototype was the English smooth-bore fowler (shotgun) or the much less common half-stock sporting rifle of the eighteenth century. Others have noted that the short-bodied, large caliber German "jaeger" style rifles in combination with English forms may have contributed to its ultimate development as a classic American firearm, which dominated sporting rifle production following the introduction of the caplock or percussion ignition system during the second quarter of the nineteenth century.

G–7b.   Detail view of the "G. F. L. RUDOLPH/FAYETTEVILLE, ARK." incuse stamp on the top flat of the barrel.

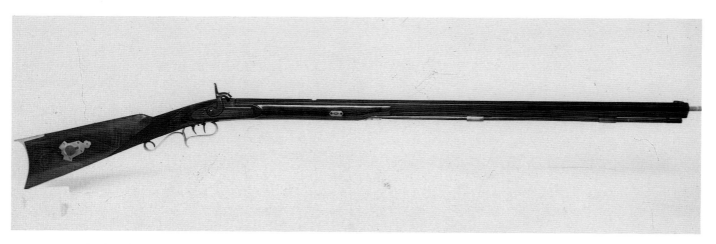

G–8a.   Caplock rifle, half stock, octagonal barrel, .38 caliber. Incuse stamped on top barrel flat "J. F. TRUMPLER/L. ROCK, ARK."

LOA: 50¼", LOB: 34". C.1870. *From the loan collection of the Arkansas Territorial Restoration.*

Bright silver and brass mounts applied to a richly grained walnut stock are the focal points for this pristine example of the work of Little Rock gunsmith J. F. Trumpler (active c. 1855–1899).

The barrel has been made with a patent, or false, breech as they were referred to in the nineteenth century.

G–8b.   Close-up view of the stamp of "J. F. TRUMP-LER/L. ROCK, ARK."

G–8c.   Detail of the patchbox on the J. F. Trumpler rifle.

G–9a.   Caplock rifle, full stock, octagonal barrel, set triggers, .43 caliber. Faintly incuse stamp "J. Draper" on top barrel flat. The side option lock plate has an intaglio cast "H" pierced by an arrow, which may be the mark of Ohio gunsmith and parts maker, J. B. Hixson, who used this mark on rifles c. 1856–60.

LOA: 57", LOB: 41 ¼". C.1850–1856. *From the collection of the Arkansas Territorial Restoration.*

Arkansas County gunsmith J. Draper (active c. 1850–56) has only one known rifle to his credit. In the midst of a plethora of half-stock sporting rifles, Draper's is one of very few documented full-stock examples to have surfaced.

Draper's walnut stock is mounted with brass nose-cap, ramrod thimbles, trigger guard, butt plate, and patchbox. The rear "buckhorn" style sight is of iron, and its front counterpart is a silver blade mounted in brass dovetailed wedge.

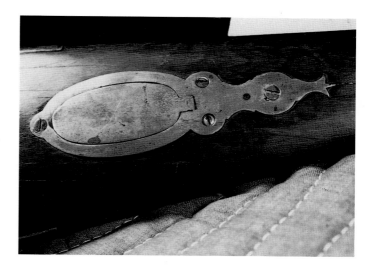

G–9b.   Detail view of the Draper rifle patchbox.

G–10.

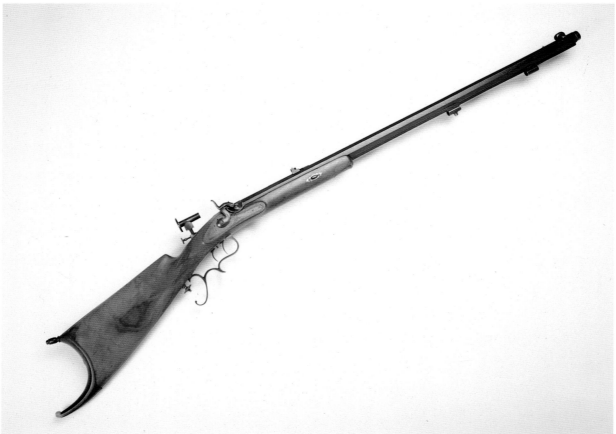

G–11.

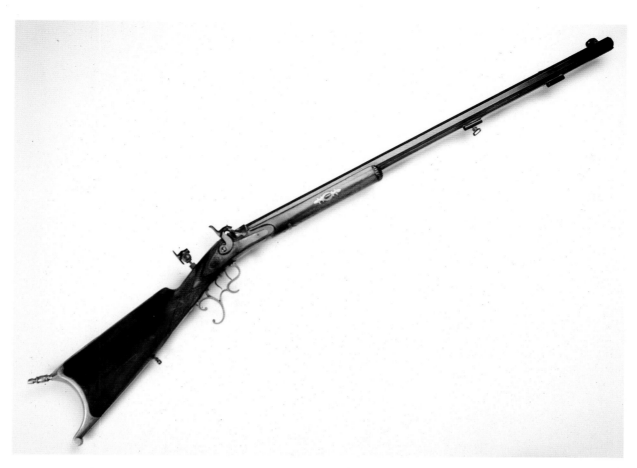

G-12.

G-10, 11, 12.   Three Caplock "Schuetzen" rifles, half stock, octagonal barrels, set triggers, walnut stocks, approximately .40 caliber. Incuse die stamped on top flat of barrels "A. E. LINZEL LITTLE ROCK." C. 1870–1880. *A. R. Condray Firearms Collection, Arkansas Territorial Restoration.*

(10) LOA: 53", LOB: 32¾"; (11) LOA: 52⁵⁄₁₆", LOB: 33⅜"; (12) LOA: 51⅞", LOB: 32".

A. E. Linzel was for three decades a popular member of the Little Rock gunsmithing fraternity. A native of Germany, he arrived in Little Rock in 1869 and immediately began cornering his share of local sporting arms patronage. These are the only known Schuetzen (German for marksman's) rifles made by Linzel. The "Schuetzen" style target rifle evolved in Germany from the short heavy barreled "jaeger" hunting rifles of the eighteenth and early nineteenth centuries. Linzel's example directly mirrors the Americanization of the Schuetzen idea, onto what is basically a nine-

teenth-century American half-stock sporting rifle. Obviously, there are notable exceptions. For example, the accuracy of Linzel's rifles is aided by the vertically mounted "vernier" rear or tang sight, which is located immediately behind the hammer. The highly scrolled trigger guard plays second-fiddle to an exaggerated "pronghorn" style butt plate, which fits tightly to the shoulder of the competition marksman. Also, all of Linzel's Schuetzen rifle muzzles are fitted for false muzzle attachment, which protected the end of the barrel from the pounding it received during each loading of a new round.

Edward Linzel was a champion shot with the local German community's Schuetzenverein (target-shooting club). In 1877 and again in 1879 Linzel was awarded prizes for his marksmanship in competitions with the largely German staffed shooting club from Fort Smith. *AG 6–7–79.*

G–13a.   Caplock rifle, full-stock, octagonal barrel, .33 caliber. Stamped on top barrel flat "J. PEARSON/ FT. SMITH"

LOA: 58", LOB: 42½". *Courtesy of the J. M. Davis Gun Museum, Claremore, OK.*

No discussion of the technological development of nineteenth-century American firearms would be thorough without mention of the Fort Smith gunsmith John Pearson (1803–1883). John Pearson was, between 1834–36, the chief gunsmith and prototype maker for Samuel Colt, one of the most successful firearms inventors on the American scene during the nineteenth century. Pearson may be credited with assisting Colt in the creation of the designs for the world's first successful revolving cylinder rifles and pistols. In addition, Pearson was almost entirely responsible for their construction, by hand, in his small, often poorly lit and heated, Baltimore, Maryland, shop. However, as is often the case, disputes between the two men over finances brought the teamwork to an abrupt end in the summer of 1836. In fact, Colt was consistently delinquent in paying Pearson's salary and keeping him supplied with proper parts or the funds to purchase needed materials.

G–13b.   Detail of Pearson mark.

John Pearson left Baltimore, and by August, 1837, he was in Little Rock, where he would remain less than two years, moving further west to Van Buren (then Ft. Smith), Arkansas, where he became well liked and widely known for his artisan skills and his relationship with Samuel Colt.

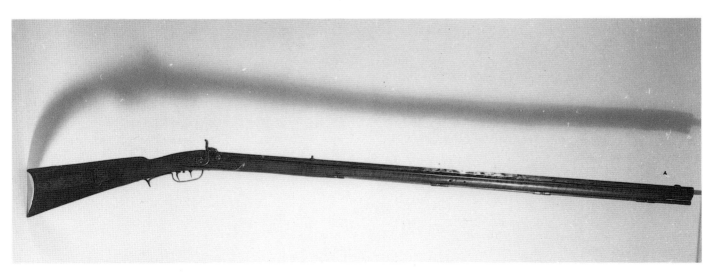

G–14.   Caplock rifle, full stock, octagonal barrel, curly maple, approximately .45 caliber. Maker unknown. Supposedly made and used in the "Pigeon Roost" community of North Pulaski County. C. 1860.

LOA: 58", LOB: 41⅞". *A. R. Condray Firearms Collection, Arkansas Territorial Restoration.*

This rifle was purchased almost forty years ago by Mr. Charles Elias, one of Arkansas's best-known collectors and authorities on Arkansas gunsmiths. According to Mr. Elias, the elderly man from whom he acquired the rifle said it had been made by a member of his family who lived in the "Pigeon Roost" community north of the city of Little Rock. The name of the maker has long since been forgotten, but thankfully this fine example of craftsmanship has survived.

The curly maple stock has the distinctive cross-grain banding known as "tiger stripe," a popular wood grain with many nineteenth-century gunsmiths. Except for the rear ramrod pipe and butt plate which are of brass, the rifle is furnished with iron mounts. The long rectangular patchbox is lightly "scratch" engraved with stylized foliate motifs.

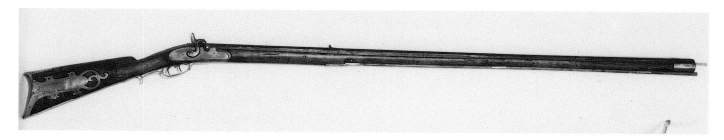

G–15a. Caplock Rifle, full stock, octagonal barrel, set triggers, .38 caliber. Stamped in script on top barrel flat "A. Carnahan." Possibly Arkansas, c. 1840–50.

LOA: 62½", LOB: 46". *Courtesy of the J. M. Davis Gun Museum, Claremore, Oklahoma.*

An A. Carnahan advertised in the *Arkansas Gazette* as a gunsmith in Little Rock for several months beginning on December 19, 1826. Carnahan's notice informed patrons that he had "taken the shop . . . lately occupied by Mr. John Sharlaville [another Little Rock gunsmith], where he proposes carrying on the Gun-Smith business, in all its various branches." Carnahan drops suddenly out of sight during the early summer of 1827.

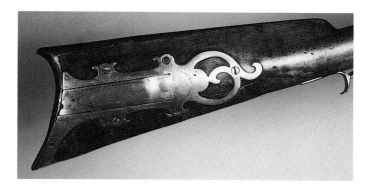

G–15b. Detail of the Carnahan rifle's ornately scrolled brass patchbox.

Glossary

APPLIQUÉ—To sew a piece of fabric onto a larger cloth ground.

BACK ACTION LOCK—A side lock used on late percussion guns. The mainspring is behind the hammer and is attached to the rear of the tumbler with a link. It was not popularly used until well into the 1850s.

BALUSTER—A vase-turned, columnar element usually used to support a stair rail; also called a bannister. Adapted as motif in furniture design.

BAR OR SIDE ACTION LOCK—In firearms, the more usual side lock type, in which the mainspring is in front of the hammer.

BARREL PIN—In firearms, a round metal pin which fastens barrel to the fore end, more usually on earlier fullstock arms.

BASE—The lowest structural element of a case piece, directly above the feet; in two-part pieces, also the lowest part of the upper section.

BEADED MOLDING—Fine, convex, half-round molding, or molding resembling a string of beads.

BEADING—A series of adjacent beadlike balls used as a decorative molding.

BISQUE—Unglazed ceramic ware that is not to be glazed but is hard-fired and vitreous.

BLANKET ROLL—Turned upper stretchers or rails between the foot posts of a bedstead are often referred to as blanket rolls. Traditionally, blankets, quilts, and/or coverlets were rolled onto these rails when not in use.

BLOCKFRONT—A furniture front which is divided vertically into alternating convex and concave panels. The center panel is recessed between the two advancing side panels.

BODKIN—A large blunt needle with a large eye used to draw thread or tape through a fabric which is being embroidered. Also referred to as a stiletto.

BRACKET FOOT—In furniture, a shaped foot that extends from a mitered corner to the front and side, may be plain scrolled or molded.

BREECH—The back of a gun barrel. In modern arms, the portion of the barrel into which the cartridge is inserted.

BREECH PLUG—A metal plug screwed into the breech end of a muzzle-loading gun.

BRIGHT CUT—A process of engraving by which silver is cut in small gouges at an angle and removed by a tool (burin) having a sharp beveled cutting edge and two cutting points (front one to cut, the other to burnish), so that the engraving is cut in narrow channels and of varying depths with variously slanting sides, thus giving a faceted and bright or sparkling appearance.

BRODERIE PERSE—An eighteenth-century appliqué technique in which motifs such as flowers and animals are cut out of chintz or another printed fabric and sewn onto a foundation, usually white, and then quilted and embroidered.

BUTT JOINT—In furniture, the simplest and cheapest type of joint. It will not take very much strain. One piece of wood is set perpendicular and at right angles to another piece of wood (the pieces butting up against each other). The two pieces are then glued, nailed, or screwed together.

BUTT PLATE—A protective metal plate on the rear of a buttstock.

CABRIOLE LEG—An S-shaped leg, with outcurving knee and incurving ankle, based on the shape of an animal's leg.

CANTED—An angled or oblique element.

CAPLOCK—Another term for a percussion firearm.

CARTOUCHE—In furniture and silver, a panel, tablet, or scroll created by embossing or engraving a border and whose plane or convex reserve thus formed can be ornamented with a monogram, inscription, or date.

CASTOR OR CASTER—A small wheel attached to the feet or base of furniture by a cuplike device or a long rod that fits into a hole; used to facilitate moving furniture.

CAVETTO OR COVED MOLDING—A quarter-circle, concave, downward curve from the ceiling to the woodwork of a wall, or in a similar position on a piece of furniture.

CHAMFERED—Having a flat area made by cutting away a corner or edge formed by two surfaces at right angles to each other.

COCK BEADING—A small convex or half-round projecting molding used around the edges of drawers.

COIN SILVER—Silver composed of roughly 900/1000 parts of fine or pure silver to 100/1000 parts of alloy.

COMB—The upper edge of a rifle or shotgun stock upon which the cheek rests.

CONE—Nineteenth-century term for a percussion nipple.

CORNICE—The horizontal molding or group of moldings at the top of a piece of furniture.

CROSS BANDING—A narrow band or wood veneer used as a frame or border design on a panel, door, tabletop, etc. The grain of the veneer wood of the band is at right angles to the grain of the panel itself.

CUT NAILED—Secured with early square machine-made nails popularly used in Arkansas furniture between c. 1830 and 1890.

CYMA CURVED—A continuous double curve, roughly S shaped, with one part convex and the other concave.

DADO JOINT—A joining technique used for supporting shelving or drawer bottoms in vertical units. It is used to stiffen or reinforce the vertical member. The edge of the vertical piece of wood fits into a groove in the horizontal piece.

DENTIL MOLDING—Classical motif consisting of a series of small rectangular blocks projecting like teeth.

DIAPER—A kind of dimity; a linen fabric (sometimes with cotton) woven with lines crossing to form diamonds with the spaces variously filled with lines, a dot, or a leaf.

DIE STAMP—A method of impressing a design on silver by forcing it with pressure into the configuration of a carved die.

DOVETAILING—A roughly triangular tenon or mortise used in the joining of two elements; so named because its shape resembles the tail of a dove.

DOWEL—A wooden rod or pin used to join two pieces of wood—usually machine cut.

DROP—Rounded extension of the stem of a spoon used as a reinforcement on the back of the bowl.

DUST BOARD—A thin wood separator between drawers to keep out the dust that might enter through the open spaces.

EARTHENWARE—Slightly porous pottery that is fired at a relatively low temperature.

ESCUTCHEON—A decorative plate that covers a keyhole—usually brass, but also bone, wood, and other metals. Or, a plate of metal to protect wood from abrasion or other injury, such as barrel pin escutcheons.

FALL FRONT—The upright lid or writing flap of a desk or secretary, which is hinged at the bottom to fall forward and form a writing surface. It is usually supported by brackets beneath the opened front.

FALSE MUZZLE—The accessory which is placed upon the muzzle of the finer target rifles during loading, particularly bench rifles, to aid in accurately starting the bullet without deforming it, and to prevent damage to the rifling at the muzzle.

FIDDLE THREAD PATTERN—A pattern used for the handle of much of American flatware during the first half of the nineteenth century. The shape somewhat resembles a fiddle or violin and often has a single or double line of incised threading running unbroken around the edges of the handle.

FIELDED PANEL—A board shaped to a tapered edge set into a frame with a raised center section, field, or panel.

FINIAL—Turned or carved ornament, ranging from simple egg to urn, shaped atop a stile or other vertical member.

FLANGE—A rim or rib for strength, guiding, or attachment to another object.

FOLIATE—To ornament with foliage; a decoration resembling a leaf.

FRIEZE—A flat band directly beneath a cornice, often decorated.

FRIZZEN—The metal arm of a flintlock mechanism, against which flint strikes to create sparks in the flashpan.

FRIZZEN SPRING—The outside spring which controls the frizzen's position.

GILDED—Decorated with a thin application of gold or gold paint.

GLAZE—A mixture of water, clay, and various metallic oxides or alkalies that is applied to a clay body before firing; during firing the glaze vitrifies, producing a water resistant surface.

GRAVER—A chisel used for engraving. *See* Bright Cut

GUN WORM—A corkscrew lip for a rod, to hold a cleaning patch, or to remove one stuck in the bore.

HOLLOWARE—Vessels such as bowls, cups, or vases usually of pottery, glass, or metal.

INCISED—Cut into a surface.

INCUSE—A mark formed by stamping or punching.

INLAY—A technique in which a design is cut out of a surface and then filled in with other materials cut to fit the opening.

JAPANNING—An eighteenth-century finishing process. Furniture and metalwork were enameled with colored shellac.

KENTUCKY RIFLE—*See* Pennsylvania Rifle

LANDS—In firearms, raised spiral ridges between grooves of rifling.

LAP-JOINT—Two pieces of wood grooved and fitted so that they make a flush X arrangement when they are put together.

LIP—The edge of a hollow vessel or cavity.

LUG—A semicircular handle that is attached to the side of a ceramic body, usually found on stoneware or redware.

MITERED—Cut at an angle.

MOCKERNUT—A type of hickory tree.

MOLDING—A continuous decorative strip, projecting or incised with profile usually convex, concave, or a combination of both.

MORTISE AND TENON CONSTRUCTION—Technique for joining two pieces of wood; the mortise is a cavity, usually rectangular, and the tenon, a protruding end shaped to fit the cavity.

NIPPLE—A small metal tube extending through the breech of a percussion weapon through which the flame is passed from the percussion cap to fire the main powder charge.

NOSE CAP—The metal cap on the front end of a muzzle loader.

OCTAGONAL BARREL—Seen on many of the earlier muzzle loaders, this is a conventional eight-sided barrel.

OGEE MOLDING—Molding characterized by a single or double cyma curve.

PANEL—A thin rectangular or square board held in place by grooves cut into the inner sides of stiles and rails.

PEG—A wooden pin, dowel, or spike used for fastening or joining furniture, wood panels, floors, etc. It is used in place of a nail. A joint which is accomplished with pegs is referred to as a "doweled joint."

PATCHBOX—An indentation with a cover in the buttstock of a muzzle-loading rifle used to carry patches or other small items.

PATENT BREECH—One in which the breech plug and nipple seat are cast in one block. This has an upturned hook on its rear which engages a slot in a separate upper tang. In a half-stock rifle, for example, one barrel lifts right out, for convenience in cleaning or transporting. Also referred to as French breech.

PENNSYLVANIA RIFLE—A generic American term referring to long, full-stocked flint or percussion lock hunting rifles. These rifles were developed from the short, full-stocked "jaeger" style of sporting rifle brought from Germany to America during the eighteenth century. Firearms historians generally agree that the classic "Pennsylvania" or "Kentucky" rifle reached its full maturity in the hands of the skilled gunsmiths of Pennsylvania during the second half of the eighteenth century.

PERCUSSION CAP—A small, metal, explosive-filled cap which is placed over the nipple of a percussion shoulder arm. As the cap is struck by the hammer, it explodes and sends a flame through the nipple to the main powder charge.

PIGEONHOLE—An open-fronted storage unit in the well of a desk or secretary.

PILASTER—Column projecting about one quarter of its ordinary depth from a surface; used as an ornamental detail on furniture.

PIN—A slender dowel or whittled peg that secures or holds together a morise-and-tenon joint.

PLINTH—A block at the base of a column; used as an ornamental detail on furniture.

RABBET—A continuous rectangular groove cut along the edge of a piece of wood or metal. It is usually cut to receive the edge of another piece of wood or metal.

RAMROD—Also called a rammer, a wood or metal rod used to impel the wad and bullet down the barrel of a muzzle-loading firearm. In the modern sense a cleaning rod is sometimes called a ramrod.

RED HAW—Hawthorn tree.

REEDING—A series of parallel, carved, rounded, and closely set ridges or beads

RESERVE—A cartouche that is formed on a piece of silver either by engraving, repose work, or casting. The blank area thus formed can be embellished with a coat of arms, scene, monogram, or presentation inscription.

RIFLING—A system of spiral grooves inside the bore of a gun.

ROULETTE—A wheeled tool which forms repeat line patterns known as roulettework.

RUNNER—A guide strip under the center or at the sides of a drawer. A term also used to describe the curved member of a rocking chair.

SCALLOPED—An edge or border that has been cut into segments of a circle. An outer perimeter which resembles the wavy contour of a scallop shell.

SCROLL—A spiral form resembling a partially rolled scroll of paper, often in a C or S curve, as on the skirt of a piece of furniture.

SERPENTINE—Contour of a wavy surface, particularly one having a convex center flanked by concave end.

SET TRIGGER—Although a few single set triggers are known to exist, most of them are comprised of two triggers. In these there is a delicate spring, which gives the sear a sharp impact when the set trigger is released. The relayed action through the triggers permits a more sensitive release than if only one trigger is used.

SHOULDERS—The nineteenth-century addition to the stem at the base of the bowl of a spoon.

SKIRT—The bottom independent element of a piece of furniture, plain or shaped, running between two vertical members; also called an apron.

SLAT—A horizontal bar connecting the upright members of a chair back.

SLIP—A suspension of ceramic materials in water.

SPANDREL—In furniture, a triangular piece spanning the space between a vertical support and a horizontal piece or rail.

SPINDLE—A long, slender rod often used in chair backs, usually turned.

SPLINT—Thin oak or hickory straps interlaced to form a chair seat; Popular since the seventeenth century.

STEP-BACKED—Refers to cupboards with a shallow work top between the upper and lower sections of the piece. This makes the upper section appear to be "stepped" or set back.

STILE—Vertical structural member usually trimming the back of a chair or sofa; often called a post if turned.

STONEWARE—A high-fired ceramic body of great density and hardness that is partially vitrified; it ranges in color from a blue-gray or off white to a dark brown; often covered with a salt glaze.

STRETCHER—The turned rods or flat boards used to reinforce furniture legs.

SWAGING—Putting conical projectiles through a precise die under pressure, to bring them to an exact diameter and shape.

TENON—*See* Mortise and Tenon Construction

THIMBLES OR PIPES—Short tubes fixed to the underside of a rifle barrel to support the ramrod.

TOE-PLATE—A metal band on the bottom edge of a gun stock adjoining the butt plate.

TONGUE-AND-GROOVE CONSTRUCTION—Construction technique for joining two pieces of wood. The groove is a long narrow channel, the tongue, a projection shaped to fit the channel.

TORUS—In furniture, a convex, semicircular molding.

TRIGGER GUARD—The metal bow which guards against accidental trippings of a trigger.

TRIGGER PLATE—A metal strap set into the bottom of the stock to control lateral motion of the trigger. Sometimes trigger assembly is attached to it, sometimes not.

TURNBUCKLE—A small rectangular wooden section attached to cupboard doors to keep them closed.

TURNING—Shaping wood by applying a chisel bit while rotating it on a lathe. Common turned shapes are: ball, box, cup, ring, spiral, sausage, rope, spool, trumpet, vase, and combinations of these.

TWILL—A basic weave, and also the fabric produced by this weave. It has a distinct diagonal line owing to the weft yarn passing over one or more warp yarns, then under two or more.

VERNIER OR TANG SIGHT—A precise, adjustable, rear aperture sight, developed in the mid-1800s. Often applied to "Schuetzen" rifles like those made by A. E. Linzel.

WARP—Stationary thread that runs the length of a loom and through which the horizontal weft passes.

WEDGE OR BARREL KEY—A flat key which holds barrel and fore-end together on many half-stock rifles and shotguns.

WEFT—Threads that are passed horizontally over and under the warp.

WHITEWORK—A textile decorated with white thread on a white ground.

WRIST—The small of a gun stock, grasped by the firing hand.

Key to Abbreviations

A.—Age
AHA—Arkansas Historical Association
AHC—Arkansas History Commission
AHQ—Arkansas Historical Quarterly
AIC—Arkansas Industrial Census
Ark.—Arkansas
A.T.—Arkansas Territory
ATR—Arkansas Territorial Restoration
bds or bldgs—buildings
Benj.—Benjamin
B.—Place of Birth
Bro.—Brother
CDV—carte-de-visite
Co.—company
Co.—county
C.—circa
CSA—Confederate States of America
c. workman—cabinet workman
DC—District of Columbia
Dept.—department
do.—ditto
Ed.—Editor
e—east
etc. or &—et cetera
ft.—feet
Ft.—Fort
LRCD—Little Rock City Directory
Lt.—Lieutenant
Maj.—Major
MCR—Manuscript Census Records

Misc.—miscellaneous
N.B.—nota bene—note well
NYC—New York City
NYCD—New York City Directory
(pt.)—part of a series or category
res.—residence
Sec.—secretary
SMC—Small manuscript records
TR or CTR—tax records or county tax records
UALR—University of Arkansas at Little Rock
UDC—United Daughters of the Confederacy
U.S.—United States
Vol.—Volume

Newspapers

BATESVILLE

DS   *Democratic Sentinel*
NAT *North Arkansas Times*
BG   *Batesville Guard*
BE   *Batesville Eagle*
BN   *Batesville News*
IB   *Independent Balance*

BENTON

DD *Daily Democrat*

CAMDEN

OH   *Ouachita Herald*
OCJ   *Ouachita Conference Journal*

CHARLOTTESVILLE, Va.

CC   *Charlottesville Chronicle*

CINCINNATI, Ohio

CR   *Cincinnati Republican*

DES ARC

DAC   *Des Arc Citizen*

FAYETTEVILLE

A or *FA*   *Arkansian*
SWI   *Southwest Independent*
AS   *Arkansas Sentinel*

FORDYCE

FWN   *Fordyce Weekly News*

FORT SMITH

FSH   *Fort Smith Herald*
FSNE   *Fort Smith New Era*
FSTWB   *Fort Smith Tri-Weekly Bulletin*
FST   *Fort Smith Times*
FSWNE   *Fort Smith Weekly New Era*
AP   *Arkansas Patriot*
SA   *Southwest American*

HELENA

SS   *Southern Shield*
HWC   *Helena Weekly Clarion*
ASD   *Arkansas State Democrat*
HDS   *Helena Democrat Star*
HC   *Helena Constitutional*

HOT SPRINGS

HSC   *Hot Springs Courier*

JACKSONPORT

JE   *Jacksonport Era*

LITTLE ROCK

ATA   *Arkansas Times and Advocate*
AG   *Arkansas Gazette* or
              Arkansas State Gazette
UU   *Unconstitutional Union*
AB   *Arkansas Banner*
TD   *True Democrat*
AA   *Arkansas Advocate*
DP   *Daily Pantograph*
AD   *Arkansas Democrat*
AM   *Arkansas Methodist*
ER   *Evening Republican*
DC   *Democrat Conservative*
ND   *National Democrat*

VAN BUREN

VBP   *Van Buren Press*
WFW   *Western Frontier Whig*
AI   *Arkansas Intelligencer*

WASHINGTON

WT   *Washington Telegraph*

OTHER NEWSPAPERS

Commercial Advertiser   New York, N.Y.
Spirit of the Times   New York, N.Y.
Picayune   New Orleans, La.

Acknowledgments

This book is based on a research project of the Arkansas Territorial Restoration, which is an agency of the Department of Arkansas Heritage.

Thanks are extended to three special sponsors who assisted in the final preparation of the manuscript: Edwin B. Cromwell, Fred K. Darragh, and William Poston Bowen.

Special thanks are also extended to the many people who worked on this project: for editorial assistance, Jim Lester and Wendy Taylor; for photography, Sandy McGuire, Cindy Manchilov, John Watson, Jan Young, John McDermott, Rebecca Lambdin, Royce Grimes, Louise Terzia, Alan Abbot, Brett Lile, Larry Hacker, Dub Allen, and Lana Crews Nunley; for advice and consultation, Brad Rauchenburg, Brock Jobe, Townsend Wolfe, Pat Butler, and Beaumont Newhall; for research, Jackie Daugherty, Lana Crews Nunley, Anne Crow, Judy Sevier, Allison Meador, Linda Gentry, Meredith Rooney, Susan Newlin, Sandra Sapp Bennett, Julie Hale Head, Roberta Muelling, Jan Young, Lynn Eubanks, Russell Baker, Mignon Wilson, Sandy Jones, Sandra Todaro, Priscilla McArthur, Cinda Baldwin, and Carol Phelps; for typing, Becky Christy, Linda Ulrich, and Patty McSwain.

Simple thanks seem not to suffice as an adequate expression of our gratitude to the following individuals who have helped with this project, often allowing us to invade their homes with cameras, lights, and a seemingly inexhaustible battery of questions pertaining to the history of their cherished heirlooms:

Mike Angelo, John Banks, Mrs. Willard David Beckenholdt, Fannie Bell, Jeff Blakely, John Bragg, Dr. Roberta Brown, Sarah Brown, Mrs. Ben Bullock, Mrs. Leo Bullock, Mr. and Mrs. Bunn Bell, Bud Burkett, David Byrd, Helen Byrd, James Morgan Byrd, Mrs. Joseph Carner, Juliet Speers Cartinhour, Jeff Cato, Victoria Churchill, Mrs. James Cobb, Mr. and Mrs. Sterling Cockrill, Mrs. Ryan Condray, Jeanne Conte, Curtis Cox, Mr. and Mrs. Fadjo Cravens, Jr., Katherine Cravens, Florence Toney Cummins, Michael J. Dabrishus, Marsha Daniels, Mae Lancaster Dobbins, Betty Dunn, Ann Early, James Reid Eison, Henry Lynn Eldridge, Charles Elias, Charlenne Etter, Jane and Daniel Fagg, Mrs. Norman Faust, Rogers Faust, Mrs. James Ford, Mary Glover Formsy, Mary L. Clingan Gray, Mrs. Henry Gregory, Louise Hall, Mr. and Mrs. Roger Hannan, Glen Harris, Fred Harrison, Sallye B. Herring, Marilyn Hicks, Mary Frances Hill, Mrs. Henry Hollenberg, Dula Wood Hook, Mrs. Vernon A. Hook, Dollie Jackson, Mrs. Ewing Jackson, Frances Hook Jernigan, Donald R. Jones, Mrs. Louis Kiene, Elmer and Virginia Kirk, Mr. and Mrs. William A. Laing, Greer Lile, Brett Lile, Bill Long, Bo Long, Glenn Mallett, Mrs. Louis Mashburn, Henri Mason, Skip Mayorga, Zula McCauley, Leonard J. McCown, Mrs. L. C. McCrary III, Chapman McGaughy, Judge and Mrs. J. P. McGaughy, Ray McKnight, Greg McMahon, Charles McNair, Mr. and Mrs. Charles W. McNair, Mr. and Mrs. Henry Means, Ginger and Steve Meeks, Minnie and Patty Moffat, Dr. Walter Moffat, Carl Moneyhon, Don Montgomery, Mrs. Edwin Victor Moore, Maurguarite Moses, Susan Condray Norton, Nona V. Ogle, Mariane Williams Olson, Mr. and Mrs. Carl Olsson, Dr. and Mrs. Ralph Patterson, David Perdue, Frances Philip, Susie Pryor, Mary Ratcliffe, Mrs. James D. Reed, Peyton and Caty Rice, Elizabeth Richardson, Hebe Riddick, Walter Riddick, Bobby Roberts, Virginia Rhode, F. Hampton Roy, Mrs. Joe Saxon, Fannelle Shepperson, Sam Shepperson, Laurie D. Sikes, Mr. and Mrs. V. A. Silliman, Pat Simpson, Burt Smith,

Mrs. Griffin Smith, Mrs. Kendall H. Smith, Mr. and Mrs. Stephen Harrow Smith, Peg Newton Smith, Florence Spore, Elizabeth Stanley, Mrs. Stephen Stanley, Elsie and Howard Stebbins, Mr. and Mrs. Harold Stockton, Mr. and Mrs. Robert Stroud, Averell Woodruff Reynolds Tate, Donya Thompson, Dodie Thompson, Sue Thweatt, Mr. and Mrs. George Toney, Lucy Marion Reaves Utterback, David Vance, Bufford C. Van Winkle, Anita and Garrett Vogel, Mrs. Frank E. Wait, Mrs. George Walsh, Maxine Washbourne, Kyle Washbourne, Beverly Watkins, Lucille Westbrook, Parker Westbrook, Ruth Wharton, Fran Vinsonhaler Williams, Mary Sue Williams, Mrs. E. C. Witham, Becky & Charles Witsell, Willie Woodruff, Kathy Worthen, Mary Fletcher Worthen, Rachel Louisa Worthen, Elizabeth Wright, and the volunteers, commission, and staff of the Arkansas Territorial Restoration.

The authors would also like to express their thanks to the following collecting institutions that have been most courteous in allowing this project to include specific examples of Arkansas-related decorative, mechanical, and fine arts:

The Academy of Natural Sciences, Philadelphia, Penn.; the American Antiquarian Society, Worcester, Mass.; the Arkansas Arts Center/Arkansas Commemorative Commission; the Arkansas History Commission; the Arkansas Museum of Science and History; the Arkansas Quilters Guild; the Chidester House, Camden, Ark.; the City of Rogers Historical Museum; the Dixie Gun Works; the Drew County Museum, Monticello, Ark.; First Methodist Church, Washington, Ark.; Henderson State University Museum; Historic New Orleans Collection; Hot Spring County Museum, Malvern, Ark.; Illinois State Genealogical Society; the J. M. Davis Gun Museum, Claremore, Okla.; the Jefferson County Clerk's Office; the Jefferson County Court House; Joslyn Art Museum; Marian Koogler McNay Art Museum, San Antonio, Tex.; Metropolitan Museum of Art Photography Library, New York; National Archives; New York Historical Society; New York Public Library (Phelps Stokes Collection); Oklahoma Historical Society, Manuscripts and Archives Division; Old Washington State Park; Pennsylvania Academy of the Fine Arts, Philadelphia, Penn.; Pioneer Washington Foundation; Prairie Grove Battlefield Park; Siloam Springs Museum; Smithsonian Institution; Southwest Arkansas Regional Archives, Texas Tech University Museum, Lubbock, Tex.; University of Arkansas Museum and Special Collections, Fayetteville; and the University of Arkansas at Little Rock Archives (Heiskell Collection).

Bibliography

Introduction

This project's research into the available primary documentary evidence has been both thorough and voluminous. Our investigation sought to uncover the names of as many of the artists and artisans who worked in Arkansas in or before 1870 as possible.

The two most obvious primary resources were newspapers and the United States Census returns.

Page by page, the research staff examined every extant newspaper printed in Arkansas through 1870. Those newspapers are listed in the bibliography, and they include papers that are on microfilm primarily and can be found in the collection of the Arkansas History Commission, the archives of the University of Arkansas, Fayetteville, Special Collections, and the Southwest Arkansas Regional Archives, Washington, Hempstead County. In addition, the Arkansas Territorial Restoration's collection of newspapers includes original bound volumes of territorial period issues of the *Arkansas Gazette* (Little Rock) and the *Arkansas Advocate* (Little Rock).

Our investigation of the surviving newspapers was followed by a page after page review of the United States Census returns from all Arkansas counties for 1830, 1840, 1850, 1860, and 1870. This included an examination of the schedules for both population and the products of industry for 1840, 1850, 1860, and 1870 (nomenclature varies for each census). The returns were available on microfilm at the Arkansas History Commission. The 1850 manuscript census schedules for products of industry included not only the names of individual artisan shop owners, but also asked other questions, such as how much and what

kind of raw materials were used, as well as the number and types of finished products and their values. Motives of power and the number of workmen in each shop were requisitely enumerated. In all, fourteen different questions relating to the operation of each shop were given to individual enumerators to ask. This procedure persisted with both the 1860 and 1870 returns. Many artisans were not enumerated since one of the basic criteria was that to be included, a shop had to annually produce goods worth five hundred dollars or more.

The census records provided the project the names of hundreds of artisans and artists, with some information on their birthplaces, ages, places of residence, family makeup, and indices of wealth. The newspapers contained a multitude of advertisements placed by many of the documented cabinetworkmen and silver and gunsmiths. Editorials would later inform the reader about the quality of workmanship a person exhibited. The frequency or longevity of ads makes it possible, at times, to figure out how long a person worked or was active in a particular locale.

All extant microfilmed county tax assessment and payment records at the Arkansas History Commission for each artisan working prior to 1871 were inspected once again page-by-page to help determine both their economic place and length of stay in a particular locale. This was especially valuable for those who were not active in Arkansas during a census year, but had been identified in an advertisement or secondary source, such as the numerous county histories prepared by the Goodspeed Company during the last two decades of the last century. In addition, county probate records in the form of estate inventories taken at the time of an individual's death to ascertain the worth of the estate's real and personal property were surveyed for each documented artist and artisan, along with extant will and marriage records. These too were available for most counties on microfilm, at the Arkansas History Commission, and in original form for Hempstead County, at the Southwest Arkansas Regional Archives. Unfortunately, some county records have been lost through courthouse fires, and the probate records from many have yet to be indexed.

The rule-of-thumb procedure for tracking an individual was to take our earliest reference for a person, usually from a census or newspaper ad, and inspect the tax records for that year and five years before and after. The results can be illuminating. Bailey Chandler was a Pulaski County cabinetmaker, at least according to the 1850 census, but a review of the county tax records for that year and five years before and after 1850 did not reveal that he was a resident of the county at anytime during the period. It was not uncommon for a person to be overlooked on the census, but county tax assessors were not nearly as lax when it came to filling county coffers. Chandler was likely here but a short time, since no other tax or census references were located.

This was an especially valuable technique in following the whereabouts of individuals who were documented only in one census year or in an advertisement, or were in the state only between decennial years.

An additional survey was added to the individual manuscript collections of the Arkansas History Commission, the University of Arkansas, Fayetteville, Special Collections, the University of Arkansas, Little Rock, Archives, and the Southwest Arkansas Regional Archives, Washington, Hempstead County. Literally hundreds of letters were read along with many well-kept and informative diaries and business papers relating to the domestic and business lives of Arkansans from ca. 1820 through 1870. Again, each repository has a complete itemized index to their collections. The specific references to any particular items retrieved and used in this work are contained in the individual notes. The same holds true for the citations for specific United States census, county tax, deed, and probate records. Reference is often made to the biographical appendices.

Due to the limitations of staff, funding, and ultimately time, much that could have been said about the economic and social mobility of the artist and artisan classes could not be included.

Census Records

Census of Population 1810

> Note: The 1800, 1810, 1820, and 1830 Censuses of Population are all found on the same reel in the microform collection.

1800–1810–1820–1830

Reel 1

1810.1   Treasury Department
Aggregate amount of each description of persons within the United States of America, and the Territories thereof, agreeably to actual enumeration made according to law, in the year 1810.
(Washington, 1811) 90 numb. leaves.

[1810.2]   Census Office. 3rd Census, 1810
Third census of the United States. Illinois Territory. 1810. (Presumably covering the county, population, 7,275). n.p., n.d. (2), 59.

Census of Population 1820

> Note: The 1800, 1810, 1820, and 1830 Censuses of Population are all found on the same reel in the microform collection.

1800–1810–1820–1830

Reel 1

1820.1   Census Office. 4th Census, 1820
Census for 1820. Published by authority of an act of Congress, under the direction of the Secretary of State. Washington, Printed by Gales & Seaton, 1821. 80 leaves.

Census of Population 1830

Note: The 1800, 1810, 1820, and 1830 Censuses of Population are all found on the same reel in the microform collection.

1800–1810–1820–1830

Reel 1

1830.1
Census Office. 5th Census, 1830
Fifth census; or, enumeration of the inhabitants of the United States, 1830. To which is prefixed, a schedule of the whole number of persons within the several districts of the United States, taken according to the acts of 1790, 1810, 1820. Washington, Duff Green, 1832. 27, vi, 163 p.

[1830.1–1]
Census Office. 5th Census, 1830
Fifth census; or, enumeration of the inhabitants of the United States, as corrected at the Department of State. 1830. Published by authority of an act of Congress, under the direction of the secretary of State. Washington, Duff Green, 1832. 165 p.

1830.2
Census Office. 5th Census, 1830
Abstract of the fifth census of the United States, 1830. Washington, F. P. Blair, 1832. 43 p.

1830.3
Census Office, 5th Census, 1830
Abstract of the returns of the fifth census, showing the number of free people, the number of slaves, the federal or representative number; and the aggregate of each county of each state of the United States. Prepared from the corrected returns of the Secretary of State to Congress. (Doc. no. 263. 22nd Cong., 1st sess. House). Washington, Duff Green, 1832. 51 p. [Contains discrepancies in the results compared to those returned in 1830.1 and 1830.2]

1830.4
Department of State
Statistical view of the population of the United States from 1790 to 1830, inclusive. (Doc. no. 505. 23rd Cong., 1st sess. Senate). Washington, Duff Green, 1835. 216 p.

Census of Manufactures 1840

Note: The 1810, 1820, and 1840 Census of Manufactures are all found on the same reel in the microform collection.

1810–1820–1840

Reel M–1

M 1840.1
Census Office. 6th Census, 1840
Statistics of the United States of America, as collected and returned by the marshall of the several judicial districts under the thirteenth section of the act for taking the Sixth Census; corrected at the Department of State. June 1, 1840. Published by authority of an act of Congress, under the direction of the Secretary of State. Washington, Printed by Blair and Rives, 1841. 409 p.

Census of Population 1840

1840

Reel 1

1840.1
Census Office. 6th Census, 1840
Sixth census or enumeration of the inhabitants of the United States, as corrected at the Department of State, in 1840. Published, by authority of an act of Congress, under the direction of the Secretary of State. Washington, Blair and River, 1841. 476, [3] p.

1840.2

Census Office. 6th Census, 1840
Compendium of the enumer-
ation of the inhabitants and statistics of the United States, as
obtained at the Department of
State, from the returns of the
sixth census, by counties and
principal towns, exhibiting the
population, wealth, and resources of the country; with
tables of apportionment. . . . To
which is added an abstract of
each preceding census. Washington, Thomas Allen, 1841.
379 p.

[1840.3]

Census Office. 6th Census, 1840
Compendium of the enumer-
ation of the inhabitants and statistics of the United States, as
obtained at the Department of
State, from the returns of the
sixth census, by counties and
principal towns, exhibiting the
population, wealth, and resources of the country; with
tables of apportionment. . . . To
which is added an abstract of
each preceding census. Washington, Blair and Rivers, 1841.
375 p.
[Differs from 1940.2 in that it
includes minor variations in
paging of tables.]

Census of Manufactures 1850

Note. The 1850 and 1860 Censuses of Manufacturers
are all found in the same
reel in the microform
collection.

1850–1860

Reel M–1

M 1850.1

Census Office. 7th Census, 1850
Message of the president of
the United States, communicat-
ing a digest of the statistics of
manufacturers according to the
returns of the Seventh Census.
Washington, U. S. Government
Printers, 1859. 143 p. (In: 35th
Congress, 2nd session, Senate.
Ex. Doc. 39.)

Census of Population 1850

1850

Reel 1

1850.1

Census Office. 7th Census, 1850
The seventh census of the
United States: 1850. Embracing
a statistical view of each of the
states and territories, arranged
by counties, towns, etc., under
the following divisions . . . with
an introduction, embracing the
aggregated tables for the United
States compared with every previous census since 1790; schedules and laws of Congress relating to the census in the same
period; ratio tabled of increased
and decrease of cities and states,
etc., by sex and ages, and color;
table of population of every
county, town, township, etc. in
the United States, alphabeti-
cally arranged, together with
some explanatory remarks and
an appendix embracing notes
upon the tables of each of the
states, etc., (Congressional
series: 32nd Cong., 2nd sess.
House, Misc. doc. unnumbered).
Washington, Robert Armstrong,
Public Printer, 1853. cxxxvi,
1022 p.

1850.2

Census Office. 7th Census, 1850
Statistical view of the United
States, embracing its territory;
population, white, free colored
and slave; moral and social con-
dition; industry; property; and
revenue; the detailed statistics
of cities, towns, and counties:
being a compendium of the seventh census, to which are added
the results of every previous
census beginning with 1790, in
comparative tables. Washington, A.O.P. Nicholson, Public
Printer, 1854. 400 p.

1850.3

Census Office. 7th Census, 1850
The seventh census. Report
of the Superintendent of the
Census of December 1, 1852: to
which is appended the report
for December 1, 1851. Washing-

ton, R. Armstrong, Printer,
1852. 160 p.

Census of Manufactures 1860

Note: The 1850 and 1860 Censuses of Manufactures are all found on the same reel in the microform collection.

1850–1860

Reel M–1

M 1860.1

Census Office. 7th Census, 1850
Manufactures of the United States in 1860; comp. from the original returns of the eighth census. Washington, U.S. Government Printers, 1865. ccxvii, 745 p.

Census of Population 1860

1860

Reel 1

[1860.0]

Census Office. 8th Census, 1860
Preliminary report on the eighth census, 1860. (Congressional series: 37th Cong., 2d sess. House. Ex. doc. 116) 1862. xvi, 294 p.

1860.1

Census Office. 8th Census, 1860
Eighth census of the United States: 1860. Volume I. Population of the United States in 1860; comp. from the original returns of the eighth census . . . Washington, Government Printing Office, 1864. xvii, 694 p.

1860.2

Census Office. 8th Census, 1860
Statistics of the United States, (including mortality, property, &c.) in 1860; comp. from the original returns and being the final exhibit of the eighth census . . . Washington, D.C., U. S. Government Printing Office, 1866. lxvi, 584 p.

Census of Population 1870

1870

Reel 1

Census Office. 9th Census, 1870
Ninth census: Census reports. Compiled from the original returns of the ninth census (June 1, 1870) . . . (Congressional series: 42nd Cong., 1st sess. House. Misc. docs. unnumbered). Washington, D.C., U.S. Government Printing Office, 1872. Volumes I–III.

1870.1

Volume I. The statistics of the population of the United States, embracing the tables of race, nationality, sex, selected ages, and occupations. To which are added the statistics of school attendance and illiteracy, of schools, libraries, newspapers and periodicals, churches, pauperism and crime, and of areas, families, and dwellings . . . xlix, 804 p.

1870.2

Volume II. The vital statistics of the United States, embracing the tables of death, births, sex, and age, to which are added the statistics of the blind, the deaf and dumb, the insane, and the idiotic . . . xxxiii, 679 p.

1870

Reel 2

1870.3

Volume III. The statistics of the wealth and industry of the United States, embracing the tables of wealth, taxation, and public indebtedness; of agriculture; manufactures; mining; and the fisheries. With which are reproduced, from this volume on population, the major tables of occupations . . . v. 843 p., map.

1870.4–1870.6

[Note: These items have been omitted from the microfilm collection since they are reprints of individual chapters already contained in 1870.1]

1870.7   [Note: this item has been omitted from the microfilm collection since it is a reprint of a chapter already contained in 1870.2]

1870.8   Census Office. 9th Census, 1870 A compendium of the ninth census (June 1, 1870) . . . (Congressional series: 42nd Cong., 1st sess. House. Misc. doc. unnumbered). Washington, D.C., U.S. Government Printing Office, 1872. vii, 942 p.

1870.9   Census Office. 9th Census, 1870 Statistical atlas of the United States based on the results of the ninth census 1870 with contributions from many eminent men of science and several departments of the government. (New York) J. Bien, lith., 1874. Various paged, maps and diagrams.

Primary

"Account Book Ordnance Department," Arkadelphia, Arkansas: Photocopy in place file, Arkadelphia, AHC.

Arkansas Gazetteer and Business Directory. St. Louis: R. L. Polk, 1884.

Ball, William McK., and Samuel C. Roane, revised. *Revised Statutes of the State of Arkansas.* Boston: Weeks, Jordan and Co., 1838.

Branner, John C. *Annual Report of the Geological Survey of Arkansas for 1891.* Volume II. Little Rock: Brown Printing Co., 1894.

Branner, John C. *The Clays of Arkansas.* Washington: Government Printing Office, 1908.

Carter, C. E., ed. "The Secretary of War to Jesse Bean, June 16, 1832." *The Territorial Papers of the United States.* Washington, D. C.: U. S. Government Printing Office, 1954.

Durand, Elias, "Memoir of the Late Thomas Nuttall." From the *Proceedings of the American Philosophical Society,* Vol. VII., C. Philadelphia: Sherman & Son, 1860. Reprint.

Langley, Elizabeth B., transcribed. *Population Schedule of the United States Census of 1860.* (Eighth Census) *Benton County Arkansas.* Billings, Missouri: Geneological Research, 1967.

"Little Rock City Directory 1871." Little Rock: Henderson and Albertson, 1871.

Little Rock Records 1862–63 in the Civil War: Arsenal Records Misc. Records National Archives. General Manuscript file, Roll 1, AHC.

Little Rock, The City of Roses and Argenta, Arkansas, With Rambles in the Path of Industrial and Commercial Circles. Descriptive Review. Memphis, Pittsburg, and London, England: Historical and Descriptive Publishing Co., 1888.

Love, Fanny. "Diary of Miss Fanny Love." Van Buren County, Arkansas, 1861–63, collection of the Arkansas Territorial Restoration.

"Monthly Report of Abandoned or Confiscated Lands." Nov. 30, 1865, Dec. 31, 1865, and Monthly Report of Lands, October, 1865. National Archives Records, Assistant Commissioner, Arkansas Freedmen's Bureau Manuscript file, Roll 30.

Moore, Dwight Munson. *Trees of Arkansas.* Little Rock: Arkansas Forestry Commission, 1972.

Nuttall, Thomas. *A Journal of Travels into the Arkansa Territory.* Philadelphia: Thomas H. Palmer, 1821. Reprint. Ann Arbor: University Microfilm, 1966.

Owen, David Dale. *First Report of a Geological Reconnoissance of the Northern Counties of Arkansas 1857–58.* Little Rock: Johnson & Yerkes, 1858.

Pfeiffer, Ida. *A Lady's Second Journey Round the World.* In two volumes. London: Longman, Brown, Green, & Longman, 1855.

Pike, Albert. "Letters from Arkansas, No. II." *American Monthly Magazine* reprinted in the *Arkansas Historical Quarterly.* Fayetteville, Arkansas: Arkansas Historical Association, Spring 1951.

Reilly and Thomas. *Commercial and Statistical Review of Little Rock, Arkansas.* Little Rock: Reilly and Thomas, 1883.

Ross, Margaret Smith, ed. *Letters of Hiram A. Whittington 1827–1834.* Little Rock: Pulaski County Historical Society, 1956.

Schoolcraft, Henry R. *Journal of a Tour Into the Interior of Missouri and Arkansas.* London: Bride-Court, 1821.

"Silas T. Toncray and his wife . . ." Record of Deeds (T1–132), Office of the County Clerk, Shelby County, Kentucky, January 22, 1817.

Shull, Louise Demby. Small Manuscripts Collections. Box VII, 8, AHC.

Tyler Texas Arsenal Records 1863–64: Misc. Records National Archives. General Manuscript file, Roll 1, AHC.

Washburn, Cephas. *Reminiscences of the Indians.* Richmond: Presbyterian Committee of Publication, 1869. Reprint by Press-Argus: Van Buren, Arkansas, 1955. Introduction by Hugh Park.

Whipple, Lieutenant A. W. *Report of Explorations for a Railroad Route . . . The Mississippi River to the Pacific Ocean.* Washington: 1854.

White, Margaret. *A Sketch of Chester Harding, Artist: Drawn by His Own Hand.* Boston/New York: Houghton Mifflin & Co., 1890.

Williams, Leonard, ed. *Cavorting on the Devil's Fork: The Pete Whetstone Letters of C. F. M. Noland.* Memphis: Memphis State University Press, 1979.

Secondary Sources

Books and Catalogs

A View of Tennessee Silversmiths, A Loan Exhibition. Memphis: The Dixon Gallery and Gardens, 1983.

Bartlett, Irving H. *The American Mind in the Mid-Nineteenth Century.* New York: Thomas Y. Crowell Company, 1967.

Beckman, Elizabeth D. *Cincinnati Silversmiths, Jewelers, Watch and Clockmakers.* Cincinnati, Ohio: B&B Company, 1975.

Benton County Bicentennial Committee. *Cemeteries of Benton County, Arkansas.* Rogers, Arkansas. Northwest Arkansas Genealogical Society, Summer 1975.

Binney, Edwin III, and Gail Binney Winslow. *Homage to Amanda: Two Hundred Years of American Quilting.* San Francisco: R. K. Press, 1984.

Boultinghouse, Marquis. *Silversmiths, Jewelers, Clock and Watch Makers of Kentucky 1785–1900.* Lexington, Kentucky: Marquis Boultinghouse, 1980.

Bridenbaugh, Carl. *The Colonial Craftsman.* Chicago: The University of Chicago Press, 1950.

Brown, Stuart E., Jr. *The Guns of Harpers Ferry.* Berryville, VA: Virginia Book Co., 1968.

The Bulletin of the Association for Preservation Technology. Vol v. 1. Ontario, Canada, 1973.

Butler, David F. *United States Firearms: The First Century 1776–1875.* New York: Winchester Press, 1971.

Caldwell, Benjamin H. *Tennessee Silversmiths.* Winston-Salem, Museum of Early Southern Decorative Arts, 1988.

Cann, Zella, and Eugene Gibson. *A History of Summers Community.* Washington County: Summers Community Club, n.d.

Carey, Merwyn A. *American Firearms Makers.* New York: Thomas Y. Crowell Co., 1953.

Carlisle, Lilian Baker. *Vermont Clock and Watchmakers, Silversmiths, and Jewelers. 1778–1878.* Burlington: Lilian Baker Carlisle, 1970.

Cary, Lucian. *The Colt Gun Book.* New York: Arco Publishing Co., 1961.

Confederate Women of Arkansas in the Civil War. 1861–65: Memorial Reminiscences. Little Rock: The United Confederate Veterans of Arkansas, 1907.

Currier, Ernest M. *Marks of Early American Silversmiths.* Watkins Glen, New York: The American Life Foundation, 1938.

Davis, James D. *History of Memphis.* Memphis: Memphis State University Press, 1873.

DeArmond, Rebecca. *Old Times Not Forgotten: A History of Drew County.* Little Rock, Arkansas: Rose Publishing Co., 1980.

Edwards, William B. *The Story of Colt's Revolver.* New York: The Stackpole Company, 1957.

Eno, Clara. *History of Crawford County, Arkansas.* Van Buren, Arkansas: Press-Argus, 1951.

Ferrero, Pat, Elaine Hodges, and Julie Silber. *Hearts and Hands. The Influence of Women and Quilts on American Society.* San Francisco: Quilt Digest Press, 1987.

Gardner, Robert. *Small Arms Makers.* New York: Crown Publishers, 1963.

Garrett, Wendell. "The Matter of Consumers' Taste." John D. Morse, ed. *Country Cabinetwork and Simple City Furniture.* Winterthur Conference Report. 1969. Charlottesville: University Press of Virginia, 1970.

Goodner, Norman. *A Scott County Scrapbook.* Mansfield, Arkansas: Frank Boyd, 1982.

Goodspeed Biographical and Historical Memoirs of Central Arkansas. Chicago, Nashville, and St.

Louis: The Goodspeed Publishing Company, 1889. Reprint. Easley, South Carolina: Southern Historical Press, 1978.

Goodspeed Biographical and Historical Memoirs of Eastern Arkansas. Chicago, Nashville, and St. Louis: The Goodspeed Publishing Co., 1889. Reprint. Easley, South Carolina: Southern Historical Press, 1978.

Goodspeed Biographical and Historical Memoirs of Northwestern Arkansas. Chicago, Nashville, and St. Louis: The Goodspeed Publishing Co., 1889. Reprint. Easley, South Carolina: Southern Historical Press, 1978.

Goodspeed Biographical and Historical Memoirs of Southern Arkansas. Chicago, Nashville, and St. Louis: The Goodspeed Publishing Company, 1890. Reprint. Easley, South Carolina: Southern Historical Press, 1978.

Goodspeed Biographical and Historical Memoirs of Western Arkansas. Chicago and Nashville: The Southern Publishing Company, 1891. Reprint. Easley, South Carolina: Southern Historical Press, 1978.

Greer, Georgeanna H. *American Stonewares. The Art and Craft of Utilitarian Potters.* Exton, Pennsylvania: Schiffer Publishing. Ltd., 1981.

Guilland, Harold F. *Early American Folk Pottery.* Philadelphia: Chilton Book Company, 1971.

Haberstein, Robert W. and William M. Lamere. *The History of American Funeral Directing.* Milwaukee, Wisconsin: Bulfin Printers, 1955.

Hindle, Brooke, and Stephen Lubar. *Engines of Change.* Washington D.C.: Smithsonian Institution Press, 1985.

Hood, Graham. *American Silver.* New York: Praeger Publishers, Inc., 1971.

Hummel, Charles F. *With Hammer in Hand.* Charlottesville: The University Press of Virginia, 1968.

Johnson, Boyd. *The Arkansas Frontier.* Pine Bluff: The Perdue Printing Co., 1957.

The Kentucky Quilt Project. *Kentucky Quilts: 1800–1900.* New York: Pantheon Books, 1982.

Kirkland, Turner. *Southern Derringers of the Mississippi Valley.* Union City, Tennessee: Union Press, 1972.

Leslie, James. W. *Saracen's Country.* Little Rock: Rose Publishing Co., 1974.

Mackie, Carey T., H. Parrott Bacot, and Charles L. Mackie. *Crescent City Silver.* New Orleans: The Historic New Orleans Collection, 1980.

Mackie, Carey Turner, and Charles LeJune Mackie. *New Orleans Silversmiths, Goldsmiths, Jewelers, Clock and Watchmakers. 1720–1870.* New Orleans: Carey T. Mackie and Charles L. Mackie, 1979.

Mary Lee Chapter #87, UDC, Small Manuscripts Collections (hereafter cited as Smc) AHC.

Masterson, James R. *Arkansas Folklore: The Arkansas Traveler, Davy Crockett and other Legends.* Little Rock: Rose Publishing Co., 1974.

McArthur, Priscilla. *Arkansas in the Gold Rush.* Little Rock: August House, 1986.

McDonough, Nancy. *Garden Sass: A Catalog of Arkansas Folkways.* New York: Coward, McCann and Georghegan, 1975.

Medaris, Mary, ed. *Sam Williams: Printers Devil.* Hope, Arkansas: Etter Printing Company, 1979.

Natchez-Made Silver of the Nineteenth Century. Baton Rouge, LA: Louisiana State University.

Orlofsky, Patsy and Myron. *Quilts in America.* New York: Hill Co., 1974.

Otto, Celia Jackson. *American Furniture of the Nineteenth Century.* New York: Viking Press, 1965.

Randolph, Vance. *Ozark Magic and Folklore.* New York: Dover Publications, 1964.

Renwick Gallery Exhibit Catalog. *American Pieced Quilts.* Washington D.C.: Smithsonian Institution Traviling Exhibition Service, 1972.

Ross, Margaret. *Arkansas Gazette: The Early Years.* Little Rock: Arkansas Gazette Foundation, 1969.

Safford, Carleton L., and Robert Bishop. *American Quilts and Coverlets.* New York: Weathervane Books, 1974.

Seale, William. *The President's House.* Washington D.C.: The White House Historical Association, 1986.

Seidler, Jan M. "A Tradition in Transition: The Boston Furniture Industry, 1840–1880." Kenneth L. Ames, ed. *Victorian Furniture.* Philadelphia: The Victorian Society in America, 1982.

Sikes, Jane E. *The Furniture Makers of Cincinnati 1790 to 1849.* Cincinnati: Jane Sikes, 1976.

Silver in Maryland. Baltimore: Museum and Library of Maryland History, Maryland Historical Society, 1983.

Smith, James Webb. *Georgia's Legacy.* The University of Georgia: Georgia Museum of Art, 1985.

Smith, Maggie Aldridge. *Hico a Heritage Siloam Springs History.* Siloam Springs, Arkansas: Maggie Smith, 1976.

Stroud, Hubert B. and Gerald T. Hanson. *Arkansas Geography, The Physical Landscape and the Historical-Cultural Setting.* Little Rock, Arkansas: Rose Publishing Co., 1981.

Students of Umpire High School. *The Unfinished Story of North Howard County.* Umpire, Arkansas: North Howard County Youth Group, 1982.

Talbot, Page. "Philadelphia Furniture and Manufacturers 1850–1880." Kenneth L. Ames, ed. *Victorian Furniture.* Philadelphia: The Victorian Society in America, 1982.

Teacher, Lawrence, ed. *The Unabridged Mark Twain.* Philadelphia: Running Press, 1976.

Thwaites, Ruben Gold. *Early Western Travels 1748–1846. A Series of Annotated Reprints . . . Nuttall's Travels Into the Arkansas Territory, 1819.* Volume XIII. Cleveland, Ohio: The Arthur H. Clark Co., 1905.

Turner, Frederick Jackson. "The Significance of the American Frontier in American History." Madison, WI: State Historic Society of Wisconsin, 1905.

Vernon, Walter N. *Methodism in Arkansas 1816–1976.* Little Rock: Joint Committee for the History of Arkansas Methodism, 1976.

Victor, Stephen K. "From the Shop to the Manufactory, Silver and Industry, 1800–1970." *Silver in American Life.* New York: The American Federation of Arts, 1979.

Warren, David. *Southern Silver.* Houston, Texas: The Museum of Fine Arts, 1968.

Williams, Derita Coleman. *A View of Tennessee Silversmiths.* Memphis: Dixon Gallery and Gardens, 1983.

Williams, Harry Lee. *The History of Craighead County Arkansas.* Little Rock: Parke-Harper Co., 1930. Reprint. Craighead County Historical Society, 1977.

Wilson, R. L. *The Colt Heritage.* New York: Simon and Schuster, 1979.

Periodicals

Arkansas Historical Quarterly. Vol. XIV., 1. Fayetteville: The Arkansas Historical Association, Spring, 1955.

Caldwell, Benjamin H., Jr. "Tennessee Silversmiths Prior to 1860: A Check List." *Antiques.* December, 1971.

Coffee, Barbara. "Antebellum Arkadelphia." *The Clark County Historical Journal.* Arkadelphia, Arkansas: Clark County Historical Association, Spring, 1981.

Ingerman, Elizabeth A. "Personal Experience of an Old New York Cabinetmaker." *Antiques.* November, 1963.

Johnson, Wilma, ed. "1883 News." *The Journal.* Fort Smith, Arkansas: Fort Smith Historical Society, September, 1983.

Key, Vera. *The Benton County Pioneer.* Bentonville: Benton County Historical Society, 1955.

Logan, Herschel C. "H.E. Dimick of St. Louis." *The American Rifleman.* April, 1958.

Martin, Wanda, and H. B. Arnold. "Col. Joseph Allen Whitaker and the 'Rosedale' Plantation." *Clark County Historical Journal.* Arkadelphia: Clark County Historical Association, Winter 1979–1980.

McKenzie. H. B. "Confederate Manufactures in Southwest Arkansas." *Publications of the Arkansas Historical Association.* Fayetteville, Arkansas: Arkansas Historical Association, 1908.

Miller, Lucille. "The Alexander Miller Home." *Rivers and Roads and Points in Between.* Vol. I. Augusta: Woodruff County Historical Society, Summer, 1973.

Smith, Samuel D. "Arkansas Kiln Sites." Monthly Newsletter. Fayetteville, Arkansas: Arkansas Archeological Society, November, 1972.

Sullivan, David M. "John Albert Pearson, Jr.: Arkansas Soldier and Confederate Marine." *Arkansas Historical Quarterly.* Fayetteville, Arkansas: Arkansas Historical Association, 1968.

Waters, Deborah Dependahl. "From Pure Coin, The Manufacture of American Silver Flatware 1800–1860." *Winterthur Portfolio 12.* Charlottesville: University Press of Virginia, 1977.

Wolfe, J. J. "Background of German Immigration to Arkansas." *Arkansas Historical Quarterly.* Fayetteville, Arkansas: Arkansas Historical Association, Summer, 1966.

Unpublished

Bennett, Swannee. "The Development of Industry in Arkansas Prior to 1836." Unpublished Research Paper, 1972.

Blakely, Jeffrey A. "The 19th Century Pottery Industry in Sebastian County, Arkansas." Unpublished Research Paper.

Bolton, Charles. "Inequality and Social Change in the Arkansas Territory." Unpublished paper presented to the annual meeting of the Southern Historical Association, November 13, 1981.

Johnson, Bernard III. "Fort Smith Furniture Manufacturers of the Late 19th Century." Fort Smith, Arkansas: Old Fort Museum, 1982.

LeDuc, Susan. Letter to Judith Stewart-Abernathy. (ATR Registrar). Hermitage, TN: May 29, 1988. LeDuc tells of her relative Welcome Boy Covey's idea of making bedsteads detached from the walls so they could be moved about the room.

Thweatt, Sue. Family Typescript. Mentions Lawrence Thompson's chest of drawers that now belongs to the Arkansas Territorial Restoration. N.d.

Watkins, Beverly. "The Bird, Welch and Culberson Potteries: Local Industry in Nineteenth Century Dallas County, Arkansas." Unpublished grant report to the Arkansas Endowment for the Humanities (grant #248–062–82M, 30 July 1982).